Demographic Research Monographs

A Series of the Max Planck Institute
for Demographic Research, Rostock, Germany

Editor-in-chief: James W. Vaupel

Demographic Research Monographs

E. Barbi, S. Bertino, E. Sonnino (Eds.)
Inverse Projection Techniques
2004. XI, 137 pages. 3-540-20931-X

G. Doblhammer
The Late Life Legacy of Very Early Life
2004. X, 204 pages. 3-540-22105-0

Roland Rau

Seasonality in Human Mortality

A Demographic Approach

With 60 Figures and 22 Tables

 Springer

Dr. Roland Rau
Max Planck Institute for Demographic Research
Konrad-Zuse-Straße 1
18057 Rostock
Germany

Diss., Univ. Rostock, 2005

Printed with the financial support of the Max Planck Society

Library of Congress Control Number: 2006934117

ISBN-10 3-540-44900-0 Springer Berlin Heidelberg New York
ISBN-13 978-3-540-44900-3 Springer Berlin Heidelberg New York

Springer is part of Springer Science+Business Media

springer.com

© Springer-Verlag Berlin Heidelberg 2007

Production: LE-TeX Jelonek, Schmidt & Vöckler GbR, Leipzig
Cover-design: Erich Kirchner, Heidelberg
The front cover photo – top right-hand corner – includes a photograph by Harald Wenzel-Orf (www.wenzel-orf.de) and has been reproduced with his permission.

SPIN 11867562   88/3100YL - 5 4 3 2 1 0   Printed on acid-free paper

To Magda

Foreword

This volume, "Seasonality in Human Mortality: A Demographic Approach" by Dr. Roland Rau, is the third book of a series of Demographic Research Monographs published by Springer Verlag. Dr. Rau is now a research scientist at the Duke University Population Research Institute (DuPRI), but at the time of his writing the book he was a research scientist at the Max Planck Institute for Demographic Research. The book is a slightly-revised version of his doctoral dissertation, which he completed at the Max Planck Institute and submitted to the University of Rostock. He was awarded highest honors, summa cum laude, for his dissertation and he was later awarded the Otto Hahn Medal of the Max Planck Society for his contribution. Rau's research has three exceptional strengths.

First, the book is meticulously researched. This is a superb example of careful reading and assessment of the corpus of relevant literature. More than 400 references are listed in the bibliography. Existing knowledge is judiciously evaluated, cogently organized and lucidly described. Rau presents all the relevant findings, pointing out when they are contradictory and when caution is needed. The result is a balanced, nuanced, comprehensive account of the state of current knowledge. Rau is clearly a dedicated, diligent scholar interested in pursuing the truth, rather than a story-teller or an advocate pushing some theory.

Second, the book includes important original contributions to knowledge. Rau has not only assessed current knowledge, he has also substantially advanced it. In particular:

- His critical appraisal of existing methods for measuring seasonality is much more than a review: it provides new insights into the comparative advantages and disadvantages of the various methods.
- Based on his understanding of the deficiencies of existing methods, Rau develops a novel approach to incorporate "changes in the trend, the seasonal component and unobserved heterogeneity."

- His analysis of data for the United States provides interesting findings for an important country that has been neglected in research on seasonality in mortality.
- His study of the data for Denmark is based on exceptionally accurate and complete information, analyzed using sophisticated statistical methods.
- Socio-economic status and marital status are known to have major impacts on mortality. Rau presents the first careful study of their impacts on seasonal mortality. Using U.S. data, he finds no significant effect of marital status, but he does find a social gradient by education in seasonal mortality. This, he notes, "is an effect which has not been discovered elsewhere".
- Using Danish data, Rau uncovered another significant finding: people living alone have higher relative mortality risks in winter than people living with someone else.
- Another important contribution to knowledge is Rau's estimate of the gain in life expectancy if seasonal increases in mortality could be eliminated. The gain, based on U.S. data for 1998, would be about 0.8 years for women and 1 year for men. Although seemingly modest, such a gain would have a large absolute impact on national well-being.
- Based on his new findings and on his careful review of previous findings, Rau is able to make the convincing recommendation that public health policies should focus on three groups that are especially vulnerable to cold-related mortality: "old people, people who are living alone and people of lower socio-economic status".

The third exceptional strength of this book is its single, clear focus—seasonality in mortality. Rau appropriately addresses this issue from various perspectives, but always with the single, clear underlying focus.

Rau starts with discussion of the causal chain linking seasonal fluctuations with mortality, emphasizing the importance of social as well as biological factors. He reviews the history of seasonal mortality, with a fascinating account of the modern elimination of the summer peak. He then turns to an analysis of alternative measures of seasonality, including an innovative comparative evaluation of different approaches. The next two chapters analyze U.S. data and Danish data. Finally, there is an interesting "outlook" chapter. Lengthy appendices that provide supplemental material for various chapters are available in the online edition of the book.

Many doctoral dissertations present a bouquet of research flowers, loosely bound together. Rau's work has a unitary theme; it is indeed a monograph. The cumulative impact is impressive. By concentrating on a single topic, by carefully and comprehensively assessing existing knowledge about it, and by adding important new knowledge, Rau has written a magisterial work that will become a key book on the subject. Rau notes that the last monograph on seasonal mortality was published more than 25 years ago (in 1977). This monograph may be the major work on the topic for the next quarter century.

The series of Demographic Research Monographs is under the editorial supervision of the Max Planck Institute for Demographic Research. Prof. James W. Vaupel, Founding Director of the Institute, is Editor-in-Chief. He is advised by an Editorial Board that currently consists of Prof. Elisabetta Barbi (Messina University, Italy), Prof. Gabriele Doblhammer (Rostock University, Germny), Dr. Jutta Gampe (Max Planck Institute), Prof. Jan M. Hoem (Max Planck Institute), and Prof. Bernard Jeune (University of Southern Denmark). Additional members of the Editorial Board will be appointed as needed to review manuscripts submitted for possible publication. The current manuscript was reviewed and accepted by James Vaupel, Gabriele Doblhammer and Jutta Gampe, based on advice from a group of referees.

The Demographic Research Monographs series can be considered the successor to the series called Odense Monographs on Population Aging, edited by Bernard Jeune and James Vaupel. The volumes in this now-terminated series were first published as hardcover books by an academic publisher, the Odense University Press, and subsequently made available online at www.demogr.mpg.de/books/odense. The nine Odense Monographs on Population Aging include two collections of research articles that focus on specific subjects on the frontier of demographic research, three volumes by senior researchers that present path-breaking findings, a review of research on a topic of emerging interest, a presentation of a new method for analysis of demographic data, an out-standing doctoral dissertation, and a unique collection of important demographic data on non-human species.

The new series of Demographic Research Monographs will continue this mix, with books that are often under 200 pages in length, that have a clear focus, and that significantly advance demographic knowledge. Research related to population aging will continue to be a prime focus on the new series, but not the only one. The new series will embrace all of demography, broadly defined. As indicated by the first volume, an important subject will be historical demography. We also plan to highlight research on fertility and family dynamics, especially in Europe. Mathematical demography is the core of the population sciences and we will strive to foster monographs that use mathematics and statistics to further develop the theories and methods of demography. Biodemography is a small but rapidly growing and particularly innovative branch of demography: we will seize opportunities to publish monographs at the intersection of biology and demography, pertaining both to human and other species, and including demographic research with ties to such fields as epidemiology, genetics, evolutionary biology, life-history biology, experimental demography, and paleodemography.

Each volume in the Demographic Research Monograph series will have a substantial link to the Max Planck Institute for Demographic Research. As well as being published as hardcover books by Springer-Verlag, the volumes of the Max Planck series of Demographic Research Monographs will subsequently be available at www.demogr.mpg.de/books/drm. The online version may include color graphs, supplemental analyses, databases and other ancillary or enhanced material. Parallel publication online and in print is a significant innovation that will make the monograph series particularly useful to scholars and students around the world.

James W. Vaupel
Editor-in-Chief

Preface

This dissertation has been written at the Max Planck Institute for Demographic Research. During this time I highly benefited from my colleagues, especially from James W. Vaupel and Gabriele Doblhammer. Gabriele Doblhammer initiated my interest in the seasonal pattern of mortality. I would like to thank her for the advice and support she provided over the past few years while supervising the progress of my dissertation. I am equally grateful to James W. Vaupel. Besides monitoring my work, he created an excellent working atmosphere as head of the "Survival & Longevity-Lab" at the Max Planck Institute for Demographic Research, where helpful colleagues are the rule, and not the exception. Among these many colleagues, I would like to express particular gratitude to Jutta Gampe for her help with many of my statistical questions.

Associated with the Max Planck Institute for Demographic Research is the International Max Planck Research School for Demography giving training for doctoral students. The dissertation benefited from courses given by James W. Vaupel, Gabriele Doblhammer, Jan M. Hoem, Francesco C. Billari, Heiner Maier and Antonio Golini.

Apart from the support provided by people from the Max Planck Institute and its Research School, I would like to thank Gavin Donaldson, Paul Eilers, William R. Keatinge, Marc Luy, and Jim Oeppen.

Considerable parts of this dissertation are based on work conducted at Statistics Denmark in Copenhagen. Otto Andersen, Jørn Korsbø Petersen, Morten Lindboe and Jørgen Leif Jensen gave me valuable advice on technical details to analyze the Danish data.

This monograph benefited greatly from Yvonne Sandor's meticulous language editing.

Rostock,   *Roland Rau*
July 2006

Contents

1

Introduction

> "Whoever wishes to investigate medicine properly,
> should proceed thus: in the first place to consider
> the seasons of the year, and what effects each of
> them produces for they are not at all alike, but differ
> much from themselves in regard to their changes."
> — Hippocrates in "On Airs, Waters, and Places", ~ 400BC

Seasonal mortality was a hot topic in the media in the summer of 2003 when more than 10,000 people died of the heatwave in France in August [55, 157]. Nevertheless, the real "grim reaper" [172] in most countries is winter. Periodically, winter excess mortality emerges in the popular media especially in countries such as the UK where cold related deaths are a serious public health issue. Headlines like "Cold killed 20,000 elderly people last winter, says charity" [362], "Cold kills 'thousands' in a week" [25] and "Britain is a rich nation; its old people should not be dying of the cold" [363] are reflected in official statistics. The national statistical office of the UK (ONS) estimates that during the last ten years between 23,000 (1997/98) and 48,000 (1999/2000) more people died annually during winter than would be expected from death rates at other times of the year [266].

Seasonality in morbidity and mortality has been of interest to scholars for a long time. At least since Hippocrates' seminal work "On Air, Waters and Places" written almost 2500 years ago, people are aware of the impact of the seasons throughout the year on diseases.[1] The first modern investigations into seasonal mortality have been conducted in the middle of the 19th century by British statisticians [eg. 368].

---

[1] Sometimes Wong Tai is credited to be the first to mention the variation of diseases with the seasons about 4700 years ago [237].

Nowadays, seasonal effects in demographic variables are rarely the center of attention in population studies[2] — although most basic indicators such as births, deaths, marriages,... are subject to annual fluctuations. The last monograph on seasonality in mortality has been published more than 25 years ago [324]. The multi-disciplinary approach taken in this dissertation is typical for demographic analyses. Demography is based on a solid foundation of methods derived from mathematics and statistics. It takes biological as well as social forces into account to arrive at conclusions which could be transmitted as policy recommendations into the political arena [cf. 202, 379]. This dissertation incorporates all of these aspects in its chapters. It focuses, nevertheless, on social strains of explanations using modern statistical methods.

The current state of knowledge of seasonal mortality will be presented after this introduction in Chapter 2 (starting at page 5). First, the biomedical causes of increased mortality risks during cold weather conditions are outlined. Such an approach would not be sufficient to take the differential in winter excess mortality between various countries into account. In a second step, social and cultural forces need to be included to obtain a more complete picture. This description of a causal chain of events is followed by a historical literature review which describes the seasonal mortality pattern from the past up until the present. Special attention is given to the influences of social and cultural factors in mediating the amplitude in seasonality of mortality.

To make any meaningful quantitative analysis of a phenomenon of interest, one has to be able to have a valid measurement of this phenomenon. The subsequent chapter (Chapter 3, starting at page 39) is therefore more methodological: On the one hand, various indices and tests for seasonality will be described, discussed and tested with hypothetical data as well as with real data. The chapter gives recommendations for which index one should use to describe seasonality, and which statistic should be employed to test for seasonality in data. On the other hand, several standard time-series methods will be evaluated whether they are suitable to analyze demographic data which often come as count data with variable trends, a changing seasonal figure and overdispersion.

The potential impact of social and cultural factors on seasonal fluctuations in deaths and mortality in current populations are analyzed in the two subsequent chapters. The study of seasonality in deaths in the United States in Chapter 4 (page 83) covers the years 1959–98. The wealth of data, large social differences, the wide variability in climatic conditions, and the lack of research for this country make the US an important case study. In addition, a new method for the time-series analysis of seasonal count data will be introduced, as previous methods did not yield satisfactory results. With the analysis of Denmark in Chapter 5 (page 125), a more homogenuous country is

---

[2] A recent exception is the second monograph in Springer's "Demographic Research Monographs" series "The late life legacy of very early life" by Gabriele Doblhammer-Reiter where month of birth is the key factor [70].

presented. The base of these data, the population registers, is the main reason for the demographers' widespread interest in Scandinavian data. These registers allow the availability of information for almost any given point in time, and are of unmatched quality.

Before the dissertation is concluded, a small chapter (Chapter 6, page 169) gives an outlook how much gain in life expectancy could theoretically be expected if people did not have to experience adverse environmental conditions during winter, yet rather faced summer mortality conditions throughout their lives.

Despite this wide scope it should be pointed out that this dissertation is specialized in two dimensions:

- The analysis does not cover the entire age range; it focuses on seasonal mortality among adults — especially at advanced ages. Due to its completely different causality, seasonality in infant and child mortality has been deliberately left out.
- Developing countries often display a seasonality pattern which is reminiscent of European countries of about 150 years ago. As this dissertation intends to focus on the latest developments in combatting seasonal mortality, it only takes developed countries into account.

2

Literature Review

2.1 Introduction

This literature review is divided into two major parts. First, a causal chain is constructed which outlines how a change in temperature triggers certain biomedical reactions in the body, which may lead to morbidity and ultimately to mortality, and how social factors can mediate this impact. Secondly, an overview of the development of seasonal mortality over time is given. It starts with studies on Roman Egypt, and presents results from the 16th to the 19th century, based on family reconstitution data. Results are shown from the first studies based on census data in the middle of the 19th century and, finally, points at recent development in Western countries. The Appendix starting on page 177 gives a sketch on how the literature review has been conducted methodologically.

2.2 Causal Chain

2.2.1 Introduction

The influence of the seasons on human mortality has been known since Hippocrates' seminal essay "On Airs, Waters, and Places" written more than 2000 years ago. Surprisingly, misconceptions are still commonplace. For example, in the summer of 2003, excess mortality from heat was heavily covered in the media. While the number of cold-related deaths typically receives less attention, although the latter far outnumbers the former in many countries in almost every year. It has been noted, for instance, that in Great Britain 40,000 cold-related deaths occur annually [16]. Also noteworthy is the often predicted risk of an increase of heat-related mortality due to global warming during the following decades is unlikely. "Populations in Europe [...] can be expected to adjust to global warming predicted for the next half century with little sustained increase in heat related mortality." [190, p. 670]. On the contrary, the number of excess deaths can even be expected to shrink. In the words of Keatinge et al: "Our data suggest that any increases in mortality due to increased temperatures would be outweighted by much larger short term declines in cold related mortalities" [190, p. 672].

Besides the timing of deaths, mistaken ideas also prevail about the causes of deaths. It is a widespread belief in the general public that deaths peak in winter because of the high suicide rate. This assumption is wrong for two reasons: suicides only make a small contribution to the overall death pattern: between one and two percent of all deaths are attributable to that cause.[1] This contribution is not enough to cause the observed differences between the seasons. Secondly, Durkheim's well-known studies in the 19th century show that suicides do not peak (late) in winter but in late spring and early summer. Another cause of death often put forward to explain seasonal mortality are deaths from influenza. This might have been true for long periods of time.[2] In Western countries in recent decades, however, the influence of influenza on cold-related mortality is highly overestimated. Donaldson and Keatinge calculated that only 2.4% of all excess winter deaths during the last 10 years were directly or indirectly due to influenza [78].

This section should therefore outline which causes of deaths are responsible for the observed pattern, which biomedical reactions are happening in the body and what we do know so far to fight the annual cold-related death toll.

2.2.2 A Simple Chain of Causality for Seasonal Mortality: Biomedical Factors

A relatively naive approach would assume a very short chain of causality: the cold decreases the body temperature under a certain level below which the body ceases functioning and then dies of hypothermia. Only a very small proportion of all cold-related deaths are induced by hypothermia, though. In the year 1998, more than 2.34 million people died in the US aged 50 years or older. Only in 316 cases the stated cause of death was hypothermia. This makes it an even less likely cause of death than dying of breast cancer for men.

A view which is a bit more elaborated takes only natural/biological forces and their consequences into account. This causal chain, where climate (and most notably cold temperatures) triggers a biomedical reaction in the body which may lead to an elevated mortality risk and, ultimately, to death, is outlined in Figure 2.1. Although the detrimental influence of cold on the body is known for ages, the actual underlying mechanism is not yet fully understood. As pointed out by Bull and Morton: "The studies to this point have not established a clear chain of events leading from a change in external temperature to

---

[1] All results are based on own calculations if no explicit reference is given.

[2] See, for example, Vaupel et al. (1997) where the effect of the Spanish Flu in various countries in the years 1918 and 1919 is easily visible on Lexis surface maps [388].

death. Nevertheless, it remains very likely that changes in external temperatures *cause* changes in death rates especially in the elderly" [37, p. 223]. More
than 20 years have passed since this assessment and many studies on seasonal
mortality have been conducted in the meantime. Yet, James Mercer and Sigurd Sparr come to the unsatisfying conclusion in their editorial to a special
issue of the "International Journal of Circumpolar Health" dedicated to understanding excess winter mortality in the elderly: "The mechanisms by which
seemingly mild exposure to cold ambient conditions can increase the risk of
death does not seem to be much clearer today than when Bull & Morten were
investigating the problem in 1978" [258, p. 152].[3] Thus, the exact mechanism
can not be described here, but only the current state of knowledge.

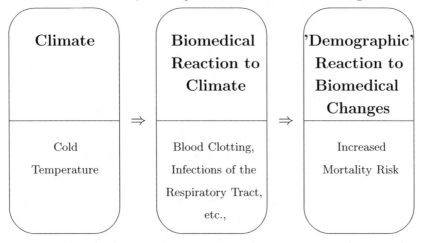

Fig. 2.1. A Simple Chain of Causality for Seasonality in Mortality

Many studies confirm the provocative judgement of Kunst et al. [209,
p. 338]: "Man is a tropical animal". Lowest mortality is usually recorded when
the ambient temperature is between 18° and 20°C. Despite dependencies on
the geographic location ("Europe": 18°C [98], Germany: 20°C [220], Southeast England 18°C [77], Netherlands, nursing home patients: 15-19°C [232],
Barcelona, Spain: 21°C [322], England and Wales [37]), the "optimal" temperature is also determined by humidity [322] and by the age of the people [57].
The World Health Organization, for example, mentions that sedentary elderly
face lowest mortality risks if the temperature is 2–3°C higher. If the temperature drops below or rises above this optimal level, death becomes more likely.
This increase in mortality is well-documented [e.g. 209]. The most thorough
investigation in this direction is the so-called "Eurowinter" study headed by
William Keatinge. Table 2.1 shows how mortality increases in percent for each
1°C fall from 18°C. Mortality in this model is lowest at 18°C, yet, there is still

---

[3] In this article, the name "Morten" (instead of Morton) has been misspelled in
the source document.

considerable variation concerning the proportional increase in mortality with a drop in temperature.The most moderate increase in mortality is observed in southern Finland where mortality rises 0.27% for each drop of 1°C in temperature below 18°C. The steepest increase is recorded in Athens (increase higher than 2%). It should be mentioned, however, that this phenomenon can not be applied universally. In Yekaterinburg, Russia, mortality increased only at temperatures below 0°C [81], in Yakutsk (Russia), the world's coldest city, mortality was completely independent in the temperature range of 10.2°C to −48.2°C [76, 185].

Table 2.1. Increase of Mortality by Fall in Temperature in Selected European Regions

Region	Deaths per 10^6 Population (per day at 18°C)	Percent Increase in Mortality for Each 1°C Fall from 18°C
North Finland	42.8	0.29
South Finland	43.0	0.27
Baden-Württemberg	31.0	0.60
Netherlands	36.5	0.59
London	40.3	1.37
North Italy	34.3	0.51
Athens	34.4	2.15
Palermo	—	1.54

Source: Eurowinter Study 1997 [98, p. 1343]

It has already been mentioned that the often associated causes of death, influenza and suicides, play only a negligible or no role at all for the increase in mortality late in winter. The causes of deaths which are of crucial importance to explain the mortality peak in winter are cardiovascular, cerebrovascular and respiratory diseases. The latter group has the strongest seasonal pattern among all major groups of causes of death [102, 148, 319]. Aubenque et al., for example, standardized mean annual mortality in France for the years 1968–72 to an index of 100 [13]. All cause mortality varied between 120 (January) and 87 (August) whereas deaths from respiratory diseases showed a peak of 172 (January and February) and a trough of 51 in August. However, respiratory diseases are not the leading cause of death in Western developed countries [e.g. 264]. Thus, they do not the largest share to the number of excess winter deaths — despite their highly seasonal pattern. About half of the cold-related mortality can be attributed to ischaemic heart disease and cerebrovascular diseases [82, 98, 376]. If all cardiovascular diseases are included, the share of circulatory diseases increases to about 2/3 of the whole cold-related mortality based on estimates for the Netherlands in the years 1979–1987/88 [208, 235]. Consequently, research on seasonal mortality mainly focused on cardiovascular, cerebrovascular and respiratory diseases. Deaths from circulatory diseases peak usually one or two days after the peak of a cold spell; respiratory deaths rise more slowly, peaking about ten days after the peak of cold period [37, 185]. Section A.2.1 in the Appendix gives an overview which study analyzed which disease/cause of death.[4]

So far, the first and the last box in Figure 2.1 have been discussed, namely the change in temperature and the elevated mortality risks for various causes of death. The following paragraphs explain the biomedical reactions in the body caused by detrimental environmental conditions, resulting in a higher chance of dying from those aforementioned diseases. It is probably best to differentiate between the triggering effects for cardio- and cerebrovascular diseases on the one hand and for respiratory diseases on the other hand.

If respiratory diseases lead to death during winter, two effects are usually mentioned [eg. 97, 98, 169]: On the one hand, low temperatures facilitate the survival of bacteria in droplets. On the other hand, cold has adverse effects on the immune system's resistance against respiratory infections. As a result from breathing cold air, the risk for a pulmonary infection rises due to bronchoconstriction [169]. "Bronchospasm precipitated by breathing cold air is now well recognised, and the finding of inflammatory cells in sputum after breathing cold air has raised the possibility that cold air breathing might induce this by causing inflammatory changes in the airways" [97, p. 155].

Deaths due to circulatory diseases is a large group consisting of cardio-vascular diseases on the one hand and cerebrovascular diseases on the other hand. Cold stress acts on the body in two ways: either on the blood vessels ("vasoconstriction" [e.g. 97, 169]) or on the composition of the blood ("haemo-concentration" [e.g. 76, 81, 98, 169, 187]). Several indicators which cause these changes in blood viscosity have been singled out: an increase in white blood cells and red blood cells [97, 169, 188], hypertension [187, 199, 322, 340, 412], platelet [97, 188], plasma fibrinogen [16, 81, 97, 169, 199, 411], and plasma cholesterol [169, 188, 322, 340] — and especially high density lipoproteins [413].

2.2.3 A More Advanced Chain of Causality for Seasonal Mortality: Social and Biological Factors

The causal model, so far, is still too simple. At this point it would be logical permitted to conclude: if cold temperatures determine excess winter deaths, then countries where a colder climate prevails have to face higher seasonal fluctuations in mortality. The opposite is true, though. Figure 2.2 shows a scatterplot based on results of the study by McKee [252]. Similar findings have been also described in [135] or [147]. On the x-axis, the minimum monthly

---

[4] For sure, the literature mentioned there is not a complete bibliography on cause-specific seasonal mortality among adults in developed countries during recent decades. It provides, nevertheless, a good starting point on cause-specific studies on winter excess deaths.

temperature is plotted, and the y-axis displays "Excess Winter Deaths". This "[e]xcess winter mortality was defined as the percentage by which observed deaths exceeded those which would be expected if the death rate during June to September pertained throughout the year" [252, p. 179]. A country specific scatterplot shows the paired values of the two variables for 18 Western and Central European countries for the years 1976–1984.[5] What could be observed in this graph is seemingly a seasonality paradox: the higher the minimum monthly temperature, the larger the extent in cold-related deaths as indicated by the gray dashed linear regression line.[6] Countries with relatively warm or moderate climate like Spain, Portugal, and Italy or the UK and Ireland experience much larger excess winter mortality than countries with harsh climatic conditions during winter such as Finland and Norway.

This leads to a more advanced chain of causality which is outlined in Figure 2.3. The three elements of Figure 2.1 have been preserved. Still, the triggering event is the fall in temperature; also the increased mortality risk is, finally, caused by some biomedical reactions to the cold in the body. Intervening social factors, however, play a crucial role in mediating the effects of the cold on the body — otherwise this "seasonality paradox" as depicted in Figure 2.2 would not have been possible. As Gemmell et al. [121] point out in their analysis of Scotland: "[. . .] the strength of this [seasonal mortality] relationship is a result of the population being unable to protect themselves adequately from the effects of temperature rather than the effects of temperature itself " (p. 274).

These intermediate factors can be alternatively also described as "man-made" influences. Most of them can be modified on the individual level. The only true exception is tackling the detrimental effects of air pollution.[7] The amount of literature giving evidence for the impact of air pollution on mortality is overwhelming as reflected in the two review essays by Tenías Burillo et al. [361] and Holland et al. [152]. The pollutant most often analyzed is particulate matter (PM) [e.g. 8, 33, 42, 137, 175, 191, 206, 282, 327, 328, 337, 364, 365, 366, 397]. Especially "fine suspended particulates, smoke and fume" (diameter of matter $< 10\mu m$) are of interest to researchers, as their "settling velocity in circulation of ambient air is negligible and [they] can be inhaled" [152, p. 534]. Sulfur dioxide (SO_2) [e.g. 42, 152, 175, 217, 327, 364, 365], nitrogen dioxide (NO_2) [e.g. 42, 361], carbon monoxide (CO) [e.g. 361, 364, 365], and ozone (O_3) [e.g. 8, 42, 329, 361] were the pollutants most frequently analyzed besides particulate matter. While high ozone concentrations are rather

---

[5] A more recent cross-country analysis for the years 1988–1997 is given by [147] but it has the disadvantage that fewer countries are covered and that the excess mortality measurement is more complicated. Nevertheless, the same trends are covered in both publications.

[6] Results from the linear regression of Minimum Monthly Temperature (MMT) on Excess Winter Deaths (EWD): EWD = $\alpha + \beta$ MMT are $\alpha = 7.72$, $\beta = 0.67$, $p_\beta < 0.0014$, $r^2 = 0.4502$.

[7] Another exception is the impact of "space proton flux" in seasonal mortality [359]. This effect is considered by me (R.R.) to be only of marginal importance if at all.

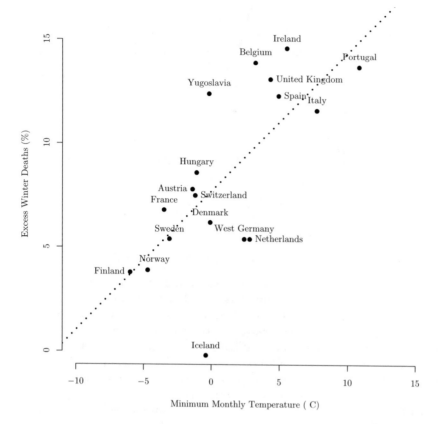

Fig. 2.2. Excess Winter Mortality in Several European Countries
Data Source: McKee 1989 [252, p. 179]

common during summer, the other substances can be labeled "winter type" air pollution [365, p. 547]. As nicely presented in Touloumi et al. [364] for SO_2, smoke and CO_2, the emission of these pollutants peaks typically in winter. The main reason for these peaks is the extensive usage of fossil fuels during the cold season for heating. The two causes of deaths which are most often associated with air pollution are also the two main causes of winter excess mortality: respiratory diseases [e.g. 33, 92, 93, 94, 137, 175, 206, 282, 328, 338, 364] and cardiovascular diseases [e.g. 33, 92, 94, 137, 175, 206, 328, 338]. The effects that "[s]mall particles penetrate deeply into sensitive parts of the lungs and can cause or worsen respiratory disease, such as emphysema and bronchitis, and aggravate existing heart disease" [92, p. 2] is questionable, though. Keat-

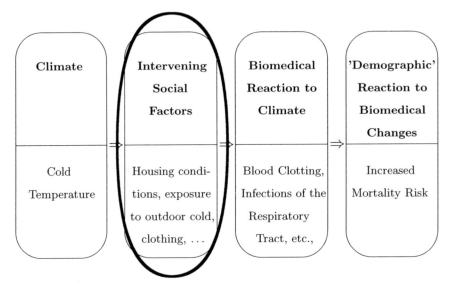

Fig. 2.3. A More Advanced Chain of Causality for Seasonality in Mortality

ing and Donaldson, arguably the two most prominent reseachers on seasonal mortality, point out in their study "Mortality Related to Cold and Air Pollution in London After Allowance for Effects of Associated Weather Patterns" that an "analysis on our data confirmed that the large, delayed increase in mortality after low temperature is specifically associated with cold and is not due to associated patterns of wind, rain, humidity, sunshine, SO_2, CO, or smoke" [189, p. 214]. Of course, it depends on the subjective point of view to decide whether an increase in mortality is due to cold or due to higher concentrations of air pollutants that have been emitted to heat houses and flats during exceptional cold spells.

Less controversially discussed is the impact of influenza vaccinations on seasonal mortality [235]. It has been shown that "vaccination against influenza is associated with reductions in the risk of hospitalization for heart disease, cerebrovascular disease, and pneumonia or influenza as well as the risk of death from all causes during influenza seasons" [273, p. 1322]. As these vaccinations are effective and cost effective to reduce influenza deaths [68], it is not surprising that an important part is attributed to them for the decreasing incidence of influenza during recent decades [e.g. 75, 78].

The remaining social factors influencing seasonal mortality can be summarized as avoiding indoor as well as outdoor cold. Various factors have been associated with a positive influence on reducing the annual cold-related death toll. Some researchers remained relatively general about the exact causes. Kunst et al. argue "that a fundamental role is played by factors closely related to socioeconomic progress" [208, p. 971]. This point of view is reiterated by Gemmell et at. [120]. Most other studies have focussed on factors associated with housing conditions [e.g. 18, 54]. The spread of central heating is argued to be the main cause for the decline in seasonality of mortality during recent decades [e.g. 16, 75, 77, 188, 251, 324, 325, 340]. District heating schemes as common in Russia [253] where heating is provided for a fixed annual sum might serve as an explanation for the small fluctuations in mortality in Russia.[8] With a heating system where your apartment can be heated as much as wanted irrespective of the costs, would avoid the often cited "fuel poverty" (=a household has to spend more than 10% of its disposable income to keep the home heated) in the UK [121, 178, 280].[9] People suffering from fuel poverty often find themselves in a vicious circle. They tend to live in houses of lower quality with poor insulation which means that they have to invest proportionally more in fuel for heating than higher quality apartments. The risk of dying during winter is further increased as dampness, condensation and mould in those apartments are more likely [121, 245, 404]. Fighting fuel poverty including poor housing conditions might not be enough, though. The behavioral component of the people should not be neglected. As shown by Keatinge for elderly people with unrestricted home heating, mortality rose for them during winter in the same manner as for individuals without this possibility — due probably to the "residents' preference for open windows and no heating at night" [187, p. 732].

But "warm housing is not enough" [186, p. 166]. It is equally important to avoid exposure to outdoor cold as its impact is independent of indoor cold [98]. From a public policy perspective, this can be performed by building windproof bus shelters and in extreme cases heated waiting rooms [186]. On the individual level, increased car ownership has probably also influenced the decrease in seasonal mortality fluctuations over time [75, 77, 188]. The most influential component on the individual level is adequate clothing worn outdoors. Several articles give evidence that people in colder regions wear warmer clothes when they leave the house during winter than their counterparts in warmer regions [76, 80, 81, 97, 98, 186]. In addition, on extremely cold days, the mortality risk is lowered if the time spent outdoors is reduced [76].[10]

Surprisingly, there is not much literature in the field of seasonal mortality on the "classical" social mortality determinants such as income, deprivation, wealth, marital status, education, occupation, . . . [e.g. 124, 168, 195, 210, 234, 314]. To my knowledge no study at all so far has addressed the question whether married people experience smaller annual fluctuations in mortality

---

[8] I would like to thank Arseniy Karkach for explaining to me the Russian system of heating. Another reason for the minor differences between winter and summer mortality in Russia is, unfortunately, the relatively high summer mortality due to accidents [253].

[9] The British government started a programme that by 2010 "no vulnerable household [. . .] need to risk ill health, or worse, because of a cold home" [178, p. 510].

[10] Again, British people present divergent behavior: the study of Goodwin et al. [127] showed that the duration of outside excursions of younger as well as elderly people did not differ between summer and winter.

than divorced, widowed or single individuals, an association which could be expected from previous studies on mortality in general [e.g. 125, 129, 163]. The analyses in Chapters 4 and 5 include besides other factors also marital status. They represent therefore a novel approach in seasonal mortality research.

While the negative social gradient is well known for mortality in general, the impact of economic factors such as deprivation, income, wealth, social class, etc. is still discussed ambiguously [16, 79, 147, 213, 214, 215, 342, 376]. Surprisingly most of these analyses — regardless of whether they support or oppose an effect — studied the same country (UK) using similar methods based on ecological data.

Literature on the influence of nutrition on seasonal mortality is sparse. Woodhouse and Khaw hypothesize that low Vitamin C intakes during the cold season may increase cardiovascular risk by raising fibrinogen levels in the blood [194, 411]. As pointed out in the review article of Ness and Powles [272, p. 1], "[a]lthough null findings may be underreported the results are consistent with a strong protective effect of fruit and vegetables for stroke and a weaker protective effect on coronary heart disease." Thus, the seasonal consumption of fruits and vegetables (lower in winter than in summer) may also play an important role for seasonal mortality [60]. The other side of the coin is highlighted by Kloner et al [199]. They assume that "overindulgence" in food, salt and alcohol consumption during the Christmas period might contribute to excess winter mortality.

2.2.4 Summary

The influence of seasonal factors on mortality has been well-known for more than 2000 years. Surprisingly, the exact mechanism of how a change in ambient temperature increases mortality is not yet full understood. Only a negligible proportion of these excess winter deaths is actually caused by hypothermia. The causes of death that contribute most to the seasonal mortality pattern are cardiovascular, cerebrovascular, and respiratory diseases. Contradicting intuition, the often cited influenza (which belongs, of course, to respiratory diseases) causes less than two percent of excess winter deaths either directly or indirectly. The major biomedical reactions to cold temperature in the body which have been singled out so far are increased risks for blood clotting via higher haemoconcentration (⇒ cardiovascular and cerebrovascular diseases) and for infections of the airways (⇒ respiratory diseases). This approach, however, could not explain the "seasonality paradox": countries with relatively cold winter temperatures (e.g. Sweden, Canada) experience consistently lower excess winter mortality than countries with warm or moderate climate (e.g. Portugal or the UK). Therefore, social factors have be referred to. Influenza vaccinations may have helped to reduce seasonal mortality over time. But as this cause of death is only of borderline significance nowadays and inoculations are available all over Europe, this can not be used as an argument to explain the observed large differences within Europe in the 1990s.

Also the impact of air pollution is questioned. If there is any agreement at all in the literature on seasonal mortality, it is the positive impact of a warm indoor climate in connection with central heating and a high standard in the quality of housing. This constitutes a "conditio sine qua non" as no scientist in this field denies the importance. It is usually supplemented by the advice to also avoid cold stress outdoors by wearing adequate clothing, reduced time spent outdoors and using bus shelters or possibly a car. The impact of socio-economic factors measured, for example, as social class or deprivation, finds support as well as opposing opinions in the literature on cold-related mortality. Other factors, such as lack of exercise, smoking [246], or the amount of public spending on health care [147] have not been investigated in detail so far. The impact of marital status has not been investigated so far at all. The question whether people who are living alone face higher excess mortality risks during winter has only been addressed once so far — without any significant finding [405]. Although many studies have been completed up to this point, further research is required in order to reduce the annual number of excess winter deaths — a figure, which outnumbers heat-related deaths considerably.

2.3 Seasonal Mortality from a Historical Perspective

2.3.1 Introduction

The following sections review the literature on seasonal mortality from a historical perspective. The main results are briefly presented over time and by age. Special attention is given to the potential impact of social factors already in historical times. The division of sub-chapters is driven by the origins of data:

Seasonal Mortality before 1400. No written records are available for the time before 1400. Therefore, mainly archaeological studies exist.

Seasonal Mortality between 1400 and 1800. Most studies using parish register data to disclose the annual fluctuations in mortality start in the 15th or 16th century.

Seasonal Mortality from 1800 until the Present. With the introduction of modern censuses, the quality of the data improved greatly. Therefore, it was useful to make another distinction for the turn of the 19thcentury. Since the middle of the 20th century, these aggregate level government statistics have been gradually supplemented and or substituted with retrospective surveys, prospective follow-up studies, register data, etc. Both kinds of data sources have greatly improved our understanding of seasonal mortality.

2.3.2 Seasonal Mortality before 1400

Introduction, Data & Methods

The main problem researchers face when analyzing (seasonal) mortality patterns for this period is the lack of written death records. Two data sources, which have been extensively studied by Walter Scheidel [330, 331, 332, 333, 334] provide, nevertheless, a sound basis for the analysis of seasonal mortality: for Roman Egypt, information can be derived from mummy labels or from funery inscriptions. Several samples have been collected there covering between 109 and 172 individuals. Data from the ancient city of Rome provide the best data-source for the analysis of antique seasonal mortality: Below the streets, thousands of inscriptions were found in the Chrisian catacombs, where the early Christians buried the deceased in niches. The trustworthiness of these data stem on the hand from the large sample-size: depending on the study between 568 and 3,725 inscriptions originating from the 3rd to the 6th century were analyzed [331, 343]. On the other hand, the reported dates of death and/or burial are expected to be considerably accurate. As Scheidel points out "[T]hese early Christians were anxious to record precise days of death and/or burial of the deceased since the moment of death was considered the beginning of true life in eternity" [331, p. 139]. These early Christians did not only report date of burial, they also frequently denoted the approximate length of life. Therefore a rough analysis by age-group can be performed as well.

In contrast to these studies set in countries with a warm, Mediterranean climate, Fichter and Volk analyzed a population with harsher environmental conditions in a region which would now be part of South-West Germany and France [106].

Results

We can see in Figure 2.4 that Roman Egypt, as well as the ancient city of Rome, both exhibit a summer peak. The one in Ancient Rome (Figure 2.4) is mainly generated by infectious diseases. It has been argued before and is now verified by modern biomolecular methods that the single most important cause of death in Rome was endemic falciparian malaria [326, 330, 333]. In addition to the relatively high temperatures in the Mediterranean climate, the spread of these diseases was facilitated by the poor sanitary standards in conjunction with a high population density [339].

The earlier peak in Egypt as shown in Figure 2.4 is misleading. At a first glance, it would suggest that the same infectious diseases of Rome — which are dependent on stable high temperatures — "would have spread, killed, and run out of steam earlier in the year than in Italy" [331, p. 153]. There is little doubt that the population in Egypt also had to suffer from high mortality in summer. However, we now know that the peak was even earlier

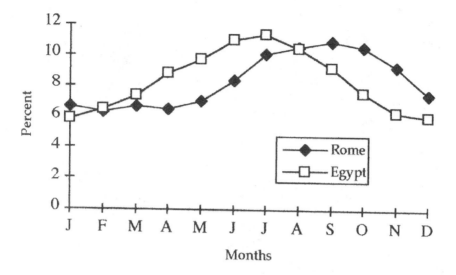

Fig. 2.4. Seasonal Distribution of Deaths: Rome and Egypt
Source: Scheidel 1996 [331, p. 155]

than Figure 2.4 suggests: While the date of death has been recorded in the Roman catacombs, the dates on the mummy labels in Egypt usually indicate the end of the mummification process [332]. This means that the actual death occurred about 70 days before the given date, implying a peak in mortality not in summer but in April/May. One can only speculate about the main causes of death: dysentery, typhoid, and tuberculosis. The main "killer" in Rome - malaria - seems to be unlikely as Walter Scheidel pointed out [334]: The annual onset of Malaria usually coincided with the fall of the Nile which happened in the fall and not in sping. However, we are far from being able to generalize that this peak is a general population pattern: adult ages are over-represented while children and elderly people are hardly among the mummies.[11]

With the presence of some information on age, we are able to further investigate the seasonal pattern, at least for Ancient Rome. Figure 2.5 shows the seasonal distribution of deaths for 20–49 year old people in the upper picture and in the lower picture for people above age 50 and 60, respectively. Elderly people still exhibit a peak in summer. However, the extent is less pronounced than at younger ages (cf. Fig. 2.5: 20–49years: 180; 50+years: 140). The risks for the elderly lurk in other months: While their younger counterparts show a below-par mortality in winter, mortality is elevated for people above age 50 during that period. Brent Shaw attributes this rise in winter to the higher susceptibility of elderly people to "winter" diseases such as respi-

---

[11] I would like to thank Prof. Walter Scheidel, now at Stanford University, for the valuable information he gave in our e-mail correspondence.

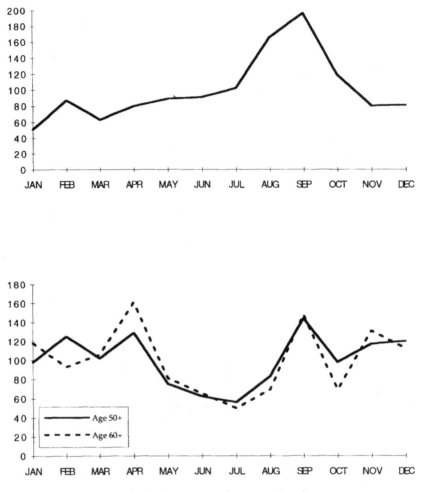

Upper Graph: Ages 20–49 (N=857);
Lower Graph: Ages 50+, 60+ (N=313);

Fig. 2.5. Seasonal Mortality in Ancient Rome by Age
Source: Shaw 1996 [343, p. 120]

ratory infections [343]. It is interesting to note that the differences between men and women have been fairly small. Figure 2.6 shows that both sexes have highest mortality late in summer. With the exception of the months August to October, mortality is evenly distributed throughout the year.[12] The only difference we have observed is that women's susceptibility towards the environmental hazards of summer begins earlier and is not as excessively high as men's fluctuations.

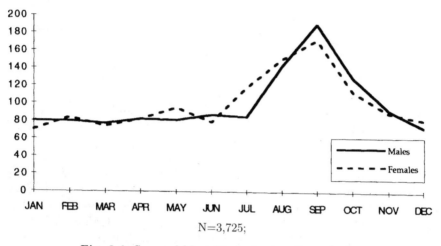

Fig. 2.6. Seasonal Mortality in Ancient Rome by Sex
Source: Shaw 1996 [343, p. 117]

The study of Fichter and Volk of the cemeteries in Sasbach-Behans and Bischof-fingen-Bigärten had to be conducted carefully [13] and resulted in a peak in winter. More specifically, the mortality maximum was reached "in the last phase of winter and in the portions of spring and autumn closest to winter" [106, p. 57]. Similar to the Roman findings, no significant differences could be detected for women and men.[14] The authors suggested that the peak in winter was probably caused by infectious diseases. However, their reasoning is founded on a vague basis: especially bones with a "winter orientation" showed malformations which are typical of severe anemia. "This blood disease causes a deficiency of those components which convey in the blood the vital oxygen

---

[12] The less stable pattern of women may be explained by a smaller sample size. A separate number of women and men in addition to the whole sample size is not given in the literature.

[13] They had to overcome several methodological problems since the date of death has been derived from the angle people have been buried. According to Fichter and Volk [106], people in that region during that era were buried in the direction where the sun rose in the morning on the day of the interment. Consequently, people could have been buried in the same direction although the burial seasons were different. The maximum difference is 6 months, when person A died on 21 March and person B on 21 September.

[14] Also children showed the same pattern.

to the tissues. The chronic oxygen deficiency in the tissues leads to a severly increased susceptibility to infection as a consequence of lowered resistance" [106, p. 56].

Problematic Studies

Besides these studies with relatively large sample sizes, there are several, mainly archaeological, approaches using indirect methods to estimate the seasonal distribution of deaths in pre-historic populations.

The study for the period that is probably the longest time ago is the analysis by Klevezal and Shislina of cementum annual layers in teeth from human skeletons [198]. They analyzed five skeletons from the Bronze Age found in Kalmyckia. Two out of them had no cementum layers. The remaining three individuals are supposed to have died in spring/early summer (2) and in late winter (1). This approach can be questioned in several perspectives. Obviously, a sample of three does not allow to for any conclusions to be drawn about the general seasonal pattern in a population. One may also doubt the methodological approach. This so-called Tooth Cementum Annulation (TCA) Method allows to estimate the age of the subject better than previous morphological methods [409, 410]. As shown in Figure 2.7,[15] teeth display similar patterns as trees. The biological basis for these rings is still questioned. According to Lieberman [222] it is related to seasonal variation in diet and growth. Consequently, Klevezal and Shislina tried to use this method to assess the season of death of humans, as done successfully before for several mammalian species [100]. The opinion of experts on the TCA method for human seasonal mortality studies [100, 408] and the fact that only one study has been conducted so far raises serious doubts about the validity of the method.

Another indirect approach has been performed by Christine White in 1993 [401]. She analyzed the hair of 15 mummies found in the Nubian desert (part of The Sudan) dating from AD 350–1300. The rationale of the study is the differential carbon composition of C_3- and of C_4-plants which are seasonally cultivated and consumed.[16] These C_3 and C_4 diets have a strong influence on the $\delta^{13}C$ content of hair. Analyzing the $\delta^{13}C$ of hair near the root and the skin of these mummies reflects relatively accurately the diet at about the time of death [401]. "The point in the seasonal cycle when the individual died is determined by how the $\delta^{13}C$ value closest to the scalp relates to values representing previous months. An individual whose $\delta^{13}C$ becomes increasingly lighter from the first to the fourth segments must have died well into the season when more C_4 plants were consumed" [401, p.664]. Christine White's

---

[15] I would like to thank Prof. Dr. Ursula Wittwer-Backofen, Dr. Alexander Fabig and Uta Cleven from the Tooth Laboratory at the Max Planck Institute for Demographic Research for the picture.

[16] C_3 such as wheat, barley as well as most fruits and vegetables are eaten in winter; C_4-plants such as sorghum and millet are part of the summer diet.

Fig. 2.7. Human Tooth Cementum under the Light Microscope

results echo the previous results for Rome and Roman Egypt, though on a less statistical foundation due to the small sample size. First, 11 out of 15 mummies died in summer indicating a peak in mortality during the warm season. Secondly, no substantial differences between women and men could be detected.

Summary

The available evidence lets us conclude that during these early historical times, there were two opposing seasonal mortality regimes: In rather warm regions (Roman Egypt, Rome, The Sudan) mortality peaked during the warm season. This peak was probably caused by infectious diseases such as falciparian malaria. Higher temperatures caused an earlier spread of diseases and, consequently, hotter regions experienced the peak earlier in the summer. Cold regions, contrastingly, showed maximum mortality in winter. The season with the least number of deaths was spring and early summer.

Demographic phenomena can be explained by three mechanisms: bad data (Level-0), direct effect (Level-1) and compositional effects (Level-2) [382, 383]. One must be very careful to avoid Level-0 and Level-2 effects when interpreting and, especially, generalizing the results of the archaeological studies. There are too many potential trapdoors for an unrepresentative sample [155]: First, samples with less than 100 analyzable individuals are unlikely to yield satisfactory interpretations of mortality patterns. Secondly, does the sample really resemble the population in its age-structure? As we have seen briefly (ancient Rome), people at different ages show different seasonal patterns. Thirdly, is the sample representative for the whole period? Maybe it was a special burial site for people with certain characteristics? "Given that most samples will be subject, differentially, to biases at a variety of levels, comparative studies based on palaeodemographic data cannot realistically be considered reliable *without careful control for those biases.*" [155, page 151, emphasis in original document].

2.3.3 Seasonal Mortality Between 1400 and 1800

Introduction

The first modern census has been conducted in Sweden in 1748 [360]. Most European countries did not follow until the beginning or the middle of the 19th century. Statistical analyzes of seasonal mortality, however, did not have to rely on archaeological data and methods any longer to study (seasonal) mortality between (about) 1400 and 1800. The introduction of parish registers enabled researchers to investigate historical population patterns. Two approaches have been used since: First, parish registrations have been aggregated to give weekly figures for vital events. These counts have been published in England as *Bills of Mortality* [154, p. 145]. The scientific value of these numbers had been recognized as early as 1662, when John Graunt first published *Natural and Political Observations Mentioned in a Following Index and Made Upon the Bills of Mortality* [130], which displays "all of the characteristics of modern, empirical research" [406, p. 5][17]. These bills of mortality did not only include the number of deaths but also the cause of death.The second approach started after World War II, when "French scholars began to apply a new technique to nominative records of the période préstatistique, i.e. the period for which government statistics were not readily available" [323, p. 537]. The most prominent among these researchers was Louis Henry. His method of applying the method of family reconstitution to parish registers has been named after him, the *Henry method* [318]. Even the critics [320] acknowledge that the approach to reconstruct the population history by using parish registers provides valuable results [146]. Depending on the country and region one could estimate the seasonal variation in mortality starting in about 1400.

---

[17] Peter Laslett actually wrote "To the trained reader Graunt writes statistical music"[212].

Seasonal Mortality over Time

Figure 2.8 shows the results of seasonal mortality over time in England between 1580 and 1837 by [415]. Each line — with the exception of the first
and last interval — represents 50 years of pooled data. The first thing we can
recognize is the relative stable pattern over time where we observe a winter
peak and a summer trough. Mortality usually peaks late in winter and reaches
a trough around July/August. Similar results have been reported for medieval
times for Westminster Abbey by Harvey and Oeppen [144]. This basic pattern
— with relatively high winter and relatively low summer mortality — is not
only stable over time but also across different geographic locations as studies
from Canada, Estonia, Finland, and France suggest [27, 45, 182, 216, 298].
The stability of seasonal mortality is even more surprising when one keeps
in mind the general mortality pattern during the *ancien régime*: First, death
rates were relatively high during that period reflected by a low level of the
parameter e_0 of about 35 years. Secondly, these high levels of mortality were
subject to immense annual fluctuations [109, 143, 161] caused by "Epidem-
ical Diseases" superimposing "Chronic Diseases" as already pointed out by
Graunt [130].

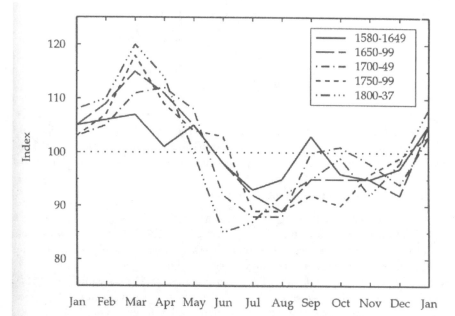

Fig. 2.8. The Seasonality of Deaths by Half-Century Periods
Source: Wrigley et al. 1997 [415, p. 325]

By comparing this modern pattern, with a peak in winter and trough in summer, to results from Italy [331], Spain [353] and parts of France [27], we detect that the following finding of Dobson for south-east England can not be attributed to being a universal phenomenon. She wrote: "The seasonal rise and fall of burials worked in the opposite direction of the movement of the thermometer — an inverse relationship that was maintained throughout the seventeenth and eighteenth centuries" [73, p. 203]. These more southern countries displayed a seasonal pattern similar to the one found in Rome 1500 years earlier: highest mortality in summer and lowest mortality in winter. Although this might lead one to assume that the main influence was the Mediterranean climate, it should be stressed that social factors were also of crucial importance in that period. By looking at Philadelphia's (Table 2.2) differences in seasonal mortality between blacks and whites, we can see that climate could not possibly shape two totally different patterns for the same time and place [197].

Table 2.2. Seasonal Mortality Ratios for Blacks and Whites in Philadelphia, 1722 and 1730

	Standardized Numbers		Standardized Ratio	
	White	Black	White	Black
Winter	81	22	86	166
Spring	75	10	86	75
Summer	122	7	130	53
Fall	98	14	104	106

Source: Klepp 1994 [197, p. 479]

While blacks seem to suffer from the highest mortality during the cold season (standardized ratio in winter and fall 166 and 106, respectively), whites experience the largest risk of death during summer (standardized ratio in summer: 130).

Two causal explanations come to mind:

- The relatively low summer mortality among blacks might by linked to a *selection effect*: Many blacks were brought to the US as slaves and have already survived some contagious diseases which typically occur during summer. As a consequence, they were immune to them.
- It can be expected that a larger proportion of this seasonal mortality differential can be explained by *social factors*: Keeping in mind the poor socio-economic conditions blacks had to suffer from during that period, one can easily imagine that blacks had insufficient protection against the

cold in winter: they were more likely to work outside and to have bad or no heating at all in their homes compared to whites.[18]

The importance of other factors other than climate on seasonal mortality during that period is also supported by other sources. As Bideau et al. showed in Dupâquier's monograph series *Histoire de la population française* [27], France varied largely in its seasonal mortality fluctuations geographically. However, the major cleavage was not between north and south but between urban and rural areas.

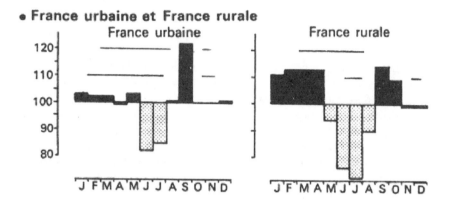

Fig. 2.9. Urban vs. Rural Seasonal Mortality Patterns in France 1740–89
Source: Bideau et al. 1988 [27, p. 240]

Rural areas in France showed a relatively modern pattern with maximum mortality during the colder half of the year and minimum mortality in summer. "Pour la France urbaine au contraire, les indices de saison froide dépassent à peine de moyenne, le creux d'été est moins marqué, mais la pointe de septembre est exceptionellement forte, sans doute parce que la conservation des ailments est encore pire en ville qu'à la campagne" [27, p. 242].[19]

This pattern and its causal explanation is not exclusively present in France. Studies from the United Kingdom point in the same direction as well: The studies from the "Cambridge Group for the History of Population and Social Structure", which focussed on the countryside of England, show a shape similar to *France rurale* [416, p. 294], whereas Landers' analysis of London resembles, rather, *France urbaine* with its summer peak until the middle of the

---

[18] Theresa Singleton's review article gives an overview of historical living conditions of blacks in the United States [348].

[19] Author's translation: "In urban France, on the contrary, the indices of the cold season were above the average, the summer trough is less pronounced, but the peak in September is exceptionally strong, without any doubt because the conservation of food was even worse in towns and cities than on the countryside".

eighteenth century [211, p. 206]. As indicated by Bideau's quotation above, we can recognize that the higher temperatures during summer were not the actual cause of death for the people. The hot weather only provided the basis for certain bacteria to develop. Only in conjunction with social factors such as high population density and bad hygienic and sanitary conditions, diseases could spread among humans and actually wipe out considerable proportions of the population. For example, during the epidemic of 1665–66, 70,594 individuals died of plague in London [12], a typical summer disease [353] transmitted by rats and flies. By the end of the 1670s, the plague was almost non-existent in London. Slack gives three possible explanations for this [350]:

- Rats, as the main carrier of the disease, became immune to the bacterium *Pasteurella Pestis*. But he considers this to be rather unlikely. He favors two other explanations:
- On the one hand, improvements had been made in the housing and living conditions such as building brick houses instead of wooden houses. There, rats had more problems spreading. But also on the individual level, major improvements had been made such as the increased usage of soap and changing bed linen more frequently.
- On the other hand, public health policies were — as surprising as it may sound — also in effect. For example, in Edinburgh 1664 restrictions were imposed on ships coming from infected ports. Almost simultaneously, the number of plague deaths diminished remarkably [350].

The erosion of the summer peak in urban areas can be nicely illustrated by the example of London. Fig. 2.10 shows the development of seasonal mortality in the capital of the British Empire between 1670 and 1779 by 25-year-periods. In the first period 1670–99 (solid black line), maximum mortality was reached in September. During the next century this peak gradually transformed into a local maximum. By the end of the eighteenth century, excess mortality during summer was almost non-existent. It is quite likely that this development can also be traced back to improvements in living conditions (hygiene, public health policies, etc.).

Seasonal Mortality by Age

Besides the development over time, it is also worthwhile to investigate the trend in seasonal mortality in various age-groups. Unfortunately, not many studies have analyzed death by month and age. In addition, it is seriously doubted whether adult mortality can be accurately estimated from the existing data. Finlay, for example, assumes that this is not possible for parts of the London Parish Registers [107]. Nevertheless, I would like to present a short analysis by age as most studies showed relatively congruent results.

Figure 2.11 presents selected age-groups from [415]. One can easily recognize two features:

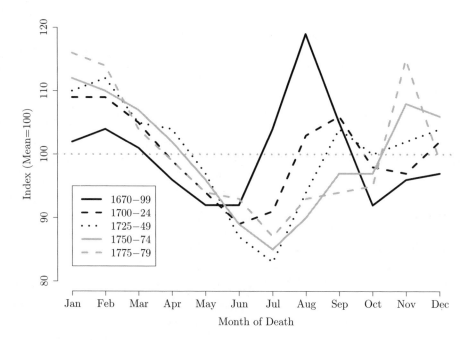

Fig. 2.10. Monthly Burial Indices in London 1670–1779 Based on Weekly Bills of Mortality

Data Source: Landers 1993 [211, p. 206]

- The older people become, the larger the differences between winter and summer.
- Except for the oldest people we can see an intermediary summer peak.

This is in accordance with Dobson who stated that the elderly were particularly susceptible to cold winter conditions [73, p. 216]. Similar results have been found for France and Canada [27, 45, 216]. The higher susceptibility of the elderly is reflected by the actual causes of death: As shown by [153] for plague mortality rates by age, younger people have a higher propensity towards summer diseases than elderly people. Whereas the proportion of plague deaths from all deaths was probably over 50 percent for children, the percentage was less than 10 percent for people aged 60 years and more [153]. The latter, however, were more affected by typical air-borne winter diseases such as tuberculosis [114, 211]. Typical diseases of winter were influenza, whooping cough, typhus, and respiratory tuberculosis. These diseases, which were mainly responsible for the winter peak, were harder to combat than just using better sanitary conditions. Duncan et al. conclude that the evolution of the whooping cough epidemics in London are directly related to two factors: pop-

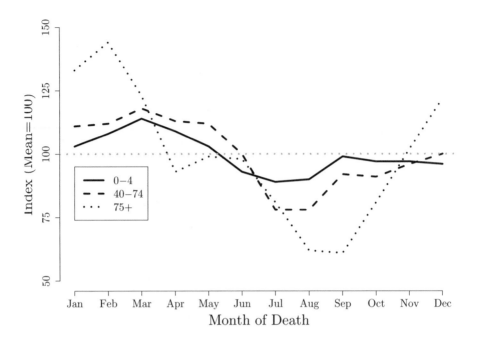

Fig. 2.11. Seasonality of Deaths by Age, England, 1580–1837
Data Source: Wrigley et al. 1997 [415, p. 326]

ulation density and malnutrition [83, p. 450]. Malnutrition is often especially singled out as one of the main causes of mortality during those times [e.g. 116, 218].[20] Richards [307], for example, estimates that the price of wheat was more important to determine mortality than winter or summer temperature. Livi-Bacci [225] also ascribes the nutritional level a clear influence on tuberculosis, whooping cough and respiratory diseases in general. This causal linkage between malnutrition, infectious diseases and high mortality has been documented well for populations during that historical period [43, 254, 399]. "Malnutrition progressively enhances infection in an individual, and [...] infection often causes further malnutrition. An ill person does not eat well, even though his metabolic needs are greater. Similarly, poorly nourished individuals rapidly exhaust protein and caloric reserves in the process of fighting infection" [43, p. 249]. It can be assumed that this mechanism did not only work during crisis years with especially poor harvest but also seasonally each year when late in winter the possibility of malnutrition was highest.

---

[20] Vladimir Shkolnikov re-iterated this assumption in a discussion during the workshop "Seasonality in Mortality", Duke University, NC, 07–08 March 2002.

Summary

The major advantage of studies examining seasonal mortality patterns between 1400 and 1800 is the basis of the data: Researchers no longer had to rely on archaeological methods to make inferences about population histories. French and British researchers (most notably Louis Henry and the "Cambridge Group for the History of Population and Social Structure") used parish registers to reconstruct demographic events of populations.

The general pattern observed for seasonal mortality in many countries resembles modern findings rather closely: deaths peak late in winter and hit a trough around July/August. English data suggest that seasonality was not equal across all age-groups. The older the people the higher the differences between winter and summer mortality.

The modern pattern with a peak in winter and a trough in summer is not found everywhere, though. Several examples show that within the same climatic region, different seasonality regimes persist which could not be explained, consequently, by climatic variation but rather by social factors: socioeconomic differences may be the root for the differential in seasonal mortality between blacks and whites in 18th century Philadelphia. Poor hygienic situations allowed a summer peak in urban regions of France and the UK ($\sim$ London). Malnutrition is the most likely cause for excess mortality during winter for the elderly.

2.3.4 Seasonal Mortality from 1800 until Present Times

Introduction

The beginning of the 19th century was chosen — similar to the previous cut-off point 1400 — rather for methodological reasons rather than for a general change in seasonal mortality regimes. Sweden started to collect demographic data resembling the first modern census [360] in 1748.[21]. Many other European countries followed in subsequent decades, so researchers no longer had to rely on archaeological methods or on parish reconsitution data to construct demographic patterns. In addition to retrospective articles using those newly available country-wide official data written during recent decades, some original articles written at that time were already analyzing seasonal mortality.

With the new wealth of available data in the 19th century, scientific knowledge expanded rapidly. It is worth adding that this time period was also heavily influenced by "back to nature" ideas exemplified by Thoreau's "Walden" [24]. It comes, thus, as no surprise that scientists became interested in the impact of nature on human health [156]. A typical example is the article "An Attempt to Determine the Influence of the Seasons and Weather on Sickness and Mortality" by Guy and Cantab in 1843 [136] or the analysis of mortality

---

[21] The population count of Quebec in 1666 can merely be called a prototype of a census [9]

in "Remote Corners of the World" by Westergaard in 1880 [400] as he called the Faroe Island and Greenland.

Since the middle of the 20th century, new data collection methods have become widespread. The introduction of retrospective surveys, prospective cohort follow-ups,... allowed to investigate phenomena in more detail. One major dimension is the analysis of individual level data. While previously, data were typically aggregated, the usage of individual level data allowed relating the phenomenon of interest with covariates without the problem of the ecological fallacy [311]. The other major dimension is the time-horizon: data have typically been cross-sectional. By following cohorts over time or by asking retrospective questions in surveys, it was possible to reconstruct individuals' life-courses which makes it easier to find out which variables (e.g. long-time smoker) change the risk for an individual to experience a certain event (e.g. death). Typical examples in the field of seasonal mortality are van Rossum et al. [376] for a cohort follow up and Donaldson et al. [81] for a retrospective survey. The various (social) factors which have been associated with excess winter mortality have been discussed in Section 2.2.

Seasonal Mortality over Time

The analysis of seasonal mortality by period exhibits two patterns and one unconfirmed recent pattern:

Pattern 1: Loss of Summer Peak An intermediary summer peak disappeared over time if it existed at the beginning of the observation period. European countries with colonies were especially prone to such a sudden increase in mortality during the hot season. McKeown and Record (1962) [255] suggest for England that typical summer epidemics such as cholera were brought to Europe from India. An illustrative example is shown in Figure 2.12. The gray dashed line displays the seasonality pattern observed for the urban French population in the middle of the 19th century. It is reminiscent of Figure 2.9 (page 25) which plotted the pattern of France observed less than one hundred years earlier: a bimodal pattern is exhibited with a minor peak in February and a maximum in September. This kind of pattern with relatively high summer mortality has been reported for London and other parts of England [11, 221, 304], too. Roughly sixty years later, summer excess mortality was no longer persistent in France as indicated by the solid black line. The highest number of deaths was observed in February, whereas September has been transformed from the month with highest mortality to minimum mortality. This shift, of course, can not be the outcome of a climatic change during such a short period of time. Clearly, social factors have to be attributed to this development. The cause for this loss of the summer peak is most likely a considerable

improvement in hygiene which almost completely eradicated intestinal
diseases, the major reason for excess summer mortality [26, p. 283].[22]

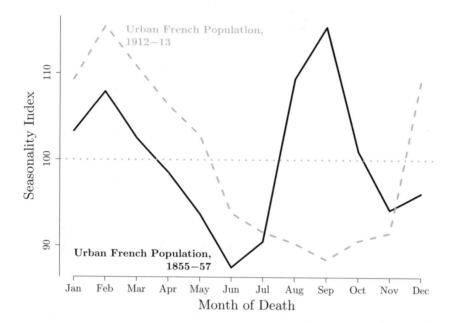

Fig. 2.12. Seasonality of Deaths in Urban France 1855–57 and 1912–13
Data Source: Bideau et al. (1988, p. 285) [26]

Pattern 2: Decline in Seasonality In 1912, March [240] noted that no European country he had analyzed showed a local summer peak.[23] Highest
mortality was found between January and March, minimum mortality
typically occured late in summer. One consequence of the disappearance of the summer peak was an increase in the differences between
winter and summer deaths. During the following decades the annual
mortality amplitude remained relatively stable. Only by the middle of
the 20[th]century did seasonal fluctuations decrease. This development has
been reported for various countries such as Japan, the United States,
Spain, the Netherlands, Germany, the GDR, Northern Italy, Finland ...
[17, 99, 119, 208, 220, 224, 231, 241, 242, 268, 269, 319, 325]. The decrease

---

[22] "Le point essentiel, c'est la disparition, pour tous les ensembles considérés et pour
tous le groupes d'âges [...], de la surmortalité d'août-septembre : l'hygiène est
venue presque à bout des maladies intestinales" [26, p. 283].
[23] Those countries were: Austria, Belgium, Denmark, Finland, France, Germany,
Hungary, Italy, Norway, Scotland, Spain, Sweden.

over time did not start, however, simultaneously in all countries. Figure 2.13 displays this by giving two examples. Both panels show a measurement of seasonality where winter mortality is related to summer mortality. Because those methods differed, one can not directly compare the results in the left panel for the United Kingdom with the right panel for Finland. This nordic country shows a decreasing trend since the 1930s whereas the differences between winter and summer mortality in the UK started to become smaller only in the 1970s [63, 251].

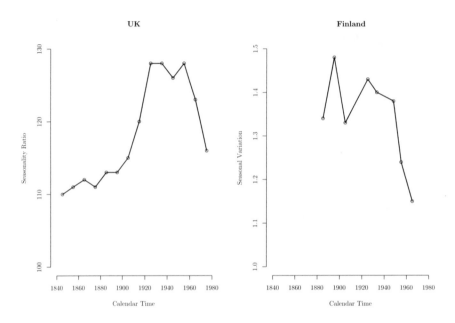

Fig. 2.13. Seasonal Mortality in the UK and Finland over Time
Coefficients for the UK and Finland are not directly comparable.
Data Source for UK: McDowall 1981 [251, p. 16]
Data Source for Finland: Näyhä 1980 [268, p. 44]

The general trend towards de-seasonalization was related to the changing composition of causes of death over time — most notably the reduction of diseases of the respiratory tract [2, 255]. Various arguments are proposed in the literature as causal factors that have influenced this decline in respiratory-related mortality. On the one hand, public health measures such as influenza vaccinations are mentioned. It is argued, though, that the remarkable declines in mortality do not coincide with the introduction of any public health measures [402]. It can be assumed, rather, that the general trend towards improved diagnosis [115] and better living conditions, especially the spread of central heating, for instance, is more likely to be the cause of this change [208, 220]. Also the possibility of less air pollution over time has been attributed to the decline in seasonality over time [e.g. 251]. Nevertheless, this decrease in seasonality did not result in a uniform distribution of mortality during the year. With the exception of Iceland, considerable differences still exist between mortality during the hot and cold season in all countries [135, 147, 252].[24]

Unconfirmed recent development: Recently, a new trend has been observed for the United States: Feinstein [102] reports an increase in seasonality of mortality for the elderly since the mid-1970s, a finding for which Seretakis et al. [340] found some indications as well in their analysis of seasonal mortality from coronary heart disease. It is argued that this is not caused by an increase of mortality during winter but by an accelerated decrease of mortality during summer: "If the reversal is real, then it could reflect the increase in use of air-conditioning" [340, p. 1014].

Seasonal Mortality by Age

The first detailed analysis of seasonal mortality by age was conducted for Belgium by Adolphe Quetelet [300] in his study: "De l'influence des saisons sur la mortalité aux différens ages dans la Belgique".[25] Data from the Appendix of his monograph were taken to produce the two panels in Figure 2.3.4. Results are shown in the left part of the figure for women and in the right part for men. A dashed gray line indicates the value for a uniform distribution ($\frac{1}{12} = 8.\overline{3}\%$). In both cases the relative contribution of the numbers of death from each month have been calculated, standardizing each month to the same length. The general trend is easily visible: seasonal fluctuations become bigger with increasing age. The youngest age-group shown here still displays a slight secondary peak during summer. Nevertheless this sudden rise is still below average mortality (=lower than the dashed gray line). At more advanced ages, this peak is non existent. Excess mortality during winter is steadily increasing with age. Although January and February make up only one sixth of the whole year, their contribution to all deaths for women as well as for men above age 90 (gray dashed line) is about one quarter of all deaths for each sex.

During recent decades, studies of seasonality in mortality have rarely focused on the influence of age — despite its paramount influence on mortal-

---

[24] The lack of differences in mortality between winter and summer in Iceland has been attributed to the widespread availability of low cost geothermal energy which makes it easy to keep a warm indoor climate [252].

[25] It is worth mentioning a few highlights of Adolphe Quetelet's biography [cf. 177]: Among his professors were Poisson and Laplace; the *Quetelet Index* was invented by him, nowadays often called *Body-Mass-Index* (BMI); while he is mostly remembered for his work as a social statistician, he started as a mathematician, changed to physics where he specialized in astronomy; this brought him to meteorology. The study of climate was the stepping stone for him to analyze the influence of the seasons on mortality.

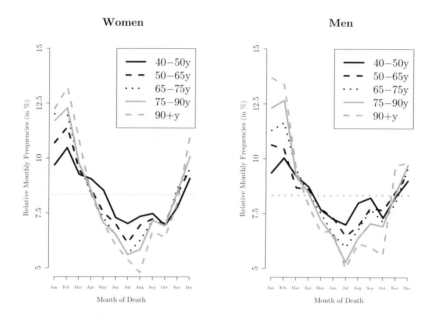

Fig. 2.14. Seasonal Distribution of Deaths, Belgium, 1830s
Data Source: Quetelet 1838 [300, p. 37–38]

ity in general [cf. 314]. Sometimes no age distinction was made at all [e.g. 13, 21, 319, 367] which turns out to be especially problematic if comparisons are made over time or across countries. If any age-effect exists, such comparisons may lead to erronenous conclusions because of the varying age-composition in the analyzed populations. Many other studies controlled for age or performed analyses for separate age-groups. Unfortunately, the highest included age or the beginning of the last, open-ended, age-category is chosen at an age after which most deaths in a population occur. For instance, Huynen et al. [169] uses a category "≥ 65 years of age", the maximum age-category in the "Eurowinter Study" was "65–74 years" [98]; at those ages, however, most people are still alive in Western populations at present [cf. 165]. The conclusions drawn from those studies are not necessarily wrong, but they may simplify or blur the relationship between age and seasonal fluctuations in mortality. Only a few studies investigated seasonal mortality into advanced ages [102, 232, 251, 262, 268]. One study [309] even analyzed seasonal mortality among centenarians and supercentenarians (110 years and older).

According to Robine, demographers assume that "mortality measures essentially the current conditions: the quality of the ecological and social environment. For biologists, mortality measures mainly the ageing process" [310, p. 911]. If we combine these two assumptions, we could postulate that during winter, when environmental conditions are especially challenging, mortality is

United States, 1994−1998

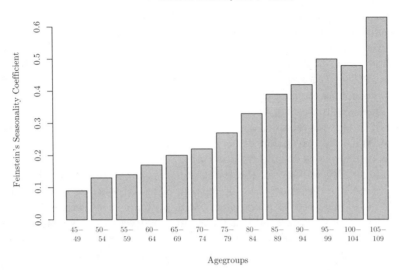

England and Wales, by Sex, 1970−72

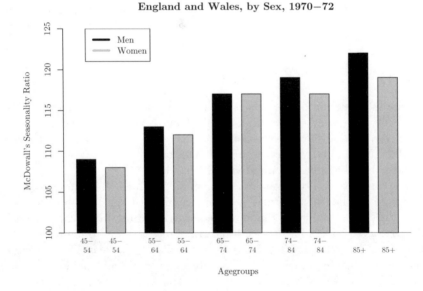

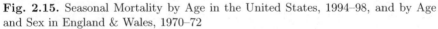

Fig. 2.15. Seasonal Mortality by Age in the United States, 1994–98, and by Age and Sex in England & Wales, 1970–72
  Data Source for the Unites States: Feinstein 2002 [102, p. 472]
  Data Source for England & Wales: McDowall 1981 [251, p. 17]

higher than in summer. In addition to the increasing mortality at higher ages, we can assume that seasonal mortality fluctuations increase with age. This hypothesis finds support in most studies which incorporated age. In Figure 2.15, results are plotted by age for the United States for the years 1994–1998 in the upper panel based on the study by Feinstein [102]. The lower panel shows data from McDowall [251] covering England and Wales during the years 1970–1972 for women (gray) and men (black). Feinstein's [102] study has been chosen as an example as it contains detailed results until 109 years of age. These estimates are based on Social Security data and are therefore considered to be very reliable. We can see that seasonality gradually increases with age. With the exception of people 100–104 years old, every age-group seems to be more susceptible to seasonal effects than women and men five years younger. By looking at the lower panel with the results for England and Wales, we can recognize that the pattern observed over age in the United States is not obfuscated by a sex effect. Still, an increase of seasonality with age is detected with women and men showing relatively similar results. This sounds puzzling to mortality researchers as women and men vary considerably throughout their whole life course in their age-specific mortality rates. Thus, one could assume that women are less susceptible to environmental effects than men and should, consequently, display smaller differences between winter and summer mortality. The lack of any significant sex differences with regard to seasonal mortality is, however, a common finding in many studies [e.g. 98, 121, 262, 419].

Summary

With the introduction of the census, it was possible to obtain more reliable information than previously with indirect methods. Starting in the middle of the 20th century, new data collection methods became commonplace like cohort follow-ups and retrospective surveys. This enabled researches to conduct longitudinal analyses based on individual level data.

Over time two major developments can be outlined. If a summer peak still existed in the 19th century, it disappeared until the beginning of the 20th century. The decline of this intermediary rise in mortality can be most likely attributed to less incidences of intestinal diseases due to improvements in hygiene. The following decades were marked by a decreases in the winter/summer mortality differences. Most articles, as already pointed out in Section 2.2, traced this development back to the widespread introduction of central heating or general improvements in living conditions. This development did not lead to an evening out of differences between mortality in winter and summer. With the exception of Iceland, remarkable differences still exist between the cold and the hot season with respect to mortality. Recent analyses for the US found an increase in seasonality again which is probably caused by an accelerated decrease of mortality during summer with the increased use of air-conditioning.

The first detailed study on the effect of the season in mortality which took the factor age explicitly into account was conducted by Quetelet in 1838 [300]. His findings are still in accordance with modern studies: With increasing age, seasonal fluctuations in mortality are gradually becoming larger. This is in accordance with the theory that mortality measures the aging process of the body as well as the subjective environmental conditions for the individual. Common sense suggests that women should have smaller seasonal fluctuations than men as their lower age-specific mortality rates throughout their whole life-course reflect less susceptibility to environmental hazards. Surprisingly, many studies could not detect any significant differences between the seasonal fluctuations in mortality of women and men.

3

Measuring Seasonality

3.1 Introduction

Public health measures aim to improve the health of the people. For that purpose, it is an absolute necessity to discover the origins of diseases. If diseases, and ultimately mortality, occur seasonally, "an environmental factor has to be considered in the etiology of that disease" [244, p. 275]. An enormous diversity of causes of death has been related to seasonal incidence: cardiovascular diseases [420], asthma [40], infectious diseases [260], diarrhea and cholera [31, 391], suicide [139], and congenital malformations [90, 184] to name only a few.

The aim of this chapter is to present the methods that have been suggested and/or employed in the literature and to discuss their advantages and disadvantages by using hypothetical and real data. From a methodological point of view, one can basically distinguish between two categories of studies. On the one hand, studies that test for the existence of seasonal trends and, on the other hand, studies that examine whether certain covariates are correlated with seasonal fluctuations in mortality. The latter group has already been briefly presented in [139]. A thorough discussion of all methods is not the scope of the present study: it is almost unfeasible to inspect all methods such as correlation analysis, regression analysis (linear, logistic, Poisson, ...), analysis of variance (ANOVA), etc., which have been employed for studies of seasonality.

This chapter is only concerned with the first group, i.e. statistical approaches to detect, measure and test seasonality. Thus, we remained in a univariate framework by not including any covariates apart from time or age. Within the methods analyzed, we can make a further distinction into three subdivisions:

- *Indices* to Measure the Extent of Seasonality
- *Statistical Tests* for Seasonality
- *Time-series Methods* for Seasonality

The rationale behind these methods will be introduced and is followed by a discussion of the their respective pros and cons. The three groups will then be faced with hypothetical and real data to evaluate how sensitive they are to various sample sizes and different distributions. The last part of this chapter will summarize the findings and give recommendations which method should be applied in which situation.

The presented and evaluated time-series methods have already been implemented by various statistical computer packages. Apart from one test (χ^2-Goodness-of-Fit test), no ready-to-use software was available for any of the indices or tests. Therefore, these indices and tests have been implemented in the R-language [170, 301]. The actual code can be obtained from the author.

3.2 Seasonality Indices

3.2.1 Introduction

Most researchers did not perform any statistical test to analyze if a seasonal pattern is present in a population or not. Instead, they used some descriptive tools to characterize the pattern they found in their data. The simplest representations are monthly death counts. This method was especially widespread among scientists of the 19th century, as they did not have any sophisticated methods or computers at their disposal. Tulloch's analysis, for example, examined the seasonality in mortality among the British Troops in the West Indies by revealing monthly death counts [368].

However, even some early researchers used some descriptive tools that are still common nowadays. In 1912, Lucien March calculated an index for which he standardized the annual number of deaths to 1,000 [240]. Thus, values above $83\frac{1}{3}$ indicated above average mortality; values below $83\frac{1}{3}$ stood for mortality less than what could be expected from a uniform distribution of deaths across the twelve months. Many recent studies used by and large the same standardization. But instead of a radix of 1,000, the preferred choice is 1,200. Thus, the expected number for each month in a uniform distribution is 100 which makes it more apprehensible for users of the decimal system to detect above- and below-par mortality.

For example, the "Cambridge Group for the History of Population and Social Structure" used this index in their explorations of English population history [415, 416]. Studies on contemporary mortality also use this "100-Index" [e.g. 101] which is easy to calculate and interpret.

Besides writing a table with the number of counts or the values of monthly mortality rates, there are also other possibilities to make the seasonal distribution of deaths comparable over time and/or across populations. The easiest way is a barplot with 12 categories representing the months on the x-axis and the usage of bars or lines to represent the actual monthly values (see Figure 3.1 as an example).

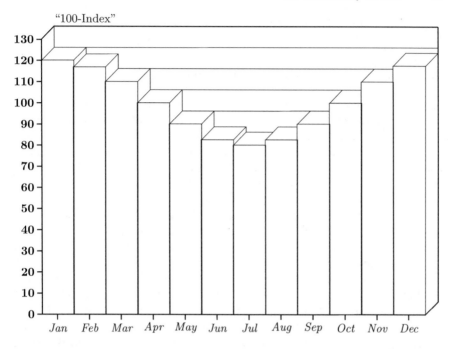

Fig. 3.1. Graphical Representation of Seasonal Mortality Data (Hypothetical Data)

3.2.2 Winter/Summer Ratio

However, a mere graphical description fails to satisfy a researcher as the judgment in comparing two populations (or one across time) depends largely on eyesight. Thus, statisticians have employed countless indices to describe data with one number (e.g. the median as measure of central tendency for an ordinal variable). An uncomplicated index for seasonality is a mortality ratio where winter mortality is divided either by summer mortality or by the average mortality during the year. With the index φ_1 in Equation 3.1, we opted to divide the number of deaths in winter by the number of deaths in summer.

$$\varphi_1 = \frac{\sum\limits_{i=JAN}^{MAR} Deaths_i}{\sum\limits_{j=JUL}^{SEP} Deaths_j} \tag{3.1}$$

Such an index has several desired properties. For example, it is easy to interpret. "1" would indicate that there is no difference between summer and winter deaths. Values above one correspond to more winter than summer deaths (and vice versa). A value of 1.24 would indicate that the number of deaths is 24 percent higher in winter than in summer. Thus, it gives a measurement of the differential between winter and summer deaths but does not take into account what happens in other months. In addition, the choice for the basis of the numerator and the denominator is somehow arbitrary.

3.2.3 Concentration/Dissimilarity Indices

Most other seasonality indices can be interpreted as a measurement of concentration or of dissimilarity. Two central concepts in that area are the Lorenz-Curve and the Gini-Coefficient. The construction and the interpretation of the Lorenz-Curve is straightforward. Assume we have a population with a certain characteristic, e.g. income (which is the typical example in textbooks). The first step is to order the population by this characteristic and give each individual a rank. For each rank, one calculates the proportion of all people whose rank is smaller or equal to that rank. Simultaneously, you also compute for each rank the relative frequency of income earned by people whose rank is smaller or equal to the specific rank [4]. If you plot these two cumulative relative frequencies, the result will be a Lorenz-Curve, as shown in Figure 3.2. If the variable of interest is uniformly distributed, the result would be the solid black curve connecting the points $(0,0)$ and $(1,1)$ with a straight line. If the variable of interest is unequally distributed, the curve still starts at $(0,0)$ and ends at $(1,1)$. But it will bend and, by definition (because of the sorting procedure), must be convex to the x-axis [192] as shown by the dotted line in black in Figure 3.2.

Several indices try to express the degree of inequality in a certain population based on the Lorenz-Curve. Among them, the Gini-Coefficient is the "best known and most widely used measure of divergence [...]. It is defined as an area between the diagonal and the Lorenz Curve, divided by the whole area below the diagonal" [346, p. 310]. Despite its intuitive appeal, the Gini-Coefficient has some important drawbacks for analyzing seasonality in deaths: it is defined for continuous data. Our data, however, are usually given in discrete units i.e. months. This shortcoming is not too problematic. It has been shown before for other discrete data, that the Gini-coefficient can be adapted to this situation [e.g. 346]. More important is the following dilemma:

- Either the monthly values are ordered according to their rank as intended by this procedure. It would then be almost certain that the original order of the months is not preserved and we could only answer the question whether our data deviate from a uniform distribution or not. We cannot make any claims about the shape of the deviation.
- The other approach one could follow is not ordering the data (i.e. the first category is January, the second category is February, ...). In that case we cannot exclude the possibility that the Lorenz-Curve is crossing the diagonal and the Gini-Coefficient would be not defined for that situation. The solid gray line in Figure 3.2 indicates this: A typical seasonal distribution in an unordered way would not only cover an area in the lower right triangle for which the Gini-coefficient is defined.

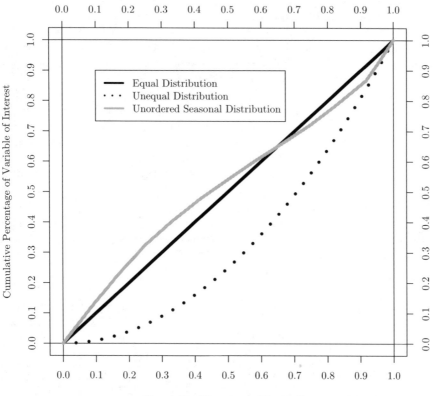

Fig. 3.2. The Lorenz Curve — Hypothetical Examples

In his study of seasonal mortality in Sweden, John Wilmoth [407] did not use the real Gini-Coefficient but a related measurement (φ_2) derived from the analysis of residential segregation [403]:

$$\varphi_2 = \frac{1}{2} \sum_{i=1}^{12} |p_i - q_i|, \tag{3.2}$$

where p_i is the *observed* proportion of deaths in month i, q_i is the *expected* proportion of deaths in month i. $\sum_{i=1}^{12} p_i = \sum_{i=1}^{12} q_i = 1$; in our case of a uniform hypothetical distribution $q_1 = q_2 = \ldots = q_{12} = \frac{1}{12}$.

As long as we use relative frequencies and a uniform hypothetical distribution, the value of φ_2 ranges from 0 in the case of equal counts in all months to 0.91666 $(= \frac{1}{2} \left(11 \times \left|0 - \frac{1}{12}\right| + 1 \times \left|1 - \frac{1}{12}\right|\right))$ in the case when events only occur in one month. Although this approach seems to be fruitful at first sight, it has a major disadvantage. For real data, the value of φ_2 does not exceed 0.1. Most emipirical distributions of deaths have a value around 0.03. Another drawback is its insensitivity to the ordering of the months. It does not take into account if a peak is followed by a trough by a peak by a trough, etc. or if there is only one peak and one trough.

Closely related to dissimilarity indices are measurements of concentration. They can also serve as an index for seasonality. The best known is entropy. This concept has been developed in information technology and measures the degree of uncertainty. It was introduced to demography in the mid 1970s by Lloyd Demetrius [65]. In popular terms, entropy tells you how safe a guess is when you do not know anything about the exact distribution of the variable of interest. In the case of a uniform distribution, your guess would be very unsafe as each category would be equally probable. Entropy, in this case, would reach its maximum value. If one uses a standardized index, entropy would be 1. If the distribution is getting closer to a monopolistic situation, entropy approaches zero. A relative entropy index (φ_3) with a defined maximum of 1 serves as our seasonality index [392, p. 22f]:

$$\varphi_3 = \frac{H(A)}{H(A)_{max}} = \frac{\log_2(n) - \frac{1}{n}\sum\limits_{i=1}^{12} n_i \log_2(n_i)}{\log_2 k} = \frac{\log_2(n) - \frac{1}{n}\sum\limits_{i=1}^{12} n_i \log_2(n_i)}{\log_2 12}, \tag{3.3}$$

where n_i is the number of events in month i and $\sum\limits_{i=1}^{k(=12)} n_i = n$; $\log_2$ is the logarithmus dualis, the logarithm to the base 2.

3.3 Tests for Seasonality

Besides these descriptive measurements, several statistics have been proposed to test for seasonality. They can be broken down into three groups: the χ^2-Goodness-of-Fit test and the "Kolmogorov-Smirnov-Type-Statistic" belong both to the group of *Goodness-of-Fit-Tests*; harmonic analyses based on Edwards' contribution [84] are members of the *Edwards' Family*. The third group consists of *Nonparametric Tests*.

3.3.1 Goodness-of-Fit-Tests

The χ^2-Goodness-of-Fit Test

The χ^2-Goodness-of-Fit Test is relatively popular for detecting seasonality because of its simple mathematical theory, which makes it easy to calculate and understand [139]. Pearson introduced the concept in 1900 [286] which can be applied to a variety of statistical problems [20]. Generally speaking, this test can be employed whenever the research question is: "In the underlying population represented by a sample are the observed cell frequencies different from the expected cell frequencies?" [344, p. 95] Thus, we test whether our empirical data can be a sample of a certain distribution with sampling error as the only source of variability [256]. Usually, this hypothetical distribution is a uniform distribution. However, there is no restriction on the underlying distribution. This test requires a sample from a population with an unknown distribution function $F(x)$ and a certain theoretical distribution function $F_0(x)$. The χ^2-Goodness-of-Fit Test examines the Null-Hypothesis $H_0 : F(x) = F_0(x)$ against the alternative hypothesis $H_A : F(x) \neq F_0(x)$. The test-statistic T is calculated as follows:

$$T = \sum_{i=1}^{k} \left[\frac{(O_i - E_i)^2}{E_i} \right] \tag{3.4}$$

where $i = 1, \ldots, k$ are the groups in the sample. For seasonality studies, the value of k is usually 12. O_i and E_i are the observed and expected cell frequencies of the ith class, respectively. If $F_0(x)$ is a uniform distribution, then $E_1 = E_2 = \ldots = E_k$.

T is under H_0 asymptotically (for $n \to \infty$) χ^2-distributed with $\nu = k - 1$ degrees of freedom [158, 321]. The χ^2-Goodness-of-Fit Test has been recently used, for instance, for the analysis of seasonality in suicide, myocardial infarction, diarrhea, pneumonia and overall mortality [110, 149, 207, 308, 345, 369, 391]. The major problem of the test is that the value of T is not asymptotically χ^2 distributed for small sample sizes. "In this case, the χ^2 statistic has positive bias, that is, it tends to be larger than the theoretical chi-square value it is supposed to estimate" [158, p. 239]. Various rules of thumb have been proposed for when the approximation is acceptable.[1]

The typical data on seasonality do not violate any of these restrictions of the use of the χ^2-Goodness-of-Fit Test. For seasonality studies, usually $\nu = 11$ and more than the suggested 5, 10, etc. cell frequencies are observed. In addition, the result of this test does not depend on the starting point (e.g. January, February, or any other month) as does the following test in its original version [278].

---

[1] For instance:

- E_i has to be ≥ 5 for each cell [344].
- Only if $\nu \geq 8$ and $n = \sum_{i=1}^{k} O_i \geq 40$ it is allowed to have expected frequencies of 1 in some classes [321].
- $k > 2$ and $n\pi_i^0 \geq 10$ for all i [392].

A Kolmogorov-Smirnov-Type-Statistic

The original Kolmogorov-Smirnov-Goodness-of-Fit Test (KS-Test) is comparable to the χ^2-Goodness-of-Fit Test in several ways. Both approaches are
designed to test if a sample drawn from a population fits a specified distribution. In addition, the tests are not restricted to a certain class of distributions.
Unlike the χ^2-Goodness-of-Fit Test, the KS-Test does not compare observed
and expected frequencies for single classes, but rather the cumulative distribution functions between the ordered observed and expected values. This test
was introduced in 1933 by Kolmogoroff.[2] Six years later Smirnoff provided a
more elementary proof of it [204].[3] Generally speaking, the KS-Goodness-of-
Fit Test has greater power than the χ^2-Goodness-of-Fit test and "is especially
useful with small samples" [354, p. 708]. As for the χ^2-Goodness-of-Fit test,
the Null-Hypothesis $H_0 : F(x) = F_0(x)$ for all $x \in \mathbb{R}$ is tested against the
Alternative Hypothesis $H_A : F(x) \neq F_0(x)$ for at least one $x \in \mathbb{R}$. However,
the ordinary Kolmogorov-Smirnov test contains some disadvantages. The first
problem we face is that this test relies on ungrouped data from continuous
distributions [393]. Also the modified method by Kuiper in 1962 is no longer
valid "once the values [...] have been grouped into months" [113]. Another
problem is the choice of the starting point. Although January is usually taken,
it is somehow arbitrary. But — as pointed out in several articles — the result
and its interpretation depends on the starting point [e.g. 250]. If one has to
choose between (the described Pearson's) Goodness-of-Fit χ^2-test and the ordinary KS-Test, Slakter advises to use the χ^2-test as it is more valid than the
Kolmogorov Test — even for small sample sizes and a uniform hypothetical
distribution [351]. Freedman proposed an improved version, which eradicates
both drawbacks: the problem of the starting point and of the grouping of
data [113]. The hypothetical cumulative distribution (in our case a uniform
distribution) is denoted by $F(t) = \frac{t}{12}$, where t equals the rank of each month
of the year (January=1, February=2, ..., December=12). The sample cumulative distribution is denoted by $F_N(t) = \frac{j}{N}$, where j is the number of events
(e.g. deaths) that have happened during all months $\leq t$. The test-statistic T
is [113, 305]:

$$T = V_N \sqrt{N} = \sqrt{N} \left[\max_{1 \leq t \leq 12} (F_N(t) - F(t)) + \left| \min_{1 \leq t \leq 12} (F_N(t) - F(t)) \right| \right]. \quad (3.5)$$

The distribution of T does not follow any specified distribution (e.g. χ^2;
$N(\mu, \sigma^2)$, ...). Therefore this distribution has been empirically determined by
performing Monte Carlo simulations and is tabulated in Freedman's article

---

[2] Spelling of Russian names (especially -ov vs. -off) differs not only in this dissertation but also in the original papers. Therefore, I opted to use the spelling in
each case from the respective source document.

[3] In this article, Kolmogoroff refers to the articles [203] and [352].

[113]. Freedman's modified KS-Type Test has been used for the study of birth seasonality [e.g. 390].

3.3.2 Edwards' Family

The first statistical test especially designed for seasonality — or more generally speaking for cyclic trends — is Edwards' Test published in 1961 [84]. It is "the most cited and the benchmark against which other tests are evaluated" [394, p. 817]. Several others modified this test in order to be valid for small sample sizes or to allow for a different alternative hypothesis. These extensions will be presented after the discussion of the original contribution. All of them use sine- and cosine-waves to approximate the observed pattern, and therefore they are methods which belong to *harmonic analysis* [142, p. 641].

Edwards' Test

The underlying idea of the original test [84] is relatively straightforward and based on a geometrical framework [263]. Given a circle whose circumference is divided into k equally long parts. In the case of months per year, $k = 12$. Thus, each month's contribution to the surface of the circle is a sector of 30 degrees: January from $0°$ to $30°$, February from $30°$ to $60°$, ... and finally December from $330°$ to $360°$. This is shown in Figure 3.3 (page 48).

A weight, N_i, is attached to the center of each segment (i.e. for January at $15°$, for February at $45°$, ...). N_i is the number of events in month i. If events were uniformly distributed, the center of gravity of this "wheel" would be the geometrical center of the whole circle as indicated by the small black circle in Figure 3.3. If, however, there is a considerable "pulse" or an underlying sinusoidal pattern, the center of gravity shifts away from the geometrical center. The small gray circle could be an example of a concentration of events in winter and, more precisely, the middle of January. If one is testing such a cyclical hypothesis against a uniform distribution, Edwards' Test has a higher power than the χ^2-Test [358]. Walter and Elwood extended Edwards' approach by allowing unequal expected numbers in each category [396]. In its original version, the Null-Hypothesis assumes to have equally spaced sectors with the same frequencies in each division. The allegation that the assumption of twelve equally spaced time intervals may cause problems in practice [139] can easily be refuted. One simply has to standardize the number of incidences according to the specific length of month. The test statistic $T = \frac{1}{2}a^2N$ is calculated as shown in Equation 3.6 (multi-line notation of T is taken from the original article [84]):

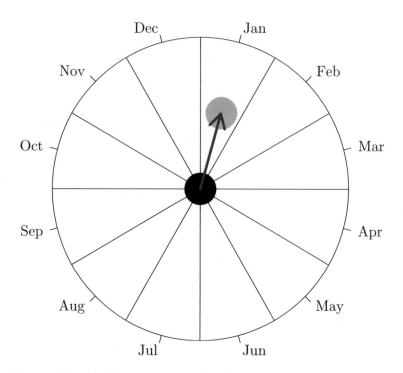

Fig. 3.3. Graphical Representation of Edwards' Test for Seasonality

$$S = \sum \sqrt{N_i} \sin \Theta_i \qquad (3.6)$$
$$C = \sum \sqrt{N_i} \cos \Theta_i$$
$$W = \sum \sqrt{N_i}$$
$$d = \frac{\sqrt{(S^2 + C^2)}}{W}$$
$$a = 4d$$

N_i corresponds to the number of events (e.g. deaths) in month i and $\sum_{i=1}^{k(=12)} N_i = N$. The parameter Θ_i indicates the position of the weight of each month on the wheel. Thus, Θ_i equals 15°for January, 45°for February, ..., and 345°for December. $\frac{1}{2}a^2 N$ is under H_0 asymptotically χ^2-distributed with two degrees of freedom [84]. Edwards' method has been employed in the study of coronary heart disease [340], myocardial infarction [131], and overall mortality [148, 268].

Roger's Test

As pointed out by Roger [312], Edwards' test does not yield satisfactory results for small and medium-sized samples. "This has the effect of making the type I errors in the test too large and hence leading to too many spurious significant results" [312, p. 153]. Roger tried to tackle the shortcoming of Edwards' Test for small sample sizes and proposed the following test statistic T [312]:

$$T = \frac{2\left[\left\{\sum_{i=1}^{k(=12)} N_i \sin\left(\frac{2\pi i}{k}\right)\right\}^2 + \left\{\sum_{i=1}^{k(=12)} N_i \cos\left(\frac{2\pi i}{k}\right)\right\}^2\right]}{n} \quad (3.7)$$

N_i represents the number of events in month i, and $n = \sum_{i=1}^{12} N_i$. T is under H_0 approximately χ^2-distributed with $n = 2$ degrees of freedom [244]. According to Roger, his test and Edwards' original test are equivalent for large samples. Roger's extension provided a useful tool for the analysis of "seasonal variations in variceal bleeding mortality and hospitalization in France" [30].

Pocock's Method

Pocock's [291] analysis of seasonal variations in sickness absence belongs also to the group of tests using harmonic analysis like [84] and [312]. While Rogerson [312] extended Edward's approach for small sample sizes, Pocock relaxed the assumption of a sinusoidal underlying pattern and "allows the alternative hypothesis of a seasonal pattern of arbitrary shape" [139, p. 49]. The test statistic T, which was originally designed for weekly values for spells of sickness absence, has been slightly adapted for our approach of monthly death counts. It tests "the seasonal sum of squares" for deviations from the Null-Hypothesis that deaths occur randomly in time.

$$T = k \sum_{j=1}^{\frac{k}{2}} \frac{(a_j^2 + b_j^2)}{2\bar{A}}, \quad (3.8)$$

where k represents the number of intervals (12 months) and $j = 1, 2, \ldots, \frac{k}{2}$. $\bar{A}$ is the mean of the monthly number of deaths A_i in month $i = 1, 2, \ldots, 12 (= k)$.

$$\left.\begin{array}{l} a_j = \dfrac{2}{k} \sum_{i=1}^{k} A_i \cos \dfrac{2\pi i j}{k} \\[2ex] b_j = \dfrac{2}{k} \sum_{i=1}^{k} A_i \sin \dfrac{2\pi i j}{k} \end{array}\right\} \quad j = 1, \ldots, \dfrac{k}{2}$$

T is under H_0 approximately χ^2 distributed with $\nu = 11$ degrees of freedeom.

Cave and Freedman's Method

Cave and Freedman proposed another modification of Edwards' test [44]. Instead of a sinusoidal curve with only one peak and one trough per year, they allowed two maxima and two minima. Their test-statistic is, thus, relatively similar to [84]. The difference is the implementation of the Θ-parameter: while for Edwards' test [84] it is required to calculate $\sin\left(\frac{2\pi\Theta_i}{360}\right)$,[4] one proceeds for the method of Cave and Freedman [44] by computing $\sin\left(\frac{2\pi\Theta_i}{180}\right)$, thus standardizing 2π to $180°$.

3.3.3 Nonparametric Tests

Hewitt's Test and Rogerson's Extension

Edwards [84] mentioned that his test was only one approach to measure seasonality. He explicitly considers also a nonparametric alternative whose construction is relatively similar to a simple Run-Test [393]. Based on that brief suggestion — two paragraphs in Edwards' original article — Hewitt et al. elaborated a nonparametric test based on rank-sums [150]. While Edwards suggested "to consider the ranking order of the events which are above or below the median number" [84, p. 83], Hewitt et al. [150] propose to use "all the ranking information rather than a simple dichotomy" [150, p. 175]. According to them, the monthly frequencies are ranked. The month with most occurrences (e.g. deaths) will have the value "12" assigned. Consequently, "1" indicates the month having the least events. Keeping the original order of the months (e.g. starting with January and ending with December), we can calculate the rank-sums of six consecutive months (January–June, February–July, ..., December–May). The test statistic T is the maximum value that one of the rank-sums attains. T can range from $21(=1+2+3+4+5+6)$ to $57(=12+11+10+9+8+7)$ and is symmetrically distributed. The authors suggest referring to the upper tail of the cumulative distribution for significance testing which they tabulated in their article based on 5,000 Monte-Carlo trials. Not surprisingly, their empirical results correspond closely to Walter's exact significance levels for Hewitt's test calculated nine years later [395]. Using such a test based on ranks has the advantage that one "avoids the problem of specifying a particular algebraic version" [113, p. 225] of what is meant by seasonal fluctuation. However, it lacks power for small and moderate sample sizes [113]. Besides, this test cannot be applied — as Reijneveld [305] points out — if there are ties. For our analysis of mortality with relatively large samples, though, ties seem to be quite unlikely. Of more relevance are the objections of Rogerson [315], Wallenstein [394] and Marrero [244] to "the assumption that the year is split into two equally wide intervals of 6 months each" [315, p. 644]. While Wallenstein and Marrero take a "one-pulse model" also into

---

[4] this applies obviously also to $\cos\left(\frac{2\pi\Theta_i}{360}\right)$

consideration, Rogerson develops a generalization of Hewitt's Test for peak periods of 3-, 4-, and 5-months [315]. Similar to taking the maximum rank sum of all possible combinations of six consecutive months, Rogerson uses the maximum rank sum of any consecutive three, four, or five month period, respectively. Because of its relative simplicity to calculate, Hewitt's Test has enjoyed widespread use [315]. However for the analysis of seasonal mortality it has not been employed as often as Edwards' Test or the χ^2-Goodness-of-Fit Test. To my knowledge, Akslen's and Hartveit's application to seasonal variation in melanoma deaths has been the only application of it so far [1]. Apart from Walter's exact specification of significance levels for Hewitt's test [395], the distributions of the respective test statistics were based on relatively few randomly generated sequences of data. The appendix (Section B.1, page 181) shows results from my own simulations.

David-Newell-Test

Another nonparametric alternative was proposed by David and Newell [64]. Their suggestions, however, have not received much attention. In contrast to Hewitt's non-parametric test for seasonality, one does not use the ranking information but the actual number of events.

$$T = \max_i \left| \frac{M_i - M_{i+6}}{\sqrt{N}} \right| \tag{3.9}$$

where N_j is the number of events in month j and $M = \sum_{j}^{j+5} N_j$; $N = \sum_{j=1}^{12} N_j$. The test statistic T does not follow any standard distribution. Therefore the critical values for two significance levels ($\alpha_{0.01}, \alpha_{0.05}$) are given in their paper [64].

3.4 Time-Series Methods

3.4.1 Introduction

The previous sections have focused on indices and statistical tests to describe seasonality and test for seasonality in data grouped into one year. Contrastingly, the following sections deal with the analysis of seasonal time-series. Typically, these data are either count data or rates over time.

Most analyses of seasonal time-series data have the opposite aim than our approach: conventionally, researchers try to "seasonally adjust" the time-series. This means that one wanted to get rid of the seasonal "distortions" to identify the "true effect". We, however, are interested in seasonality itself: How does the seasonal pattern change over time? Despite these two antagonistic theoretical starting points, the actual analyses can be carried out with the same methods because both approaches need to model the exact seasonal signal from the data.

Basically, there are two approaches for seasonal time-series-analysis: either one decomposes the time-series into several components, or one models all of these aspects simultaneously [389]. In reality, methods for analyzing seasonal time-series cannot always be clearly assigned to one of the groups as they are using methodology from both strains. In the following paragraphs, I want to briefly outline what is meant by decomposition methods and simultaneous modelling. Subsequently, I will discuss several of the methods which are actually used and also implemented in various software packages.

3.4.2 Decomposition Methods

It is argued that decomposing time-series started in the 1920s at the National Bureau of Economic Research (NBER) [417] of the United States. Starting with the first "monthly means method" and the "ratio to moving average method" [270] to modern methods, decomposition methods are based on the assumption that the observed data contain four components [335]:

Trend: The trend is the long-term change in the time-series. In the analysis of seasonal mortality two thrusts can be imagined to influence the trend over time: First, a change in the variable of interest: death rates are falling rapidly for people above age 70 at least for the last 30 years [378]. Secondly, a compositional change can either increase the effect of the variable of interest or it can be counteracted. The latter is more probable for the analysis of death counts as more and more people attain very high ages because of improved survival conditions [383].

Cycle: The cyclic component captures a fluctuation with a frequency of more than one year [335]. While they are an important part of economic analysis, e.g. the Kondratieff long economic cycles [205], they play only minor role in mortality research.[5] The cyclic component is sometimes not extracted on its own but rather as a part of the trend component.

Season: The seasonal component is an annually repeating pattern observed in the time-series, and is the feature of the data which is our main focus. While it is beyond doubt that climate shapes the basic pattern of seasonal mortality fluctuations, a large body of literature shows that the impact of climate can be mediated and alleviated. Consequently, we want to analyze how seasonal fluctuations are changing over time, which measures indirectly the influence of improvements in public health and general living conditions.

Irregular: The remainder between the aforementioned components and the observed data is summarized in the irregular component.

---

[5] I consider the analysis of Stoupel et al. [359] concerning the impact of "space proton flux" on the temporal distribution of cardiovascular deaths as negligible.

Basically, there are two approaches on how these components constitute the observed time-series: In an additive model, one assumes that the trend component y_t^t (includes the cyclic component), the seasonal component y_t^s and the irregular component y_t^{res} are working independently. Thus, the resulting model would be:

$$y_t = y_t^t + y_t^s + y_t^{res} \qquad (3.10)$$

In the majority of real-world applications, however, independent effects are rather the exception rather than the rule. Thus, a multiplicative combination of the trend and the seasonal components

$$y_t = y_t^t \times y_t^s + y_t^{res} \qquad (3.11)$$

is often preferable.

3.4.3 Simultaneous Modelling

In contrast to the decompositon approach, the time-series data can also be modelled simultaneously. This is done by so-called seasonal ARIMA-Models. This approach follows the Box-Jenkins methodology [32] of identifying parsimonious models for the data under scrutiny. A seasonal ARIMA-Model is an extended ARIMA-Model. An ARIMA-Model is an extended ARMA-Model. Thus, I want to start with the basic model: An ARMA-Model consists of an autoregressive (AR) and of a moving average (MA) part. As explained in [95], "an $AR(p)$ process is specified by a weighted average of past observations going back p periods, together with a random disturbance in the current period [. . .], an $MA(q)$ process is specified by a weighted average of past random disturbances going back q periods, together with a random disturbance in the current period."[6] The aim of ARMA modeling is a parsimonious model. This means in the words of its creators to "employ the smallest possible number of parameters for adequate representations" [32, p. 16]. Typical diagnostics to check for pickung the best model are, for example, the Akaike Information Criterion (AIC) or the Schwarz Bayesian Criterion. However, ARMA Modelling requires a stationary time-series. If the data are non-stationary which is rather the rule than the exception, the ARMA(p, q) Model is extended to an ARIMA(p, d, q) Model (ARIMA=Auto Regressive Integrated Moving Average). In such an ARIMA-Model, the time-series is first differenced finite d times until a stationary process is obtained. Seasonal ARIMA-Models represent a further extension. The general form of such a SARIMA Model is:

$$\text{ARIMA}(p, d, q)(P, D, Q)_{12}.$$

---

[6] Mathematically, the specifications may be written as given by Box et al. [32, p. 52]:

$$\text{AR(p)} : \tilde{z}_t = \phi_1 \tilde{z}_{t-1} + \phi_2 \tilde{z}_{t-2} + \ldots + \phi_p \tilde{z}_{t-p} + a_t$$
$$\text{MA(q)} : \tilde{z}_t = a_t - \theta_1 a_{t-1} - \theta_2 a_{t-2} - \ldots - \theta_q a_{t-q}$$

In addition to the previously explained parameters p, d, q, SARIMA contains the parameters P, D, Q indicating autoregressive (P) and moving average (Q) components differenced D times at a seasonal lag. In the case of an annual seasonal pattern with monthly values, the respective lag is 12 months.

3.4.4 Seasonal Time-Series Methods

The "Classical" Decomposition Method

The "classical" decomposition method uses moving averages as outlined in Brockwell and Davis [34] or Hartung [142]. The first step is an estimation of the trend "by applying a moving average filter specially chosen to eliminate the seasonal component and to dampen the noise"[34, p. 30]. The seasonal component is then estimated by computing the average deviation of the monthly values from the estimated trend. This method is, however, irrelevant for the rest of this chapter, as it contains a constant seasonal component. The aim of this research is, though, exactly the analysis of this seasonal component over time (or age).

X-11

Still the most widely used method is the so-called "X-11, Census II" method. Its development can be traced back to the "ratio to moving average method" from the 1920s. The various revisions have been labeled "X-" followed by the version number. X-11 was developed at the U.S. Bureau of the Census in 1965 by Julius Shishkin [417].

The estimation is performed in several steps [cf. 417]. Ghysels and Osborn [122] and Yaffee [417] give an overview how these steps are performed. We are following the overview given by Fischer [108] for the X-11 ARIMA variant:[7]

1. First estimate of the seasonal and the irregular component using a 12 term moving average.
2. Preliminary estimate of the seasonal factors using a 5-term moving average.
3. A 12-term moving average is applied to the preliminary factors found in the previous step.
4. The seasonal factor estimates are divided by the seasonal irregular ratio to obtain an estimate of the irregular component.
5. Detection of outliers
6. Adjustment for the beginning and the end of the time-series (necessary since symmetric filters are used).

---

[7] X-11 uses moving averages for the estimates. Since these weights are symmetric, problems arise in the beginning and in the end of the time-series. To remedy this drawback, Statistics Canada introduced the so-called X-11-ARIMA/88 to improve the fore- and back-casting possibilities of X-11 [cf. 417, 55–56].

7. Estimation of preliminary seasonal factors by applying a weighted 5-term moving average to the SI (ratio of the seasonal and irregular component) ratios with replacement of extreme values (detected two steps earlier).

8. Step 3 is repeated and applied to the factors in step 7.

9. Division of the original data by the result from the previous step to obtain a preliminary seasonally adjusted time-series.

10. The original series is divided by the result of applying a moving average to the seasonally adjusted series.

11. Applying a weighted 7-term moving average to each month's SI ratio separately. This results in a second estimate of the seasonal component.

12. Step 3 is repeated.

13. The original series is divided by the result from step 11 to obtain a seasonally adjusted time-series.

Fischer [108, p. 15] gives a flow-chart to display graphically this procedure. Despite its popularity, several serious drawbacks of X-11 have been pointed out [14, 53, 303]:

- Using X-11 can imply that a non-seasonal cycle can be wrongly specified as seasonal.
- X-11 is not very robust in the case of a sudden change in the trend. This might sound unimportant as natural processes typically do not change all of a sudden. However, in the analysis of seasonal mortality of a specific cause of death across time, relatively abrupt changes in the trend can happen after an ICD-Revision[8] — no matter how careful the preparation of the time-series.
- In the case of zero-value observations ($\neq$missing values), neither an additive nor a multiplicative X-11 approach is applicable. Zero events might happen in certain age-groups for diseases with a highly seasonal pattern like deaths from influenza.
- X-11 may over- or under-estimate the seasonal component (non-idempotency). The lack of this property is a serious shortcoming for the analysis of seasonal changes over time.
- The values for the seasonal factors depend on the beginning of the time-series. As pointed out by Raveh [303], X-11 yields different seasonal estimates for the same original values if the series is shifted forward for half a year, for instance.
- X-11 is over-sensitive to outliers. This problem of the original variant, though, seems to be eradicated by X-12.

Despite these disadvantages, X-11 is still a popular choice. The original version has been employed for the analysis of seasonal mortality in an early 20th century population [21] and more recently for examining seasonal deaths in the United States [102]. An example for X-11-ARIMA is Richard Trudeau's

---

[8] ICD is the abbreviation for "International Statistical Classification of Diseases". See http://www.who.int/whosis/icd10/ .

study on "monthly and daily patterns of death" in Canada [367]. For our analysis, we used X-12-ARIMA which is the successor to X-11-ARIMA "to handle additive outliers and level shifts" [35, p. 1]. The estimates should be at least as good as X-11 since it improves the detection and correction of outliers and estimates automatically the ARIMA-Models [108, p. 16].

SABL

William S. Cleveland and his colleagues did not only pin-point the weaknesses of X-11, they also suggested alternative procedures. Their first suggestion was the so-called SABL [50, 51].[9]. This procedure works basically in four steps [51]:

1. A power transformation of your time-series
   The power transformation is carried out as follows [52, p. 53]:

$$x^{(p)} = \begin{cases} x^p & \text{if } p > 0 \\ \log_e x & \text{if } p = 0 \\ -x^p & \text{if } p < 0 \end{cases} \qquad (3.12)$$

   The value of the power p should be chosen to minimize the interaction between the trend and the seasonal component. Fortunately, the program Splus picks the best p-value — provided a vector of possible values has been given before.
2. Additive decomposition of the transformed time-series into trend, seasonal, and irregular component. The details of this decomposition are described in [p. 15–16 51]:[10]
   a) "A combination of smoothers, which involve moving medians for robustness, is used to get initial estimates of the trend and the seasonal. Moving medians are similar to moving averages except that means are replaced by medians.
   b) The irregular, which is the series minus the trend and seasonal, is computed.
   c) Robustness weights are computed using the irregular values. Irregular values large in absolute value receive small or zero weight.
   d) Updated estimates of the trend and seasonal are computed using smoothers that are doubly-weighted moving averages. The two sets of weights are those computed in step (c) and the usual kind of weights in moving averages.
   e) Steps (b) to (d) are repeated using the updated estimates of trend and seasonal. The trend and seasonal component in step (d) on the second pass are the final trend and seasonal."

---

[9] SABL is the abbreviation for **S**easonal **A**djustment at **B**ell **L**aboratories
[10] Alternatively, one can also consult the flowchart given in [108, p. 12].

3. Seasonal Adjustment. This step is not required in our estimations since we are interested in the final seasonal component obtained in the previous step.
4. In its original version, SABL printed tables and plotted graphs. We do not need this option since we are using modern statistical software which allows for printing the results and plotting the graphs in a user-defined way.

STL

The seasonal decomposition STL was also invented by Cleveland and his colleagues [48]. As usual, the data are decomposed into three components: a trend, a seasonal part and a remainder. Among other criteria, the authors wanted to develop a procedure which has a simple design, its use is straightforward, does not have problems with missing values, has a robust trend and seasonal component, and is easily and quickly implemented on a computer. The core of the procedure are smoothing operations based on locally-weighted regression (loess). As written by Cleveland et al. [48, p. 6]: "STL consists of two recursive procedures: an inner loop nested inside an outer loop. In each of the passes through the inner loop, the seasonal and trend components are updated once; [...] Each pass of the outer loop consists of the inner loop followed by a computation of robustness weights; these weights are used in the next run of the inner loop to reduce the influence of transient, aberrant behavior in the trend and seasonal components." The inner loop consists of the following steps [48, p. 7–8]:

1. Detrending
2. Smoothing of the Cycle Subseries
3. Filtering of the Smoothed Cycle-Subseries (obtained from pervious step)
4. De-trending of Smoothed Cycle-Subseries
5. De-seasonalizing
6. Trend Smoothing

BV4

BV4 is the abbreviation of the fourth revision of the so-called "Berliner Verfahren". It is the official seasonal adjustment method of the Statistisches Bundesamt (Federal Statistical Office) in Germany. It was developed by Martin Nourney and is described in detail in [275, 276, 277]. Currently the Statistisches Bundesamt is replacing BV4 with an updated version called BV4.1 which can handle calendar effects and outliers better. According to Speth [357] three of the main advantageous characteristics of BV4.1 are:

• Low cost benefit ratio because high-quality analysis can be performed without expert knowledge and without much experience for time-series decomposition methods.

- Results are independent from the user.
- High efficiency of the seasonal adjustment which can incorporate even rapid changes in the seasonal component.

BV4.1 assumes (after a possible transformation of the data, e.g. a log-transform) an additive decomposition of the time-series of the form [104, 105]:

$$Y_t = G(t) + S(t) + \epsilon_t. \tag{3.13}$$

$G(t)$ denotes the trend-cycle component ("Glatte Komponente") which is approximated by a third-order polynomial: $G(t) = \hat{y}_t^t = a_0 + a_1 t + a_2 t^2 + a_3 t^3$. The seasonal component $S(t)$ is approximated by 11 trigonometric functions [see also 108]:

$$y_t^s = \sum_{i=1}^{5} (b_i \cos \lambda_i t + c_i \sin \lambda_i t) + b_6 \cos \lambda_6 t.$$

The irregular component ϵ_t is an independently, identically distributed random variable with mean 0 and a constant variance σ^2. The actual fitting procedure is performed by locally weighted least squares.

TRAMO/SEATS

TRAMO/SEATS has been developed by Victor Gómez and Agustín Maravall.[11] Their work is based on "seasonal adjustment by signal extraction" by Burman [39]. A detailed, technical description of TRAMO/SEATS is given in [239]. Fischer [108] summarizes the six steps of the TRAMO/SEATS procedure as follows (a flow-chart with more details is given on page 18 of [108]):

- TRAMO identifies automatically an ARIMA Model
- Simultaneously, outliers are detected
- TRAMO passes its results to SEATS
- "In SEATS, first the spectral density function of the estimated model is decomposed into the spectral density function of the unobserved components, which are assumed to be orthogonal" [108, p. 17]
- Then, the trend-cycle and the seasonal component are estimated
- In the last step, outliers are re-introduced.

3.5 Evaluation of Seasonality Indices and Tests Using Hypothetical and Real Data

3.5.1 Description of Datasets

We distinguish between *real* and *hypothetical* data. If real data were taken from publications which introduced a measurement for seasonality, the data

---

[11] TRAMO stands for **T**ime Series **R**egression with **A**RIMA Noise, **M**issing values and **O**utliers. SEATS stands for **S**ignal **E**xtraction in **A**RIMA **T**ime **S**eries.

were used to check the correct implementation of the underlying algorithm. Otherwise real data from other sources were used to analyze how the various indices and tests behave in typical situations of seasonal mortality analyses. They are briefly described in the next section and are plotted in Figure 3.4. Hypothetical data served only experimental purposes. For example, we think that any measurement should test positively if a pronounced sine wave is present. Random numbers and a uniform distribution should, conversely, not detect seasonality at all. For the hypothetical data, I have always created two data-sets: one with a small sample size and one with a larger sample size as described below. For each category, only the data based on the larger sample is plotted in Figure 3.5.

Real Data

Wrigley: These data consist of 75,398 deaths from the British parish register data between 1580–1837. These data represent standardized death counts where 100 indicates the mean number of monthly deaths. Wrigley et al. [415] provide more details.

Nuns and Monks: Marc Luy kindly provided death counts from his data collection on Bavarian nunneries and monasteries [229]. A detailed description can be found in [228]. The nuns' data-set consists of 3,919 individuals who have died during the 20th century in the analyzed nunneries. In the other data-set all 349 male deaths are included which occured in the respective monasteries during the 19th century.

Union Army: These data are taken from the *Public Use Tape on the Aging of the Veterans of the Union Army* [111]. It consists of 24,610 individuals who died between January 1862 and December 1937. Each death has been recorded by month and year of death. Thus, the aggregated data-set contains 912 records. For our analysis we only used deaths starting in 1866 to avoid distorting effects due to the Civil War.

Danish Register Data: All Danes are included who were alive on 1 April 1968 and 50 years or older and died by August 1998. The data from which these 1,176,383 deaths have been derived are explained in more detail in [72].

Respiratory Diseases: The data-set includes 25,272.56 men who have between January 1959 and December 1998 from respiratory diseases in the United States being between 80 (inclusive) and 90 (exclusive) years of age. The reason for the non-integer number of deaths is that monthly deaths have already been adjusted to the same length. The data were taken from the public use files of the *Centers for Disease Control and Intervention (CDC)*. These data are described in more detail in Chapter 4.

Anencephalics: The monthly distribution of 176 cases of anencephalics that have occurred in Birmingham between 1940 and 1947 are given in [84].

Lymphoma: The monthly distribution of 133 cases of Burkitt's lymphoma from the West Nile district of Uganda between 1966 and 1973 are given in [113].

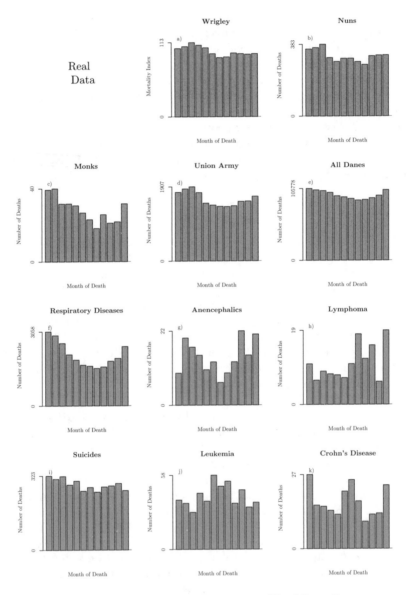

Fig. 3.4. Graphical Representation of Real Data-Sets

Suicides: The monthly distribution of adolescent suicides (3474 cases) in the United States, 1978–79, is given in [315].

Leukemia: The monthly distribution of the onset of acute lymphatic leukemia between 1946 and 1960 (506 cases) is taken from the *British National Cancer Registration Scheme* as reported in [64].

Crohn's Disease: Cave and Freedman [44] give a bar-plot displaying the monthly distribution of the onset of Crohn's disease for 211 patients in three British hospitals between 1945 and 1974. More details about the data can be found in the original article.

Hypothetical Data

Uniform Distribution: Two vectors with 12 elements — each of the 12 elements representing the numbers of death in a month —are given consisting of either 5 or 5000 cases in each month.

Sine Wave: Again, we have two vectors with 1 entry for each month. The "small" sine wave has a maximum value of 12 in January and 8 in July, whereas the large sample's extreme values are 120 and 80 in the same months.

Cosine Wave: The Cosine Waves are equivalent to the two Sine Waves with a forward shift of $\frac{3}{2}\pi$. One should expect the same results as for the Sine Wave data as we basically face the same pattern. Testing the measurements with the Cosine data can help to evaluate whether certain indices or tests are restricted to the Northern Hemisphere with a peak in the first (few) months of the year.

Local Summer Peak: The literature on seasonal mortality sometimes also refers to a second peak in summer. The data-sets are the same as the Sine Wave data apart from the minimum. Instead of values of 8 and 80 respectively in July, we have values of 10 and 100.

One-Pulse Pattern: Some causes of death do not have a sinusoidal but a "one-pulse"-pattern. This means that deaths are uniformly distributed throughout the year with the exception of some months where deaths rise rapidly. Our data have 10 (small sample) and 100 (large sample) deaths in each month. In winter, however, deaths suddenly increase, reaching a peak in January and February of 13 and 130 deaths, respectively.

Random Pattern: Randomly distributed numbers should (in general) not result in significant test results for seasonality. The random numbers are derived from the "true" random number generator at `http://www.random.org`. Integers were generated between 900 and 1100 for the larger sample; for a smaller sample we used the same numbers but divided each of them by 10.

3.5.2 Results and Discussion for Indices and Tests

Results and Discussion for Indices

Table 3.1 shows the results for the three descriptive indices $\varphi_1, \varphi_2, \varphi_3$. The upper section refers to hypothetical data, in the lower section we faced the indices with real data. In our synthetically generated data only one value is

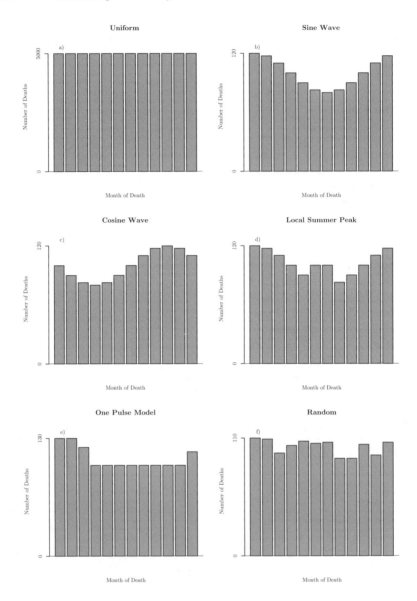

Fig. 3.5. Graphical Representation of Hypothetical Data-Sets

given for each pattern (uniform distribution, sine wave, ...) as all indices are inelastic with regard to sample size.

As mentioned in their description above, seasonality indices are closely related to measures of inequality. Goodwin and Vaupel [126] suggested several

Table 3.1. Sample Sizes and Results for Descriptive Indices φ_1 (Winter/Summer), φ_2 (Dissimilarity), and φ_3 (Entropy) for Seasonality of Hypothetical and Real Data

Hypothetical Data	Sample Size N	φ_1	φ_2	φ_3
Uniform	60 / 60,000	1.000	0.000	1.000
Sine Wave	120 / 1,200	1.375	0.062	0.996
Cosine Wave	120 / 1,200	0.833	0.062	0.996
Local Summer Peak	123.73 / 12,373.32	1.274	0.048	0.997
One-Pulse Pattern	129.5 / 1,295	1.267	0.049	0.998
Random Pattern	122.2 / 1,222	1.094	0.029	0.999

Real Data	Sample Size N	φ_1	φ_2	φ_3
Wrigley	1,199	1.165	0.032	0.999
Nuns†	3,919	1.266	0.038	0.998
Monks†	349	1.656	0.100	0.989
Union Army Veterans†	24,610	1.191	0.034	0.999
Danish Register Data†	1,176,383	1.161	0.028	0.999
Respiratory Diseases	25,272.56	1.781	0.102	0.989
Anencephalics†	176	1.605	0.139	0.978
Lymphoma†	133	0.627	0.167	0.969
Suicides†	3,474	1.191	0.034	0.999
Leukemia†	506	0.749	0.087	0.992
Crohn's Disease†	211	1.113	0.132	0.982

† Monthly values have been adjusted to equal weights

desirable properties for "Measures of Evenness". Most of them can also be applied to the field of seasonality:[12]

The Relativity Principle: The relativity principle refers to sample size. According to the principle, it is a desirable property for any index that it should be independent from the sample size, as long as the proportions of each category remain the same. An index which fulfills this condition will return the identical value for a data-set of 100 individuals and 100 million individuals if the corresponding subgroups in each population contribute the same share. All our three indices fulfill this condition. To produce the upper part of Table 3.1, we used data with the same basic distribution and only varied the sample size. When we analyzed the data, φ_1, φ_2 as well as φ_3 gave exactly the same results.

The Transfer Principle: According to this principle, a diversity measure should increase if there are any transfers from a "poor" individual to a "rich" individual. Applied to the case of seasonality in mortality, any good index

---

[12] The so-called *Anonymity Principle*, for instance, is not included. This principles states that an index should be anonymous in the sense that it does not matter which element of the underlying population has a certain trait. It is less useful for the analysis of seasonality because a seasonality index should actually take into account whether January or September shows higher mortality values.

should increase if there is a transfer from a low mortality month such as June to a high mortality month like December.[13] All indices fulfill this property as well. For instance, if a certain number of deaths occur less in summer but more in winter, the winter/summer ratio φ_1 would increase, likewise φ_2, the dissimilarity index. As entropy φ_3 is measuring concentration it decreases, consequently. It has to be mentioned, though, that not all possible transfers affect φ_1. If there are any transfers between spring and autumn months, this winter/summer ratio will remain constant.

Standardization: Standardizing an index to a certain interval, say $[0; 1]$, facilitates describing population across time or across countries. The dissimilarity index φ_2 fulfills this condition. In the case of a uniform distribution, its value is 0. If deaths occur only in one month, it reaches its maximum value (for the case of 12 possible event times) 0.91666. In the same scenario, entropy (φ_3) would be bounded by 1 (uniform distribution = "minimum safeness of a guess") and would approach 0 in the case where deaths are only possible in one month. The winter/summer index is only bounded on one side. If death is equally probable in each month, φ_1 would be 1. If deaths only occurred in summer, φ_1 would approach 0; on the other extreme if deaths exclusively happened in winter, $\varphi_1 \to \infty$.

Intelligibility: "Ideally, a measure should be easy to comprehend, intuitively meaningful, simple to explain to others, and naturally relevant to the problems addressed" [126, p. 11]. The winter/summer ratio is the only index which fulfills all these conditions, especially the explanation to other people of the dissimilarity index or of entropy is considerably more complicated for φ_2 and φ_3 than for φ_1. It also seems to be more meaningful intuitively. For example, a value of 1.26 from φ_1 (real data: nuns) can be read as: among nuns in the respective data-set, 26% more died during winter than during summer. The corresponding values of $\varphi_2 = 0.038$ and $\varphi_3 = 0.998$ can contribute only little to the understanding of the underlying phenomenon.

Based on these criteria, it is difficult to make a decision for which index is best suited for seasonality studies. It can be argued that the winter/summer ratio φ_1 is preferable because of its better intelligibility and because φ_2 and φ_3 are unfavorable due to the following reasons:

- Standardized entropy (φ_3) does not seem to be a useful index because we observed only values between 0.996 and 1 for hypothetical data and between 0.969 and 0.999 for real data in our analysis. As this index is standardized to have a value range of $(0; 1]$, φ_3 uses only roughly 3% of its potential range. The dissimilarity index φ_2 performs only slightly better than φ_3 in that respect (18% of the value range is used).

---

[13] This, of course, holds only for measurements of unevenness. If we measure concentration, the opposite direction should be true.

- Neither index can distinguish between two patterns where one has its peak in winter and the other one has its maximum value in summer (i.e. φ_2 and φ_3 would give the same results in both situations).
- A related problem is the order of the months: The indices φ_2 and φ_3 do not take the ordering of the months into account: It does not matter, for instance, for φ_2 or for φ_3 whether the values appear as in a sine wave or in any other order. Clearly, an unfavorable property of any index for seasonality.

Results and Discussion for Seasonality Tests

Figures 3.6 and 3.7 (pages 66, 68) show the results of our analysis of the tests described in section 3.3. The tests are ordered according to which group they belong to: Goodness-of-Fit tests, the "Edwards' family" or nonparametric tests. All of them are faced with the data-sets outlined in section 3.5.1. Hypothetical as well as real data were tested for two levels of significance: $\alpha_1 = 0.95$; $\alpha_2 = 0.99$. In the case of hypothetical data, we tested both sample sizes as indicated by "small" and "large". To facilitate recognizing the outcomes of these tests, they were labeled with a dark gray square and a "−"-sign in case of insignificant results at the given level. A light gray square and a "+"-sign were used for significant values.

All tests passed a minimum requirement: as displayed in Figure 3.6, none of the tests detects seasonality for a uniform distribution nor for the random pattern — regardless of the sample size. The tests developed by Cave and Freedman [44] and by Pocock [291] will be excluded from further analysis, as they did not evaluate any of the hypothetical data-sets to be seasonal [44] or only the sine/cosine-data based on a large sample [291]. An advantage of all tests presented here is that they show exactly the same results for a sine and a cosine wave if the sample size is the same in both instances. This implies that all of them can be applied on both hemispheres giving the same results. While this requirement sounds obvious, the most widely-used seasonal time-series method, X-11, does not produce the same results if data start in January or in June [303]. Nevertheless, it is quite surprising that neither any Goodness-of-Fit-test nor any test from the "Edwards' Family" tests positively for seasonality for the sine- and cosine curves when the sample size is small. Only the non-parametric tests yield significant values. Because of their definition (using ranks instead of the actual counts or rates), Hewitt's tests and its generalization by Rogerson output the same values for small and large sample sizes. For the data-sets with a local summer peak or displaying only one pulse, we again detect the sample-size dependency for the Goodness-of-Fit tests and for the "Edwards' Family": no seasonality for small samples, significant p-values for large samples. The nonparametric tests for peak periods of 3 and 4 months behave as expected by returning significant results for the hypothetical data with one-pulse.

Hypothetical Data (Part A)	Uniform				Sine Curve				Cosine Curve			
	small		large		small		large		small		large	
Test	0.05	0.01	0.05	0.01	0.05	0.01	0.05	0.01	0.05	0.01	0.05	0.01
1. Goodness-of-Fit-Tests												
1.1 Chi-Square - Goodness of Fit	-	-	-	-	-	-	+	-	-	-	+	-
1.2 Kolmogorov-Smirnov-Type-Statistic	-	-	-	-	-	-	+	+	-	-	+	+
2. Edwards' Family												
2.1 Edwards' Test	-	-	-	-	-	-	-	-	-	-	-	-
2.2 Roger's Extension of Edwards' Test	-	-	-	-	-	-	-	-	-	-	-	-
2.3 Pocock's Method	-	-	-	-	-	-	+	-	-	-	+	-
2.4 Cave and Freedman	-	-	-	-	-	-	-	-	-	-	-	-
3. Non-Parametric-Tests												
3.1 Hewitt's Test [1]	-	-	-	-	+	-	+	-	+	-	+	-
3.2 Rogersons' Generalization for												
3.2.1 a 5-months peak [1]	-	-	-	-	+	+	+	+	+	+	+	+
3.2.2 a 4-months peak [1]	-	n.a.	-	n.a.	+	n.a.	+	n.a.	+	n.a.	+	n.a.
3.2.3 a 3-months peak [1]	-	n.a.	-	n.a.	+	n.a.	+	n.a.	+	n.a.	+	n.a.
3.3 David-Newell-Test	-	-	-	-	-	-	+	+	-	-	+	+

Hypothetical Data (Part B)	Local Summer Peak				One Pulse Pattern				Random Pattern			
	small		large		small		large		small		large	
Test	0.05	0.01	0.05	0.01	0.05	0.01	0.05	0.01	0.05	0.01	0.05	0.01
1. Goodness-of-Fit-Tests												
1.1 Chi-Square - Goodness of Fit	-	-	-	-	-	-	-	-	-	-	-	-
1.2 Kolmogorov-Smirnov-Type-Statistic	-	-	+	+	-	-	+	+	-	-	-	-
2. Edwards' Family												
2.1 Edwards' Test	-	-	+	+	-	-	+	+	-	-	-	-
2.2 Roger's Extension of Edwards' Test	-	-	+	+	-	-	+	+	-	-	-	-
2.3 Pocock's Method	-	-	-	-	-	-	-	-	-	-	-	-
2.4 Cave and Freedman	-	-	-	-	-	-	-	-	-	-	-	-
3. Non-Parametric-Tests												
3.1 Hewitt's Test [1]	+	-	+	-	-	-	-	-	-	-	-	-
3.2 Rogersons' Generalization for												
3.2.1 a 5-months peak [1]	+	+	+	+	-	-	-	-	-	-	-	-
3.2.2 a 4-months peak [1]	+	n.a.	+	n.a.	+	n.a.	+	n.a.	-	n.a.	-	n.a.
3.2.3 a 3-months peak [1]	+	n.a.	+	n.a.	+	n.a.	+	n.a.	-	n.a.	-	n.a.
3.3 David-Newell-Test	-	-	+	+	-	-	+	-	-	-	-	-

1) The actual levels of significance for the non-parametric tests are:		
Levels of Significance	0.05	0.01
Hewitt	0.0483	0.0130
Rogerson 5 months peak	0.0562	0.0152
Rogerson 4 months peak	0.0470	n.a. (Max. Ranksum=42; p_{42}=0.0267)
Rogerson 3 months peak	0.0545	n.a. (Max. Ranksum=33; p_{33}=0.0545)

Fig. 3.6. Results for Seasonality Tests: Hypothetical Data

Switching to the evaluation of the tests using real data in Figure 3.7, the first impression is that significant results are the rule rather than the exception (as in Figure 3.6). This indicates that most of our hypothetical data fulfilled one of their requirements: They represented rather extreme cases one is usually not faced with in reality.

All tests produced significant results on the $\alpha_1 = 0.95$; $\alpha_2 = 0.99$ levels for the Danish Register Data and for Respiratory Diseases. As both data-sets show a pronounced sinusoidal pattern, it is obvious that the nonparametric tests yield this result. The significant values for the Goodness-of-Fit tests and the "Edwards' Family" when evaluating the Danish register data underlines their sample size dependency: If one were taking simply the relative monthly frequencies, the Danish data would show less fluctuation than the hypothetical sine wave which was tested negatively for small sample size. The χ^2-Goodness-of-Fit-Test, especially, seems to be extremely sensitive to sample size. It does not yield significant results for the monks data at all, while the nuns data are highly significant. When looking at the histograms of both data (Figure 3.4 b and c), the eye would assign the tag "seasonal" to the monks' rather than to the nuns' monthly distribution of deaths. For the five data-sets shown in the lower part of Figure 3.4, the nonparametric tests show only rarely significant results. This is probably due to the sparse data of some data-sets such as Lymphoma (Figure 3.4 h) or Leukemia (Figure 3.4 j) where assigning ranks might not be the best option.

Most of the desired properties for inequality indices do not narrow down the choice for a "best" seasonality test. Tests which are based on ranks like the nonparametric tests presented here fulfill the "relativity principle". According to that principle, the outcome should be dependent on the relative contribution of each group — regardless of the sample size. On the contrary, the nonparametric tests cannot pass the "transfer principle". If deaths were "shifted" from months with low mortality to months with high mortality, the non-parametric tests would not necessarily result in more significant ρ-values. This would, however, be the case for the Goodness-of-Fit tests and the "Edwards Family". "Standardization" poses no problem for any of these tests. They are, by definition, designed to return values between 0 and 1 for ρ. All tests are relatively "easy to comprehend, intuitively meaningful and easy to explain to others" [126, p. 11] (Intelligibility): the Goodness-of-Fit tests analyze if an observed distribution deviates too much from a hypothetical distribution which cannot be explained by chance. The tests based on Edwards' contribution have some kind of geometrical framework, where the deviation from a uniform distribution is tested. The nonparametric tests examine whether the observed data show a peak-period of either 6, 5, 4, or 3 months, respectively. The favorable properties of *Sensitivity* and *Robustness* [126] have not been introduced before. If data are described with one statistic, the first choice is often a measurement of the central tendency. Typical examples are the mean and the median. While the mean is often the preferred description, one has to be aware that it is not very robust when the data contain outliers. Likewise, some seasonality tests could be also prone to be too sensitive when faced with some outliers. Nevertheless, seasonality indices should also not be too robust: If there is one extreme outlier, for example caused by an influenza epidemic, a reasonable test should not treat this as similar to another value which might be just slightly higher than values in any other month. Thus, a seasonality index based purely on ranks is too robust. "Sensititivity" and "Robustness"

Real Data (Part A)

Test	Wrigley		Nuns		Monks		Union		Danish		Resp.	
	0.05	0.01	0.05	0.01	0.05	0.01	0.05	0.01	0.05	0.01	0.05	0.01
1. Goodness-of-Fit-Tests												
1.1 Chi-Square - Goodness of Fit	-	-	+	+	-	-	+	+	+	+	+	+
1.2 Kolmogorov-Smirnov-Type-Statistic	-	-	+	+	+	+	+	+	+	+	+	+
2. Edwards' Family												
2.1 Edwards' Test	-	-	+	+	+	+	+	+	+	+	+	+
2.2 Roger's Extension of Edwards' Test	-	-	+	+	+	+	+	+	+	+	+	+
2.3 Pocock's Method	-	-	+	+	+	-	+	+	+	+	+	+
2.4 Cave and Freedman	-	-	-	-	-	-	-	-	+	+	+	+
3. Non-Parametric-Tests												
3.1 Hewitt's Test [1]	+		+	+	+	+	+	+	+	+	+	+
3.2 Rogersons' Generalization for												
3.2.1 a 5-months peak [1]	+	+	+	+	+	+	+	+	+	+	+	+
3.2.2 a 4-months peak [1]	+	n.a.	+	n.a.	+	n.a.	+	n.a.	+	n.a.	+	n.a.
3.2.3 a 3-months peak [1]	+	n.a.	+	n.a.	-	n.a.	+	n.a.	+	n.a.	+	n.a.
3.3 David-Newell-Test	-	-	+	+	+	+	+	+	+	+	+	+

Real Data (Part B)

Test	Anenc.		Lymph.		Suicides		Leukem.		Crohn's	
	0.05	0.01	0.05	0.01	0.05	0.01	0.05	0.01	0.05	0.01
1. Goodness-of-Fit-Tests										
1.1 Chi-Square - Goodness of Fit	-	-	+	-	+	-	+	-	-	-
1.2 Kolmogorov-Smirnov-Type-Statistic	+	-	+	-	+	+	+	-	-	-
2. Edwards' Family										
2.1 Edwards' Test	+	-	+	-	+	+	+	+	-	-
2.2 Roger's Extension of Edwards' Test	+	-	+	-	+	+	+	+	-	-
2.3 Pocock's Method	+	-	+	-	+	+	+	+	-	-
2.4 Cave and Freedman	-	-	-	-	-	-	-	-	+	+
3. Non-Parametric-Tests										
3.1 Hewitt's Test [1]	-	-	-	-	-	-	-	-	-	-
3.2 Rogersons' Generalization for										
3.2.1 a 5-months peak [1]	-	-	-	-	+	-	-	-	-	-
3.2.2 a 4-months peak [1]	-	n.a.	-	n.a.	-	n.a.	-	n.a.	-	n.a.
3.2.3 a 3-months peak [1]	-	n.a.	-	n.a.	+	n.a.	+	n.a.	-	n.a.
3.3 David-Newell-Test	+	-	+	-	+	-	+	-	-	-

1) The actual levels of significance for the non-parametric tests are:		
Levels of Significance	0.05	0.01
Hewitt	0.0483	0.0130
Rogerson 5 months peak	0.0562	0.0152
Rogerson 4 months peak	0.0470	n.a. (Max. Ranksum=42; p_{42}=0.0267)
Rogerson 3 months peak	0.0545	n.a. (Max. Ranksum=33; p_{33}=0.0545)

Fig. 3.7. Results for Seasonality Tests: Real Data

are excluding principles. The nonparametric tests are very robust against outliers. Consequently, they cannot be too sensitive for sudden, abrupt changes in the distribution. The other two groups of tests behave exactly the other way around.

Our analysis does not yield "the best seasonality test". Depending on data and the relevant research question, different tests are useful. One should always keep in mind that some tests are quite sensitive to sample size. Another important feature is the distribution of the underlying data: Do we have a relatively smooth pattern or do the data look rather erratic? Last but not least, the test should be also aimed at the research question: Do we assume that the underlying data have a bimodal pattern? Only in that case, the test developed by Cave and Freedman [44] can be recommended. If it is expected that the disease/cause of death has a rather sudden prevalence throughout the year for a relatively short period of time, Rogerson's generalization of Hewitt's test for 3, 4 or 5 months should be used. In the case of smooth data structure across the twelve months, it is probably best to use Hewitt's test. As it is based on ranks, it would be probably best to use it in conjunction with a seasonality index such as φ_1 to give an indication of the extent of seasonal fluctuations. Goodness-of-Fit tests and "Edwards's Family" should only be used if the data do not show a smooth pattern.

3.6 Evaluation of Time-Series Methods Using Hypothetical Data

3.6.1 Introduction

Evaluating time-series methods aims at a different angle than the discussion of indices and tests discussed above. A general applicable tool should be able to fit a model to data with characteristics one typically observes for seasonal mortality studies [117]. One major part is the correct estimation of the trend component. It is more common in studies of seasonal mortality to have pure count data available than rates of the variable of interest. Thus, a correct estimation of the trend should be flexible enough to incorporate on the one hand changes in the variable of interest. For example, it can be expected that the overall trend in mortality is decreasing over time. On the other hand, compositional changes can push the trend in the other direction. Due to the increased survival chances, for instance, more and more old people are alive which implies an increase in death counts in absolute terms. It should be also obvious that it is necessary for a seasonal analysis of time-series that the seasonal component is not constant over time.

Not all time-series methods discussed before have been analyzed. The "classical decompostion" has been omitted as it assumes a constant seasonal component over time. Instead of X-11 and X-11-ARIMA the latest version, X-12, has been used since it should yield better estimates than the previous version due to improved outlier detection and automatic estimation of ARIMA-Models.

There are not any software package available that contain all remaining time-series methods. Therefore, we had to rely on several packages to investigate the various approaches. Table 3.2 gives an overview which software has been used for which particular method. Besides R [170, 301], we also used Splus, EViews and BV4 [38].

Table 3.2. Software for Implementation of Time-Series Methods

Method	Software	Version
X12	EViews	4
SABL	Splus	2000
STL	R	1.8.1
TRAMO/SEATS	EViews	4
BV4	BV4	4.1

3.6.2 Description of Data-Sets

In contrast to seasonality indices and tests we analyzed time-series methods only with hypothetical data. Real data are used in Chapter 4.

We used seven synthetically generated data-sets with an increasing level of complexity. The construction of these data is briefly outlined in Table 3.3. Seasonal rates are rarely available. This is why we wanted to reflect this fact in our hypothetical data by constructing them as count data. We started with a simple model being constant in the trend and the seasonal component. No residuals are put into the data (Model I). It should be expected from any seasonal decomposition/adjustment procedure to extract the trend and the seasonal component correctly. For any subsequent model (Models II–VII) we introduced a third-order polynomial to obtain a monotonously increasing trend. Starting with Model IV we modeled a linearly increasing seasonal component. The last models' seasonal components employ also a second, semi-annual wave in the data. This should test whether the seasonal procedures are also able to detect heat-related deaths during summer. We chose three distributions from which the data are drawn: (1) none for Models I, II, and IV; having no residual component at all is very unlikely in reality; (2) therefore models III, V, and VI followed a Poisson distribution; however, the Poisson distribution is sometimes inappropriate. This can be easily seen if the requirement of the Poisson distribution of $E(x) = \mu(x) = Var(x)$ is not met. One often encounters so-called overdispersion $(Var(x) > E(x))$. This can be typically caused by unobserved heterogeneity. As we use only time as a covariate it can be assumed that this proxy is unable to catch all significant influences and, as a consequence, we are faced with unmeasured factors. A pure Poisson process is therefore the exception rather than the rule. Thus, (3) we opted to use a Negative Binomial distribution [22, 41, 292].[14]

3.6.3 Results and Discussion

There are different approaches to evaluate statistical methods. We decided to base our judgment on visual inspections of the decomposition process. While

---

[14] While a Poisson distribution requires $E(x) = Var(x) = \mu$, the negative binomial distribution relaxes the assumption about the variance with $E(x) = \mu$ and $Var(x) = \mu + \frac{\mu^2}{\theta}$ [389]. In our application, we set θ to 100.

Table **3.3.** Hypothetical Time-Series Data

Model	Trend	Seasonal Component	Errors
I.	constant	constant	—
II.	monotonously increasing	—"—	—
III.	—"—	—"—	Poisson
IV.	—"—	increasing	—
V.	—"—	—"—	Poisson
VI.	—"—	increasing "heat-related mortality"	—"—
VII.	—"—	—"—	Neg. Binom.

a theoretical statistician may criticize this, the major advantage is that one can immediately recognize whether a specific method caught the important characteristics of the underlying data. The following Figures 3.8–3.14 show the results for the Models I–VII described before. For all our calculations we did not use the default settings but tried to adapt the methods as closely as possible to the actual data. In the case of X-12, for example, we linked the components multiplicatively or log-additively according to our initial assembling of the data. In real world applications, one does not have that background knowledge. Therefore, the results for X-12 might show better results for our hypothetical data than for real world data. TRAMO/SEATS did not pose any problems for the implementation, nor did SABL or the Berliner Verfahren. Applying STL was less straightforward: As pointed out in the original paper [48], there are 6 parameters to be entered into the model. Five of them can be found automatically (e.g. number of observations), for one parameter, however, there is no straightforward solution. Unfortunately, it is a crucial parameter for our purposes: the smoothing parameter for the seasonal component. We followed Cleveland et al.'s suggestion to visually inspect various parameter values [48]. Our analysis resulted in an optimal value of approximately 7 for all our models. Lower values made the seasonal component change too quickly, higher values resulted in seasonality being too smooth. [15]

The column on the left in each figure represents the "real" data (i.e. the input). Combining the trend (f) with the seasonal component (k) and the residuals (p) resulted in the "real data" (a). Those "real data" were used as input for the four different seasonal decomposition methods X-12, SABL, STL, and TRAMO/SEATS and the Berliner Verfahren ("BV4"). Perfectly working methods should decompose the input data in exactly the components we used for the composition initially. We can see the outcome of these methods in columns 2–6 in each graph for X-12 (column 2), SABL (column 3), STL (column 4), TRAMO/SEATS (column 5) and BV4 (column 6).

---

[15] Cleveland et al. advise to use odd numbers ≥ 7 [48]. We actually searched values from 1 until 50 wheres the original authors looked only from 7 until 35.

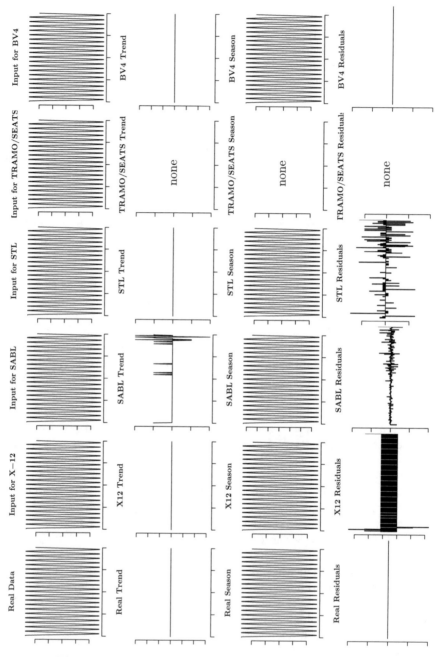

Fig. 3.8. Seasonal Decomposition of Time-Series — Model I

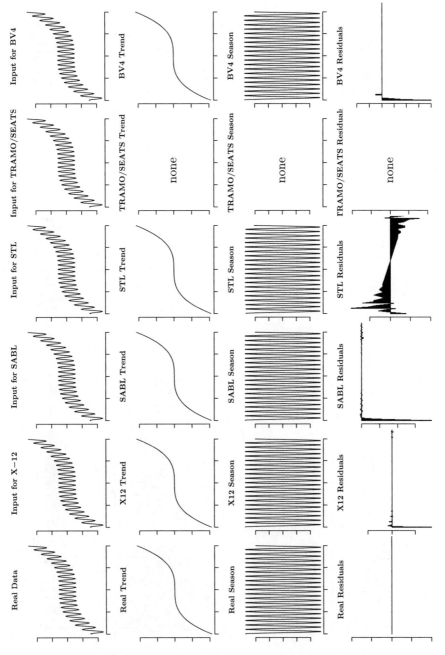

Fig. 3.9. Seasonal Decomposition of Time-Series — Model II

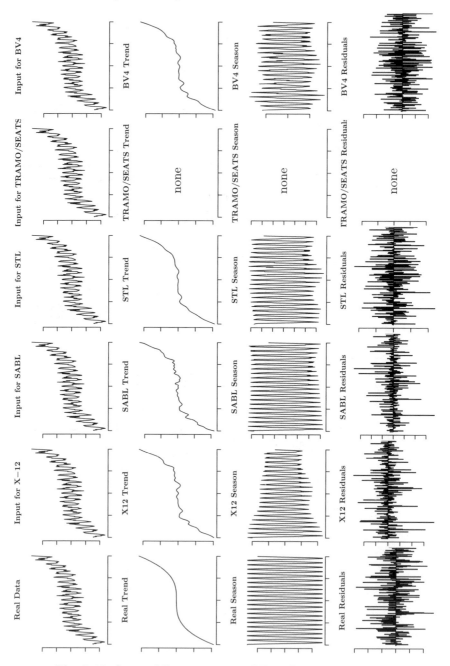

Fig. 3.10. Seasonal Decomposition of Time-Series — Model III

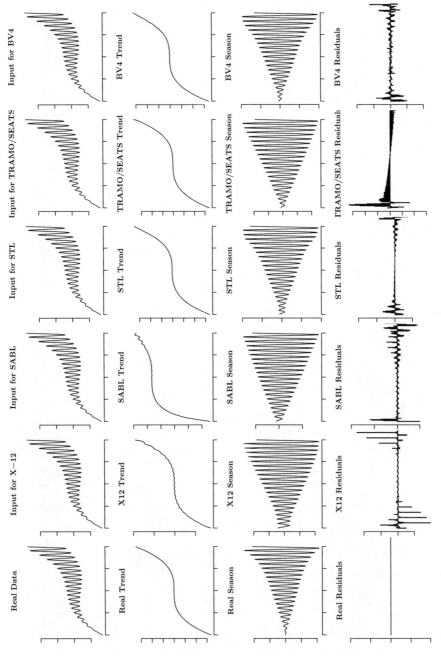

Fig. 3.11. Seasonal Decomposition of Time-Series — Model IV

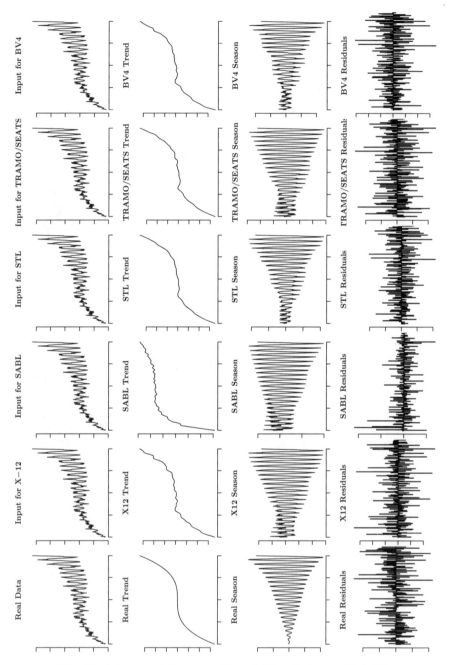

Fig. 3.12. Seasonal Decomposition of Time-Series — Model V

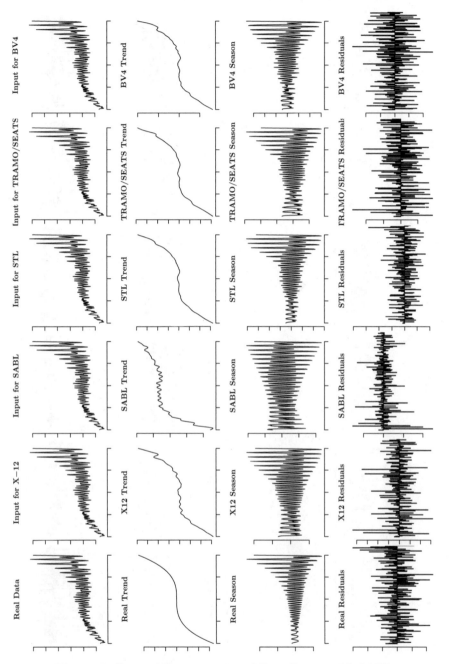

Fig. 3.13. Seasonal Decomposition of Time-Series — Model VI

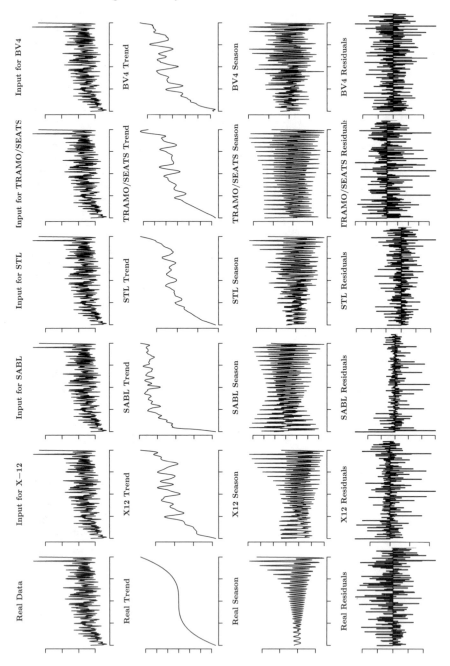

Fig. 3.14. Seasonal Decomposition of Time-Series — Model VII

For Model I (Figure 3.8), BV4 works perfectly; the methods X-12, SABL and STL perform almost as well as the procedure from the German Statistical Office. This close fit should be expected anyway, as a constant trend and a constant seasonal pattern represents the easiest seasonal pattern. The implementation of TRAMO/SEATS in EViews 4.1 did not work for Models I–III. Surprisingly the failure of this method is highly correlated with a constant seasonal pattern. Due to the lack of detailed information [299], it was impossible to determine the reason for the program's crashes.

With the exception of TRAMO/SEATS, the four other methods performed again very well for Model II. Solely STL's extraction of the residuals was slightly problematic: While no residuals should appear, STL, nevertheless extracted residuals. In addition, those residuals are highly auto-correlated, indicating that important characteristics of the data are misspecified into the irregular component. However, this is only a minor drawback: for reason of simplicity, no numbers have been put on the scales. The mean value of the trend is 400 and the amplitude of the seasonal component is 54. The residuals' mean amplitude height is 0.40 and their maximum value amounts only to 1.92. This misspecification of the irregular component is, thus, rather negligible.

Seasonal decomposition by standard methods becomes tricky when artificial noise is added to the data, as shown in Model III when the data are drawn from a Poisson distribution (Figure 3.10). All procedures contain a somehow wiggly trend. Only SABL seems to extract the seasonal component very well. X-12 shows a decline in seasonality; STL's algorithm produces a fairly shaky result. The seasonal component of the Berliner Verfahren is the least stable.

Model IV (Figure 3.11) is the first model for which TRAMO/SEATS was working. STL, TRAMO/SEATS and BV4 reproduced the trend almost identically to the input data. X-12's of the underlying third-order polynomial is only slightly worse, whereas SABL's trend is smooth but estimated wrong.[16] All methods performed remarkably well for the extraction of the seasonal signal.

The quality of the four decomposition methods declines rapidly, starting with Model V (Figure 3.12). Besides a monotonously increasing trend and seasonal component we allowed the data again (Model III) to be derived from a Poisson distribution. SABL still faces the same problems when plotting the trend as in Model IV. But the other methods (X-12, STL, TRAMO/SEATS, BV4) also do not show a clear signal extraction for the trend; it becomes rather wiggly. None of the decomposition methods is able to mirror the seasonal component exactly into the data. Although all four methods show somehow an increase in seasonality, only STL and BV4 fit the seasonality part relatively well. The results from TRAMO/SEATS, SABL and X-12 are not satisfactory.

So far we have only used one sine and one cosine term to model annual fluctuations in mortality. Model VI (Figure 3.13) introduces a more elaborated seasonal component with a sine and a cosine component of frequency of six

---

[16] The wrong estimation is not caused by using a log-transform initially and forgetting about re-transforming in the end.

months. This allows to incorporate heat-related mortality (summer excess deaths) into our models. As Model VI is equivalent to Model V with this exception, it should be no surprise that none of the four methods performs better than previously.

Model VII (Figure 3.14) is the most complicated pattern we faced our data with. In addition to a monotonously increasing trend, an annual and a semi-annual ("heat-related mortality") seasonal swing, we input unobserved heterogeneity by drawing our data from a Negative Binomial Distribution with a relatively low value of the dispersion parameter Θ.[17] None of the five methods is able to capture the trend or the seasonal component even remotely. All trend estimates show a wiggly upward tendency but neither X-12, SABL, STL, TRAMO/SEATS, nor BV4 mirror the underlying third-order polynomial correctly. Furthermore, the seasonal component is not extracted properly by any of the standard methods: X-12, SABL, TRAMO/SEATS and BV4 seem to be inadequate. The general approach of STL seems to work well for seasonality. Its estimate of this component is, nevertheless, too shaky to be declared satisfactory.

Thus, evaluating time-series methods with hypothetical data did not result in one procedure which can unanimously be recommended. For simple data patterns, the standard methods yield satisfactory results. If these approaches are, however, faced with data structures one can typically encounter in demography (i.e. variable trend, changing seasonality, overdispersion), none of them extracts the entered components well enough. We rather suggest, therefore, the method outlined in Chapter 4 which is especially tailored for those situations and returns the trend as well as the seasonal component almost identical to the simulation input.

3.7 Summary

The aim of this chapter was to present and critically evaluate indices, tests and time-series methods for seasonality. For that purpose various methods which are used in the literature have been presented, discussed and evaluated with hypothetical (indices, tests, time-series methods) and with empirical (indices, tests) data.

Three indices were presented: a winter/summer ratio, a dissimilarity index and a measurement based on entropy. Among them, the winter/summer ratio seems to be the best choice, mainly because of its easy interpretability and that it takes the ordering of the months into account.

Recommending a test for seasonality is less straightforward. Several tests have been presented and discussed which can be categorized in three classes: Goodness-of-Fit tests, the "Edwards' family", and nonparametric tests. Choosing an appropriate test should be guided by the underlying research question

---

[17] The lower the dispersion parameter Θ, the larger the variance of the data: $\mathrm{Var}(Y) = \mu + \frac{\mu^2}{\Theta}$ [cf. 389].

and by the nature of the data. For the "normal" application, i.e. a smooth pattern with one peak during the year, Hewitt's test is probably best [150]. Because this test is purely based on ranks, it should be used in conjunction with the winter/summer-ratio to have a measurement also of the height of the seasonal fluctuations. Generalizations of Hewitt's test [315] can be employed if one assumes sudden outbreaks of certain diseases throughout the year which last only a limited amount of time. If two peaks during the year are expected such as for Crohn's disease, the test proposed by Cave and Freedman seems to be appropriate [44]. If the data are rather erratic, one should use either one of the Goodness-of-Fit tests or one from the "Edwards' family" [e.g. 84].

Five common time-series methods (X-12, SABL, STL, TRAMO/SEATS, BV4) have been evaluated using seven models of simulated data with increasing complexity. The general outcome is not convincing: If any of those methods are faced with complicated data, the decomposition of the trend and the seasonal component does not return the input data. For relatively simple simulated data, the signal extraction in all methods works well. The trend and the season in the given data, and after the decomposition process, are almost identical. Sudden changes in the trend does not pose any problems. Problems arise on the one hand if the seasonal pattern is not constant over time. Methods which are unable to handle this, can not be applied as changes in the seasonal component over time (or age) is often the main interest in seasonality studies. On the other hand, the evaluated time-series methods fail to return the entered signals if the data are derived from a Poisson distribution or from a Negative Binomial distribution. In practice, especially the latter distribution appears to be the rule rather than an exception if data are not rates but counts and if relevant factors are unmeasured. It is difficult to point at the exact estimation problem of these standard methods as they are quite complicated due to the filters employed and the various iterative steps involved.

Due to these shortcomings, a new method has been developed which is able to incorporate changes in the trend, the seasonal component and unobserved heterogeneity. This novel approach is presented, evaluated and applied to real data in Chapter 4 (page 83).

4

Seasonal Analysis of Death Counts in the United States

4.1 Introduction

Demographers — as probably most other empirical researchers — prefer working with rates rather than with pure counts: growth rates, birth rates, death rates, transition rates, etc. The advantage is obvious: While count models rely only on the actual event of interest, rate models take also the units into account which are exposed to this event (e.g. person-years lived). Unfortunately, exposures are often not available. For example in the case of historical demography, the number of deaths by age and sex is regularly available. What is frequently absent, however, is the number of people who were alive (and therefore exposed to the risk of dying) in that particular age and sex. Also for the analysis of seasonal mortality, we are often faced with the situation to have death counts available but no exposures.

One way to avoid this problem is to estimate the exposures. Donaldson and Keatinge [77], for example, obtained the daily population in their study of winter excess mortality in southeast England "by linear interextrapolation from the 1981 and 1991 censuses". Also Kunst et al. [209] used linear interpolation for population estimates in their time-series analysis on the influence of outdoor air temperature on mortality in The Netherlands. Another solution in the case of absent exposures is to use only events. For those count models, it is not necessary to estimate any exposures. Typically, those studies assume an underlying Poisson process in the data like the analyses of seasonal variation in mortality in Scotland and in The Netherlands [121, 235].

The latter approach is clearly less desirable if exact exposures are available. If this is not the case, it is open to discussion whether an estimated population at risk is more favorable than pure counts. Especially in the case of seasonality studies, there are many problems associated with estimating seasonal populations (=exposures), as pointed out by Happel and Hogan [140].[1]

---

[1] It should be noted that Neale [271] already mentioned the problem of estimating monthly population counts in 1923.

This chapter presents an analysis of seasonality based on pure death counts in the United States from 1959 to 1998. Vaupel [381] once remarked that demographers should use the best possible data to study a certain phenomenon. Working with death counts as the best possible data seems to be contradictory at first sight as Scandinavian population registers, for example, offer exact event counts and precise exposure times. The *quality of the data* is, however, only one side of the coin of *best data*: it is equally important to take care of the *content of the data*. Small, egalitarian countries such as Denmark and Sweden with one common climate are less desirable than the US when one's aim is to study the impact of social factors on seasonal mortality. Thus, the "Multiple Cause of Death"-Public-Use-Files we used for the United States provide such a data-source: every individual death since 1959 is publicly available, broken down by various characteristics. The wealth of having almost 80 Mio. individual records available makes it possible to study selected causes of death for the whole period since the late 1950s across a wide age-range. More details of the data are explained in Section 4.3.

Besides the sheer amount of information, the lack of research on seasonal mortality in the United States during the last 25 years has been another reason to choose this country. Studies on seasonal mortality focused on European countries during the last 25 years. For the US, this topic has not been investigated since the late 1970s [231, 316, 319, 324, 325]. The only exception being regional studies (e.g. 199, 285) and one study on deaths from coronary heart disease by Seretakis et al. [340]. Solely, Feinstein [102] examined overall mortality in the United States recently. One important finding was that the "seasonalities of deaths have been increasing over the years [...] for older people and decreasing for younger people"[102, p. 485].

This was quite surprising. With the improved chances of people attaining high ages since the 1970s [378], we would have expected that elderly people were also better able to withstand environmental stress (i.e. cold in winter) with improvements in general living conditions.

4.2 Research Questions

There is ambivalent evidence for differences in seasonality of mortality for women and men. Some studies surprisingly found no differences for seasonality for this main determinant of mortality while others discovered remarkable differences between women and men in their seasonal mortality patterns with men showing larger seasonal fluctuations than women [98, 121, 262, 302, 419]. Therefore we decided to conduct all subsequent analyses for women and men separately.

- **Period & Cause of Death.** Do we find support for Feinstein's result of increasing seasonality for the elderly over time? Is it possible to detect different patterns for all cause mortality and selected groups of causes of death?

- **Age & Cause.** Previous studies have shown an increase in seasonality with age for various countries [251, 268, 302]. Can these findings be replicated in the US for all cause mortality and for selected causes of death?
- **Region & Period.** It is argued in the literature that socio-economic progress in general and the widespread use of central heating and air conditioning decreased seasonal fluctuations in deaths [188, 251]. We expect decreasing seasonality over time. However, regions with a high differential between winter and summer temperatures should have benefited more than regions with a moderate climate.
- **Region & Age.** How important is the region where you are living for the development of seasonal mortality? Is an assumed increase with age in seasonality of deaths larger in regions where one faces higher environmental stress than in other regions?
- **Education, Age & Cause of Death.** The question how socio-economic status — a major general mortality determinant [374] — affects seasonality in deaths is still unanswered. Few studies argue that lower social groups are disadvantaged [e.g. 79, 147]; most others found no social gradient [214, 215, 342]. Our analysis focuses on the question whether people with higher education face lower seasonality in deaths.
- **Marital Status & Age.** Another major factor in mortality research is marital status, usually showing that married people have lowest (overall) mortality. Typically, married people have lower mortality risks throughout their life courses than single, widowed or divorced persons. Men's differences are larger than women's [129, 163, 223]. These differential mortality risks are usually explained either by a protection effect or by a selection effect [125, 223]. In the case of seasonal mortality, a protection effect can be imagined in several directions: people who are married can pool their financial resources and have therefore not only better access to medical care, but can also afford a higher quality of housing which is a major determinant in avoiding cold-related mortality as previous studies have shown [e.g. 245]. While this causal pathway could be also captured by education as a proxy for socio-economic status, marital status may also work in another direction: in comparison to single, widowed and divorced people, married women and men are most likely not living alone. In the case of an emergency, the spouse is usually present to organize help. Nevertheless, no research has been published so far on the potential impact of marital status on seasonal mortality.

4.3 Data

Our analysis uses the "Multiple Cause of Death"-Public-Use-Files for the years 1959–1998 published by the "US Centers for Disease Control and Prevention" (CDC). We downloaded the data from 1968–1998 from the "Inter-university Consortium for Political and Social Research" (ICPSR) at http://www.icpsr.umich.edu/. Data for previous years have been kindly provided by the "Program on Population, Policy and Aging" at the Terry Sanford Institute for Public Policy at Duke University, NC.

We included only deaths at ages 50 and higher, because we wanted to focus on adult mortality. At younger adult ages, the number of deaths in certain age-groups for selected causes of deaths are too few to obtain robust estimates. The data consist of more than 77 Mio. individual death records. Each of the records contains information on the sex of the individual, month and year of death, age at death. For our analysis, we also extracted information on the cause of death, state of residence and state of occurence, and several social variables. Figure 4.1 gives an overview on the availability of these variables in our data over time. The following subsections explain how we divided and coded the data for our analysis.

4.3.1 Cause of Death

Table 4.1 outlines which ICD codes we used to extract the information for our selected causes of death. ICD is the abbreviation for "International Statistical Classification of Diseases and Related Health Problems" from the World Health Organization (WHO). This coding scheme gives mandatory instructions how the cause of death has to be coded. During its existence, the ICD underwent several revisions. While ICD-10 is the current revision, ICD-7, ICD-8, and ICD-9 were in use in the United States during our observation period. ICD-7 was used until 1967; between 1968 and 1978 ICD-8 was the valid coding scheme; from 1979 until 1998 deaths in the United States were coded according to ICD-9.

Table 4.2 gives an overview about the actual number of deaths for each cause. In addition, we have given information about the contribution of each cause to all deaths for the whole time-series, for the first five years, and the last five years to highlight vaguely any time trends. In the column "Winter/Summer Ratio" we divided winter deaths (January–March) by summer deaths (July–September) to find out whether our selected causes show a considerable seasonal difference in mortality. We did not give an extra-column for a test for seasonality. All causes of death presented here have passed Hewitt's nonparametric test for seasonality with significant values ($\rho = 0.0130$) [150, 395]. This indicates that all causes examined show a pattern where the six highest values of a year and the six lowest values of a year are not mixed but appear in separate halves of the year. Most people died of cardiovascular diseases during our observation period, with almost 32 Mio. deaths. In conjunction with neoplasms, cerebrovascular and respiratory diseases almost 80% of deaths are covered. Despite the regularities in the ordering of the months (i.e. significant results for Hewitt's test), the extent of seasonality differs remarkably: On average (=All Causes), the number of summer deaths is exceeded by winter deaths by roughly 16%. Neoplasms, not surprisingly, show relatively small fluctuations (1.6%), whereas respiratory diseases have 62%

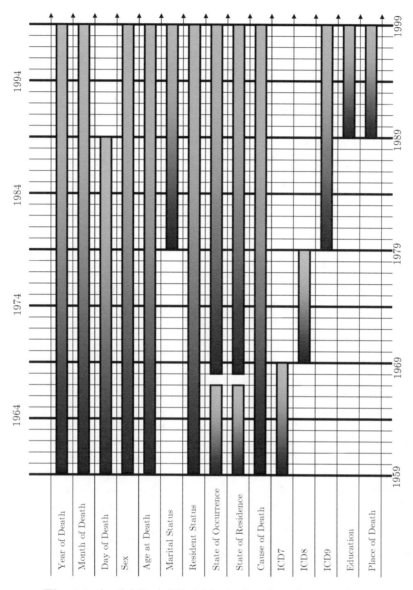

Fig. 4.1. Availability of Variables in Our Data-Set over Time

more deaths in winter than in summer. The leader in that respect is influenza with a value of 27.762 (i.e. almost an excess of 2,700%).

Although the most remarkable changes in the cause of death structure over time are usually associated with the "epidemiological transition" [281] and the vanishing of tuberculosis [402] in the 20th century, the proportions of the leading causes of death have not remained constant during recent decades either.

Table 4.1. Coding Scheme for Selected Causes of Death

Cause of Death	ICD-Codes		
	ICD-7	ICD-8	ICD-9
Cardiovascular Diseases	400–468	390–429	390–429
			440–459
		440–458	557
IHD	—	410–414	410–414
Neoplasms	140–239	140–239	140–239
Cerebrovascular Diseases	330–334	430–438	430–438
Respiratory Diseases	240; 241	460–519	460–519
	470–527		
Asthma	241	493	493
Influenza	480–483	470-474	487
Pneumonia	490–493	480–485	480–483
			486
Bronchitits	500–502	490–491	490–491
Diabetes Mellitus	260	250	250
Infect. & Parasit. Dis.	001–138	001–136	001–139
Tuberculosis	001-019	010–019	010–019
Liver Cirrhosis	581	571	571

With the exception of IHD (1968–98), all causes of death
are covered for the period 1959–1998.

Figure 4.2 gives an overview of how seven major causes have changed during
our observation period. For "both sexes", "women", and "men" there are two
columns each, showing the cause-of-death spectrum for the first (1959–63)
and last (1994–1998) five years, respectively, covered in our dataset. Cardiovascular diseases remain the leading cause of death (see also Table 4.2) —
although the contribution shrunk for both sexes from 45% to 35%. Similarly,
also cerebrovascular diseases lost in relevance between the late 1950s and the
late 1990s. Almost 12% of all people died from that group of diseases between
1959–63, whereas in the years 1994–98 only 7% died of it. Net "winners" in
this respect are mainly malignant neoplasms (17% → 22%) and respiratory
diseases (7% → 9%). Diabetes Mellitus and "Infectious and Parasitic Diseases" also gained in relevance, however their overall share is comparatively
small (Diabetes Mellitus: 1.84% → 2.66%; Infectious and Parasitic Diseases:
1.24% → 2.80%). It is interesting to note that influenza and hypothermia —
two causes of death which are often associated with winter excess mortality
— make up only a negligible part of all deaths (influenza: 0.04%; hypothermia: 0.02%). These small proportions, however, might mask the real impact
of these diseases. For example, it is well-known that "[i]nfluenza epidemics
cause deaths additional to those registered as being due to influenza, such as
deaths caused by arterial thrombosis"[78, p. 90].

Table 4.2. Number of Deaths, Proportion and Seasonal Pattern of Selected causes of Death

Cause of Death	# of deaths 1959–1998	Proportion of Cause, 1959–1998	Proportion of Cause, 1959–1963	Proportion of Cause, 1994–98	Winter/ Summer Ratio
All Causes	77,640,423	100.00%	100.00%	100.00%	1.157
Cardiovascular Diseases	31,926,214	41.12%	44.97%	34.84%	1.206
IHD (1968-98)	17,422,235	27.96%	29.23%	21.10%	1.211
Neoplasms	16,335,426	21.04%	16.84%	22.15%	1.016
Cerebrovascular Diseases	7,055,237	9.09%	11.84%	6.88%	1.197
Respiratory Diseases	5,688,290	7.33%	5.76%	9.70%	1.624
Asthma	153,338	0.20%	0.31%	0.24%	1.295
Influenza	107,048	0.14%	0.28%	0.04%	27.762
Pneumonia	2,356,304	3.03%	3.45%	3.50%	1.789
Bronchitits	174,048	0.22%	0.27%	0.14%	1.663
Diabetes Mellitus	1,599,351	2.06%	1.84%	2.66%	1.187
Infectious and Parasitic Diseases	1,226,575	1.58%	1.24%	2.80%	1.151
Tuberculosis	160,856	0.21%	0.62%	0.06%	1.201
Liver Cirrhosis	1,080,511	1.39%	1.27%	1.10%	1.098

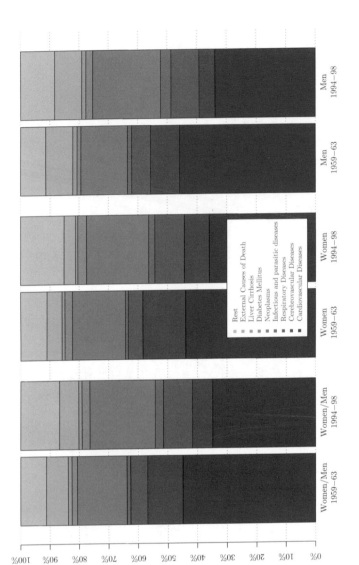

Fig. 4.2. Changes in the Cause of Death Composition of Adult Deaths in the United States Between 1959–63 and 1994–98 by Sex

4.3.2 Education

The variable education has been included since 1989. The original data are given as a two-digit code indicating years of education. We followed the re-coding advice in the coding manual with one exception: we included two additional categories which indicate whether a person has finished elementary school (8 years of education), dropped out of elementary school (less than 8 years) or has received no formal education at all (0 years). All other categories remained the same and have been given meaningful labels. The categories, their labels and the corresponding numbers of death broken down by sex are given in Table 4.3.

Table 4.3. Number of Deaths Broken Down by Sex and Level of Education

Code	Meaning	Deaths			
		Women		Men	
		Counts	%	Counts	%
0	No formal education	105,462	1.0	108,348	1.0
1	Elementary School Dropout	846,138	7.9	975,483	8.7
2	Finished Elementary School	1,390,687	12.9	1,229,727	10.9
3	High School Dropout	1,197,240	11.1	1,229,727	10.9
4	Finished High School	3,746,633	34.8	3,594,343	31.9
5	College Attendance	1,120,953	10.4	1,147,500	10.2
6	College Degree or more	857,895	8.0	1,264,765	11.2
7	Not Stated	1,502,673	14.0	1,549,632	13.8
	Σ	10,767,681	100.0	11,249,981	100.0

Finishing high school was the most common level of education achieved by both sexes (women: 34.8%; men: 31.9%). Although our decomposition in 7 categories is relatively detailed, enough people remain even in the smallest group "no formal education" with more than 100,000 deaths for each sex.

4.3.3 Marital Status

Data on marital status are available since 1979. To make comparable analyses on the impact of social factors by age, we restricted our analysis to the years 1989–98, the same period as for education. In the official codebooks six categories are given which have been converted to five: never married / single, married, widowed, and divorced remained the same. The category "not stated on certificate" has been merged together with "not stated". This residual category comprises less than one percent of each sex ($\female$: 0.3%, $\male$: 0.7%). In contrast with the variable "education", the cell frequencies differ remarkably between women and men. Most notable are the differences for married and widowed women and men. This is the result of the higher life expectancy of women. It is more likely for women at the end of their lives to be widowed than for men.

Table 4.4. Number of Deaths Broken Down by Sex and Marital Status

Code	Marital Status	Deaths			
		Women		Men	
		Counts	%	Counts	%
1	Never Married, Single	935,504	8.7	1,536,393	13.7
2	Married	2,820,570	26.2	6,487,584	57.7
3	Widowed	6,102,184	56.7	2,011,515	17.9
4	Divorced	879,450	8.2	1,136,594	10.1
9	Not Stated	29,973	0.3	77,895	0.7
	Σ	10,767,681	100.0	11,249,981	100.0

4.3.4 Region

Various studies have shown that countries with relatively harsh climatic conditions and cold winters (e.g. Canada, Sweden) show less winter excess mortality than countries with warm or moderate climate such as Portugal, Spain or the UK [135, 147, 252]. It is argued that people in colder regions are better able to protect themselves against adverse environmental conditions. One disadvantage of previous studies was that these results were based on cross country analyses. The data from the United States provide an excellent framework to analyze seasonal mortality in different climatic regions within one country. For our regional analysis we followed the state groupings given in the original coding manuals which resemble different climatic regions. Our slightly adapted division of states is presented in Table 4.5. In its original version the states Alaska and Hawaii belonged to the group "Pacific". In our analysis, these two states have been examined separately. Figure 4.3 makes it easier to locate the coding of the regions geographically. This classification resembles in most cases the "Köppen Climate Classification". In some cases, however, the regional classification does not describe states with similar meteorological conditions. For example, Arizona and Montana in the "Mountain-Group" differ considerably in their climate. Special care should therefore be taken for the interpretation if estimations from the "Mountain" and from the "Midwest" show exotic results.

We refer to the actual "state of occurrence", i.e. the state/region where the death has happened. "State of residence" is given in the data as well. In our analyses by region we only included those deaths where state of residence and state of occurrence were in the same regional division excluding the impact of "snowbirds" [140].[2] The loss of data is relatively minor. More than 98% of all deaths happened in the same region as the place of residence of the deceased.

---

[2] People who are seasonally migrating — usually to warmer regions during the cold season — are sometimes labeled "snowbirds" in the literature.

Table 4.5. Coding of Regions by State

Code	Region	States		
1	New England	Connecticut	Maine	Massachusetts
		New Hampshire	Rhode Island	Vermont
2	Middle Atlantic	New Jersey	New York	Pennsylvania
3	Midwest	Illinois	Indiana	Iowa
		Kansas	Michigan	Minnesota
		Missouri	Nebraska	North Dakota
		Ohio	South Dakota	Wisconsin
4	South Atlantic	Delaware	D.C.	Florida
		Georgia	Maryland	North Carolina
		South Carolina	Virginia	West Virginia
5	South Central	Alabama	Arkansas	Kentucky
		Louisiana	Mississippi	Oklahoma
		Tennessee	Texas	
6	Mountain	Arizona	Colorado	Idaho
		Montana	Nevada	New Mexico
		Utah	Wyoming	
7	Pacific	California	Oregon	Washington
8	Alaska	Alaska		
9	Hawaii	Hawaii		

4.3.5 Known Data Problems

Generally speaking, the "US Multiple Cause of Death"-Public-Use-Files provide a very good basis for research. Nevertheless, there are some real and some potential pitfalls in the data which will be briefly outlined here as well as the approaches used to tackle them.

ICD Revisions: During our observation period, three revisions of the ICD were in practice in the US (ICD-7, ICD-8, ICD-9). If one is not careful, the introduction of a new revision is prone to result in sudden shifts in the number of deaths. An illustrative example is Asthma. While ICD-7 was used, this disease (ICD-7 code: 241) belonged to the group of "Allergic, endocrine system, metabolic and nutritional diseases" (ICD-7 Codes: 240–289). Since the eighth revision, Asthma (ICD-8 code: 493) is one of the "diseases of the respiratory system" (ICD-8: 460–519). Therefore particular care was taken in reconstructing the time-series. Besides consulting the original coding schemes, the following procedures have been undertaken to obtain time-series with a maximum of quality:

- The first step was to plot the data to discover any breaks or otherwise strangely behaving characteristics in the data. As pointed out by Cleveland: "Data display is critical to data analysis. Graphs allow us to explore data to see the overall pattern and to see detailed behaviour;

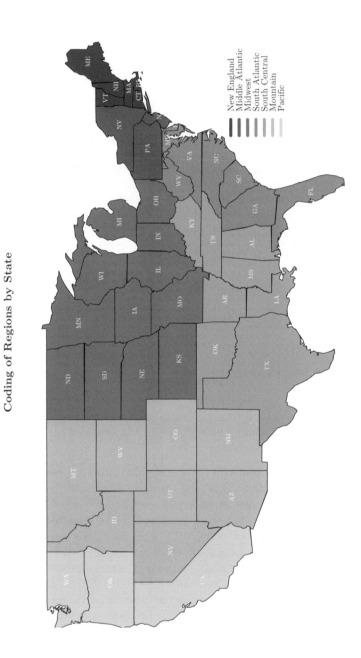

Fig. 4.3. Coding of Regions by State

no other approach can compete in revealing the structure of the data so thoroughly" [49, p. 5].

- Articles and monographs by Jacques Vallin and France Meslé were consulted (e.g. [259, 375]) who are probably *the* experts on reconstructing time series of causes of death.
- Several articles on seasonal mortality give details about the ICD codes they used for a particular cause [e.g. 98, 209]. This was valuable in finding "hidden" causes such as asthma mentioned before. The scope of some articles covered more than one ICD coding scheme. Marshall et al. [246], for example, give the ICD codes for Coronary Heart Disease for ICD-8 and ICD-9. Articles like this facilitated the transition from one ICD revision to the next.
- The statistical software package Stata with its search facilities for ICD codings (`icd9 search` and `icd9 lookup`) allowed to find all possibilities for a certain disease which would otherwise remain undetected.
- Vladimir Shkolnikov, Michael Bubenheim, Sigrid Gellers-Barkmann, Rembrandt Scholz and Markéta Pechholdová from the "Laboratory for Demographic Data" at the Max Planck Institute for Demographic Research in Rostock, Germany, have given valuable advice and suggestions for the reconstruction of the time-series.

The Year 1972: In the year 1972, the Multiple Cause of Death Public Use File contained only a 50% sample of all deaths. We simply multiplied all deaths by a factor of 2 to circumvent this problem.

The Years 1987 & 1988: We discovered a sudden drop in death counts by plotting annual deaths for selected causes for the years 1987 and 1988. After checking several possibilities as a cause, we found out that only the first 44 US states (in alphabetical order) had been included for those two years. Utah, Vermont, Virginia, Washington, West Virginia, Wisconsin, and Wyoming were missing. We tackled this problem by estimating the contribution of those states for the year 1986 and 1989 for our respective analysis (e.g. for sex, age group and educational level). With those two values we made a linear interpolation of what we would expect for the years 1987 & 1988. We then multiplied the actual counts for those states with a factor to obtain the expected number of deaths. Of course, this does not solve the problem perfectly. Nevertheless, we believe that this approach yields more satisfactory results than, for example, leaving out these 7 seven states for all analyses.

4.4 Methods

4.4.1 Model Requirements

The data used in this project have specific features that we need to take into account when selecting the appropriate models for analysis: the employed methods should allow for the count character of the data, without requiring information on the corresponding exposures. Covering a period of four decades of remarkable changes in mortality, especially at older ages, the data show considerable variation in the overall trend, both between different causes of death but also between different age-groups within the same cause. Thus, appropriate models have to allow for a flexible specification of these different trend features. We do not know how the trend and the seasonal component changes with age and/or over time. Therefore we do not want to impose any specific parametric model upon our data but rather use data-driven, non-parametric techniques to estimate our components. Last but not least, we would like to allow for overdispersion in our models as this "is the norm in practice and nominal dispersion the exception" [249, p. 124–125]. As shown in Chapter 3 (Measuring Seasonality), previously existing methods such as X-11, STL, ... were unable to extract the exact trend and the exact seasonal component. Therefore, a new method has been developed which is presented in the following sections to fulfill these requirements.

4.4.2 The Model

Basic Model Specification

Let t denote the underlying time variable which can represent calendar-time or age. For matters of convenience in this explanation, t represents calendar-time. The corresponding number of deaths, corrected for the different lengths of months, is denoted y_t. Our model resembles several characteristics from the well known field of *generalized linear models* (GLMs):

Distribution: We assumed that the y_t follow a Poisson distribution with parameter μ_t. Thus $\mathrm{E}(y_t) = \mathrm{Var}(y_t) = \mu_t$. The Poisson distribution is usually regarded as "the benchmark model for count data"[41, p. 3].

Link Function: Similar to the setting of GLMs, we relate μ_t, which are the expected values of y_t to a stimulus matrix via a link function. In our case, the stimulus matrix is time (or age) and transformations of it. While other link functions are also possible for Poisson distributed data (for example, the square-root- or the identity-link, see [389]), we use the canonical/default choice of a log-link.

The model we are estimating is:[3]

$$\ln \mu_t = f(t) + \sum_{l=1}^{L} \left\{ f_{1l}(t) \sin \left(\frac{2\pi l}{12} t \right) + f_{2l}(t) \cos \left(\frac{2\pi l}{12} t \right) \right\}. \qquad (4.1)$$

---

[3] It should be pointed out that the development of this model is based on an idea of Dr. Jutta Gampe. The model was implemented in strong collaboration between her and the author.

The model is estimated in a similar manner as a GLM. The main deviation are the parameters which are estimated. In the GLM setting, *one parameter* is estimated for each column in the covariate matrix. In our model, these scalars are replaced by functions. These functions are indicated by $f(t)$, $f_{1l}(t)$ and $f_{2l}(t)$ in Equation 4.1. The component $f(t)$ describes the varying trend in the level of counts — due to changing exposures and overall changes in mortality. The seasonal fluctuations are modeled with the latter two terms in the equation. In the most simple case with $L = 1$, two seasonal functions $f_{11}(t)$ and $f_{21}(t)$ are estimated, resulting in one(!) smoothly changing annual fluctuation. If $L = 2$, a semi-annual swing is added. Theoretically, it is possible to add higher frequencies. It is doubtful it will make sense, though, if $L \geq 3$. These kinds of models have been termed *varying coefficient models* by Hastie and Tibshirani [145]. "In contrast to the GLM, where the regression coefficients [...] are assumed to be constant, [...] this model accommodates situations in which one or more of the coefficients are allowed to vary smoothly (interact) over [...] time or space"[89, p. 760].

Technical Digression: Nonparametric Estimation of Smooth Trends Varying Coefficients

The following section, until page 101, represents a technical digression.[4] The aim is to show how a function like $f(t)$, $f_{1l}(t)$ or f_{2l} is actually estimated. The equations in this section (Equations 4.2 and 4.3) are not directly linked to Equation 4.1.

We assumed that $f(t)$, $f_{1l}(t)$ and f_{2l} are smoothly changing over time (or age). In a recent paper, Eilers and Marx [89] showed that such models, which they termed *GLASS* (Generalized Linear Additive Smooth Structures), can be estimated via *P*-Spline smoothing. This technique belongs to the family of nonparametric smoothers. *P*-Splines are cubic *B*-Splines being used as regression bases with a roughness penalty on their regression coefficients. *B*-Splines are made of polynomial pieces connected with knots. Please see Figure 4.4 for a graphical explanation.[5] In our case of cubic (degree $q = 3$) *B*-Splines, each *B*-Spline consists of $q+1 = 4$ polynomial pieces, as indicated by the four segments in gray. Each of these polynomial pieces is of degree $q = 3$. These polynomial pieces are connected at $q = 3$ inner knots (t_2, t_3, t_4). At those knots, the spline function as well as the $q - 1 = 2$ derivatives of the neighboring polynomial pieces are continuous. The *B*-Splines are positive on a domain of $q + 2 = 5$ knots. This corresponds in Figure 4.4 to the range from t_1 to t_5 on the time-axis; everywhere else they are zero [87, 132]. These *B*-Splines are bell-shaped and resemble a Gaussian density (=density of a Normal distribution) [89] without the smoothing problems when regression bases are derived

---

[4] As this approach is novel, it is appropriate to include it in the main text instead of putting it into the appendix.

[5] An extensive discussion of *B*-Splines (definition, basic properties, ... is given in [67].

from a normal distribution. For example, Gaussian smoothers cannot fit a straight line as they are not locally defined but from $[-\infty; \infty]$ resulting in a "Gaussian ripple" [86]). Such an example is given in Apppendix C on page 183.

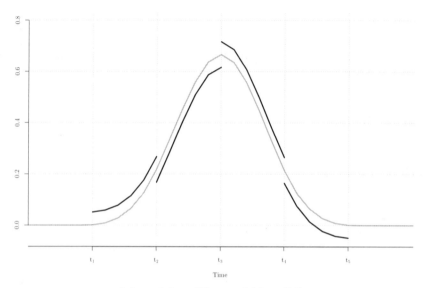

Adapted from Eilers and Marx [86].

Fig. 4.4. Construction of One B-Spline

With these cubic B-Splines as regression bases, we are working in the well known area of linear regression. The smoothed function is found by minimizing S in Formula (4.2) via the traditional OLS-fitting. In this equation, y represents the response vector, B the matrix of covariates (=our B-Splines) and α their respective regression coefficients.

$$S = |y - B\alpha|^2 \tag{4.2}$$

Figure 4.5 shows cubic B-Splines "in action" to smooth artificial data.[6] In the lower part of each of the four panels, you see cubic B-Splines which are close to normal densities as postulated. From left to right and from top to bottom, the number of B-Splines is increasing. The upper part of each

---

[6] It might be interesting to note that the use of cubic B-Splines is relatively widespread: For example, the software to design the letters of this text (META-FONT) used some cubic B-Splines to have smooth and visually appealing shapes [200].

panel shows scatterplot of the data and a line. This line is the result of the smoothing using the cubic B-Splines as regression bases.

One can easily see:

- The higher the number of B-Splines, the closer (and "wigglier") the smoothed curve is to the data.
- The lower the number of B-Splines, the smoother is the curve.

The problem one faces now is to find an optimally smoothed curve. If the curve is too smooth, important characteristics of the data are not caught. If the curve is too wiggly, the data are overfitted, i.e. we include more complexity into the model than what is actually desirable. There is no golden standard for choosing the optimal number of B-Splines and therefore of regression parameters.[7] One could follow a subjective approach to determine the optimal number of parameters. Although it may sound repulsive to the "objective" scientist, "[i]t may well be that such a subjective approach is in reality the most useful one" [132, p. 29]. We are following another approach outlined by Eilers and Marx [87] as no all-purpose scheme existed to choose the optimal number of splines automatically. The idea is simple: Building on works of O'Sullivan [283] and Reinsch [306], they proposed to choose a relatively large number of cubic B-Splines which would normally result in over-fitting. To prevent this fallacy, a penalty is put on the regression coefficients. More specifically, a penalizing constant is multiplied with the second derivative of the regression coefficients.[8] The previous optimization problem (in Formula 4.2) changes to Formula 4.3:

$$S^* = |y - B\alpha|^2 + \lambda |D_2\alpha|^2 \quad , \text{ where } D_2\alpha = \Delta^2\alpha \qquad (4.3)$$

The iterative procedure to optimize S^* has been described in [89]. Figure 4.6 shows the impact of how a change in the penalizing parameter λ affects the smoothness of the curve. In all of the nine panels we see the same artificial data as in Figure 4.5. The number of cubic B-Splines has been set to a relatively high level, which would result in over-fitting if the regression coefficients were not penalized. With a λ-value of 0.01 in the upper-left panel, the weight of the penalty-term is relatively negligible, resulting in the expected overfitted, wiggly curve. The higher the λ-values (from left to right and up / down), the smoother the curve gets. While the upper two graphs are definitely too close to the data, the last curves are — without any doubt — too smooth

---

[7] As we are actually using regression parameters, the term "non-parametric models" might be misleading. Eilers and Marx [87] pointed out that "anonymous models" is preferrable as parameters are estimated. They simply have no scientific interpretation.

[8] Eilers and Marx note that the second derivative has been used since "the seminal work on smoothing splines by Reinsch (1967)", however, "[t]here is nothing special about the second derivative; in fact, lower or higher orders might be used as well" [87, p. 91].

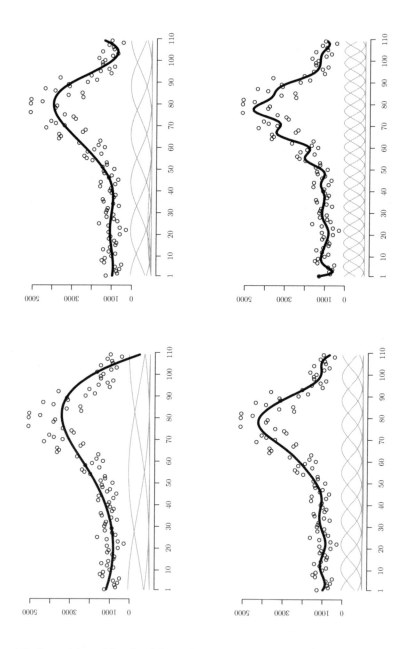

Fig. 4.5. Smoothing of Artificial Data Using Different Numbers of Cubic *B*-Splines as Regression Basis

with the outcome that important characteristics of the data are not captured. Ultimately, the smoothed curve tends to become a horizontal line for $\lambda \to \infty$.

There are several strategies to find the optimal value of λ, for example cross-validation. We followed the path of Eilers and Marx [87] and used the Akaike Information Criterion (AIC). Put in a nutshell, the AIC corrects the fit of the model for the number of parameters involved in the model's estimation.

P-Splines have several useful properties which makes Eilers and Marx [87, p. 98] "believe that P-splines come near to being the ideal smoother." For example, their foundation in linear regression and the generalized linear model makes them easy to understand and use. Also the lack of unwanted boundary effects favors P-Spline smoothers instead of other smoothing methods.[9] An exhaustive comparison of various smoothing methods, their properties and their respective pros and cons are found in [88].

Overdispersion & Smoothing Parameter Selection

After initial experiments, we discovered that our data violated one of the key assumptions of the Poisson distribution which we were using; As stated in Formula 4.4, the mean and the variance are characterized by the same parameter (we denoted the parameter by μ as the standard choice; λ is already in use for the smoothing penalty parameter).

$$\mathrm{E}(y_t) = \mathrm{Var}(y_t) = \mu_t \tag{4.4}$$

As mentioned before, this assumption of nominal dispersion is relatively strong. Regularly, one observes *overdispersion* in practical applications. Overdispersion is defined as $\mathrm{E}(y_t) = \mu_t < \mathrm{Var}(y_t)$. This case, where the variance exceeds the mean, can arise for various reasons [22]:

- if the rate μ_t is not constant within a chosen time unit t (*time dependence in the rate*)
- if the number of events in a time-interval depends on the number of previous events (*contagion*).[10]
- in the case of *unobserved heterogeneity*, i.e. there are covariates not entered into the model which affect the number of counts.

All of them are likely for our analysis of death count data — especially *unobserved heterogeneity*. We can certainly expect two sources of unobserved

---

[9] In the case of smoothing with a polynomial, it can not be excluded that some values are estimated at the boundaries which do not make sense. For example, if a quadratic curve is used for smoothing, the fitted line points on both ends go either up or down although it is possible that the resulting values do not have any theoretical meaning (e.g. lifetimes smaller than zero).

[10] It should be noted that already Greenwood and Yule stated in 1929 [133, p. 276] "the problem of the distribution arising when the chance of a happening is affected by antecedent success or failure".

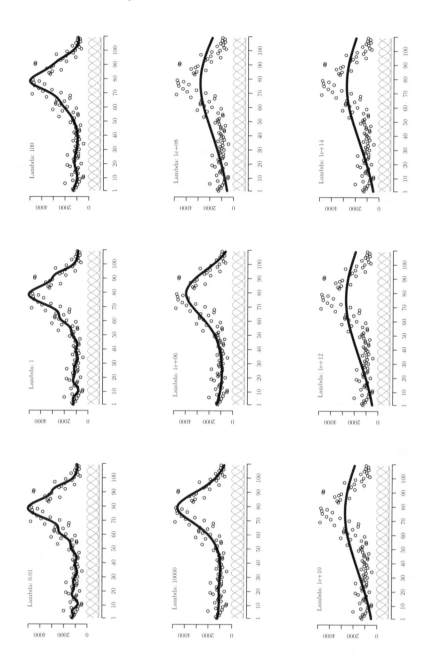

Fig. 4.6. The Impact of Changing λ-Parameters on the Smoothness of the Curve

heterogeneity in our data: one is due to the fact that the month of death is only a proxy-variable for the actual factors (e.g. temperature) which modulate the expected number of deaths μ_t seasonally. There is individual but unobserved heterogeneity in the risk of death for specific months across years. Secondly, even if we restrict the analysis to one sex, narrow age-groups, ..., people in these groups are heterogeneous with respect to other characteristics not included in the analysis.

Although we do not know what the actual reason of overdispersion is, there is a way to control for it. The typical approach still follows the suggestion of Greendwood and Yule [133] of assuming that the data follow a Poisson distribution, "but there is gamma-distributed unobserved individuals heterogeneity reflecting the fact that the true mean is not perfectly observed" [41, p. 71]. This modeling of a random effect for the mean with a gamma distribution leads to the Negative Binomial Distribution for the count [41, 160, 292].

The Negative Binomial Distribution is closely related to the Poisson Distribution as the following tabulation shows:

Distribution	Expected Value	Variance
Poisson	μ_t	μ_t
Negative Binomial	μ_t	$\mu_t + \frac{\mu_t^2}{\theta}$

The estimator for the expected value remains the same: μ_t. Using this parameterization of the variance as shown by Venables and Ripley [389], we can easily recognize that the Negative Binomial distribution depends simply on one more parameter called θ. One could argue that the Negative Binomial Distribution is a generalization of the Poisson distribution by relaxing the term for the variance. We can model the Poisson case of nominal dispersion by letting $\theta \to \infty$. The other extreme of large overdispersion can be modelled by letting $\theta \to 0$.

The problem that arises is now: which θ-value is to be chosen, as this parameter has to be entered into our model? The solution is found in the properties of the so-called *Pearson Residuals* in the Generalized Linear Model. They are defined as [see 249, p. 37]:

$$r_P = \frac{y - \mu}{\sqrt{V(\mu)}} \quad \text{and in our case and notation:} \quad r_{P_t} = \frac{y_t - \hat{\mu}_t}{\sqrt{\hat{\mu}_t + \frac{\hat{\mu}_t}{\theta^\lambda}}},$$

where y_t denotes the number of deaths at time t (for the analysis by period), $\hat{\mu}_t$ represents the estimated value at time t and Var is the estimated variance. This standardization of the *raw residuals* $(y_t - \hat{\mu}_t)$ results for an optimal model in large samples in $\mathrm{E}(r_{P_t}) = 0$ and $\mathrm{Var}(r_{P_t}) = 1$ [41, p. 141].

Our strategy for choosing the optimal model proceeds in the following steps.

1. We assume a grid of possible overdispersion parameters θ.
2. For each given θ:
   - we estimated all possible models with the given grid of all λ-permutations. In the simplest case when $L = 1$ in Equation 4.1, three separate λs were estimated.[11]
   - we estimated the AIC from all models estimated in the previous step and chose the one with the minimum AIC value.
3. We iterated the previous step for all values of θ.[12]
4. The outcome of the previous step was one "conditional optimal model" for each given θ. Then, we calculated the Pearson Residuals for these "conditional optimal models". The one model where the variance of the Pearson Residuals was closest to 1 was then chosen to be the optimal model.[13]

Using simulated data, we compared our final model which incorporates overdispersion with a model which assumed data following a poisson distribution. This approach has the advantage that we know the various components that are entered into the model and can therefore check whether the two decomposition approaches return the same components we have entered into our simulated data. Figure 4.7 shows such a simulated example in a 3 × 4 panel. The left column displays the simulated data. The trend component (Figure 4.7 d) has been constructed by using a third-order polynomial. The seasonal component is linearly increasing (Fig. 4.7 g). We assumed a value of 10 for θ in the Negative Binomial Distribution which results in high overdispersion. This is reflected in the residuals as shown in Figure 4.7 j. Apart from the linear increase in the seasonal component, this model is equivalent to Model VII in Chapter 3 presented on page 78.

The middle column represents the optimal model, which has been estimated using our approach which incorporates unobserved heterogeneity. Figure 4.7 b shows the entered time-series which is equivalent to Figure 4.7 a. It can be clearly seen that the extraction of the trend (Fig. 4.7 e) and of the seasonal component (Fig. 4.7 h) mirrors the input data almost perfectly. As demanded from our model, the variance of the Pearson residuals should be 1 for the optimal model. Figure 4.7 k shows that our estimation is reasonably close enough with a value of 1.04. The right column exemplifies a mis-specified model. Although we used a Negative Binomial Model in the middle column

---

[11] If we had given 5 values for λ_{Trend} which estimates the trend function $f(t)$, and also 5 values each for the penalty coefficient for the seasonal functions $f_{1l}(t)$ and $f_{1l}(t)$, we would have had to estimate $5 \times 5 \times 5 = 125$ models.

[12] If we had also given 5 possible values for θ, $125 \times 5 = 625$ models would be required to be estimated.

[13] If the variance of the Pearson Residuals was not close enough to 1, we started again with step 1 with an increased grid. "Close enough to 1" for the variance of the Pearson Residuals was defined as: $0.99 < \text{Var}(r_{P_t}) < 1.01$.

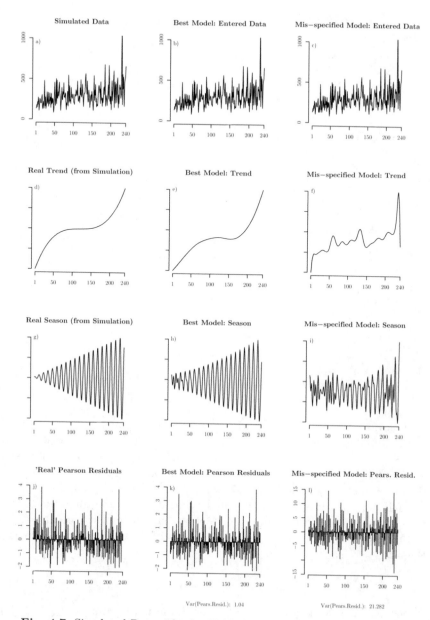

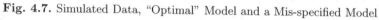

Fig. 4.7. Simulated Data, "Optimal" Model and a Mis-specified Model

as well, we have chosen a value for θ ($= 9000$), which approximates a Poisson Distribution. Without taking unobserved heterogeneity into account our model is helpless in estimating the trend (Fig. 4.7 f) and the seasonal component (Fig. 4.7 i). Not surprisingly, the variance of the Pearson Residuals in the mis-specified model (Fig. 4.7 l) is far too high (21.282) for an expected value of 1.

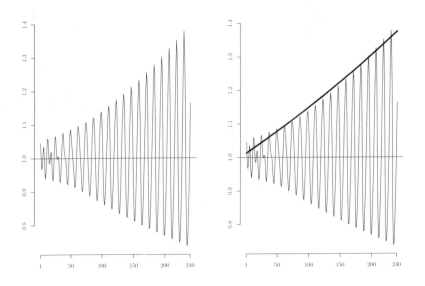

Fig. 4.8. Seasonal Component from Figure 4.7 and Its Amplitude

Based on this simulation study,[14] we concluded that our approach meets our requirements that an appropriate method should be able to work with overdispersed data having a flexible trend and a changing seasonal component.

The following section presents the results of our analysis for which we used the decomposition method outlined here. We are, however, only interested in a small part of the three components: the change in the amplitude of the seasonality over time (or age). This corresponds in mathematical notation to the smooth amplitude-modifying functions of the seasonal components in Equation 4.1 (page 96) [118]:

$$a_l(t) = \left(f_{1l}(t)^2 + f_{2l}(t)^2\right)^{\frac{1}{2}} \tag{4.5}$$

We use the resulting function $a_l(t)$ from Equation 4.5 and plot $e^{a_l(t)}$. Figure 4.8 explains this graphically. In the left panel our extracted seasonal component for an optimal parameter selection from Figure 4.7h is displayed. The difference between the left and the right panel is that in the latter we added the amplitude over time($e^{a_l(t)}$) of the seasonal fluctuations using a bold line.

---

[14] Of course, more simulation studies have been conducted. The one presented here should only serve as an example.

This line is used as indicator of the change in seasonality over time or age in the subsequent sections. A value of 1 corresponds, thus, to the case when no seasonality is present. These seasonality values should not be confused with the exponentiated regression coefficients known from event-history models and understood as relative risks. Values apart from 1 have no direct interpretation.

4.5 Results & Discussion

4.5.1 Seasonality by Period & Cause of Death

All Cause Mortality

Figure 4.9 shows the change in the amplitude for seasonality in deaths from all causes by 10-year-age-groups for the whole observation period from January 1959 until December 1998. The left panel illustrates results for women, whereas the right panel deals with men. For both sexes we see the same general trends: the older the people (=the darker the lines), the higher is the seasonal amplitude. Changes over age will be examined in subsequent parts of this section. Right now the focus is on changes over time. What we discover is some preliminary support for Feinstein's finding: Younger age-groups seem to have a constant or slightly decreasing trend as indicated by the dotted and dashed gray lines — especially for men. People who died at an age above 80 (dotted, dashed and solid lines), however, have to suffer from higher fluctuations in seasonality towards the end of the observation period.

With the progress made in survival chances — especially for older people — we would have suspected that people are better able to withstand environmental stress in recent times. A solution for this surprising finding is not straightforward. One has to keep in mind that "Seasonality for All Cause Mortality over Time, by Age-Group" is an aggregated outcome over several variables. Between 1959 and 1998 mean age at death, measured by e_0, rose from 73.24 years to 79.31 years for women (♂ 1959: 66.80 years; 1998: 73.53 years) in the United States [166]. Consequently, also the distribution of deaths within one 10-year-age-group shifted upwards. Among octogenarians, for example, the arithmetic mean for age at death increased from 83.68 years to 84.01 years for men (♀ 1959: 83.94 years; 1998: 84.54 years). This compositional effect might blur the "true" effect of changes in seasonality over time. We checked this problem by estimating seasonality for all cause mortality over time by single ages. The results (not shown here) resembled our findings for 10 year-age-groups: at least since the late 1970s, seasonalities are increasing for the elderly.

Selected Causes of Death

After ruling out the impact of the age composition, we decomposed the aggregated picture into selected causes of death and analyzed them separately for women and men by age-group as shown in Figure 4.10.

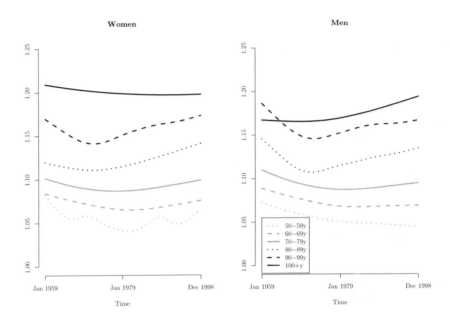

Fig. 4.9. Seasonality of All Cause Mortality over Time by Sex and Age-Group

Deaths from cardiovascular diseases are shown in the upper left panel for women and in the upper right panel for men. As this was and still is the leading group of cause of death, the fact that the two diagrams resemble the results for all cause mortality rather closely is not too surprising. Cerebrovascular diseases, as illustrated in the two panels in the middle row, are similar to the previous pictures for deaths from all causes as well as from cardiovascular diseases. The increasing trend for the elderly is even more obvious for this cause of death category. Apart from women who have died between 50 and 59 years of age from that cause (dotted gray lines), all seasonalities are increasing at least since the middle of the 1970s.[15]

If data problems can be excluded, there are always two strains of explanation which can be referred to when interpreting changes in populations [383]. First, there is a *real* difference in the variable of interest (seasonal susceptibility). In our context, this explanation would imply that people have become more susceptible to environmental stress over the years. One has to be careful with this interpretation, though: by looking at the changes in the amplitude we are using a relative measurement. An increase in the amplitude can either be

---

[15] The dashed gray line on the left, denoting deaths of women aged 60-69 years, represents an outlier. So far, it has been impossible to track down the source for this problem since several checks have been already conducted such as plotting the time series, looking for sudden changes in the number of deaths, etc. Also a completely new approach for estimation resulted in the same outcome.

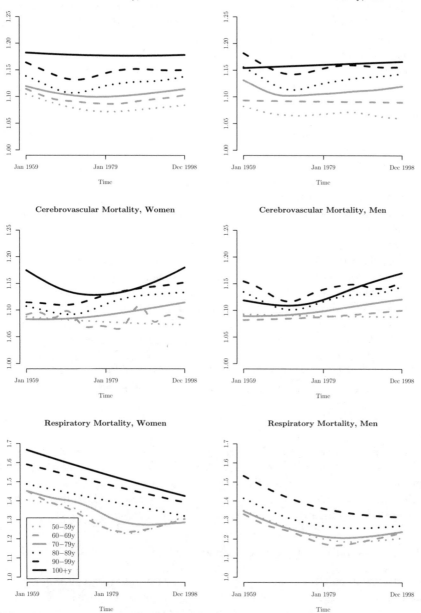

Fig. 4.10. Seasonality of Selected Causes of Death over Time by Sex and Age-Group

caused by a real increase in winter mortality or by a decrease in winter mortality over time with decreases in summer mortality at an even faster pace. The results would be the same: a larger seasonal amplitude in deaths/mortality by the end of the observation period than in the beginning. This conjecture finds support in the article of Seretakis et al. [340], who also found a decrease in deaths from coronary heart disease until the 1970s followed by a slight increase: "If the reversal is real, then it could reflect the increase in use of air-conditioning, which would have blunted the effects of occasional heat waves on coronary mortality" [340, p. 1014].

Secondly, however, there is the possibility that the change is influenced by a *compositional* difference. In the context of seasonal mortality fluctuations, it is possible that current progress against old-age mortality has the side-effect that nowadays even frail people can become relatively old. While in the past, frail individuals died early and left a relatively robust cohort of survivors who were coping well with environmental hazards in winter, frail people today may become older and are more susceptible in winter. This explanation could be, however, only applied to people at relatively advanced ages.

Not all causes of death show the same pattern over time. The two panels on the bottom of Figure 4.10 contain the development of seasonality over time for respiratory diseases. For both sexes we observe a decline in seasonality. While the decrease is almost linear for women at advanced ages, men's and "younger" women's seasonality shrank until the late 1970's, and has stalled since. Please note the different scale on the y-axis in comparison to cerebro- and cardio-vascular diseases: seasonality for respiratory diseases was much higher in the past and still is. Although this gap has become smaller, the amplitudes in seasonal death fluctuations from respiratory diseases remain higher in comparable age-groups.

In univariate analysis of time-series it is always difficult to determine causal influences of external variables. It is, however, quite likely that improvements in housing conditions played a major part. While in the US in 1960 only half of all households were heated by gas or electricity, this proportion reached 82 percent in 1990 [372]. With these improved chances to heat the house properly, chances are decreasing for people to "catch a cold". The different pattern for women and men cannot be explained by this, though.

4.5.2 Seasonality by Age & Cause of Death

Of prime interest for demographers are not only death patterns for women and men over time but — maybe even more important — with age. Previous articles state that seasonality is increasing with age. However, the data used in many studies appear to be problematic [cf. 302, p. 199]: "In several studies, no distinction by age was made at all [13, 21, 319, 367]. If the factor age was taken into account, the highest included age or the beginning of the last, open-ended, age category was chosen at an age after which most deaths in a population occur [37, 62, 76, 97, 98, 164, 169, 188, 253, 369]. The oldest people in the "Eurowinter"-study, for example, were 74 years old. Bull and Morton [37] merely made a binary distinction: younger than 60 years; 60 years and older. Thus, results from these studies may simplify or blur the relationship between age and seasonal fluctuations in mortality " [302, p. 199]. So far, there are only a few studies that have investigated seasonality in mortality or deaths into very high ages [251, 268, 302]. The highest ages that have been analyzed were centenarians and supercentenarians (110 years and older) in the study of Robine and Vaupel [309]. Regardless whether they calculated seasonality indices and ratios or log-odds, the typical outcome were higher seasonal fluctuations by the end of the lifespan than at middle ages. Even supercentenarians show higher excess winter mortality than centenarians, which indicates that also at those ages, the resistance against environmental hazards is decreasing [309].

All Cause Mortality

Figure 4.11 gives a first impression how seasonality in deaths changes with age. The left panel shows seasonality for deaths from all causes for women where each solid line indicates a 10-year-calendar period. The right panel shows results from the respective analysis for men.

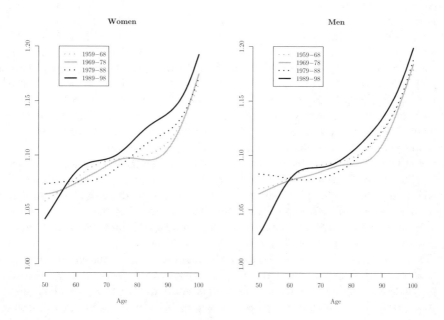

Fig. 4.11. Seasonality of All Cause Mortality by Sex and 10-Year-Calendar-Pperiod

The general trend for both sexes shows — as expected — higher seasonality with age. The increase is far from linear. We could make a distinction for women as well as for men by grouping the first three decades together (dotted gray: 1959–68; solid gray: 1969–78; dotted black: 1979-88) and contrast them with the last 10 years (1989–98 in solid black): Until age 80 the increase is relatively moderate. Then, at the highest ages, seasonality bends sharply upwards. The black solid line in both panels represents changes with age for the most recent decade in the analysis (1989–98). One can differentiate three stages: Compared to previous decades, seasonality is relatively low at age 50 and increases until age 60 where it is roughly on level terms. Between 60 and 75/80 years seasonality remains relatively constant. After age 80, seasonality in deaths from all causes is increasing, and shows higher values than in the past for the same ages.

Selected Causes of Death

To gain further insights, we decomposed the pattern for all causes again into the three major seasonal diseases. The results are shown in Figure 4.12 for cardiovascular (upper left & upper right panel), cerebrovascular (middle left & middle right panel), and respiratory diseases (lower left & right panel).

As we have seen previously for the analysis by calendar-time, seasonality of cardiovascular diseases matches seasonality from all causes almost perfectly. Especially for men during the most recent decade analyzed (1989–98), we recognize again the development of seasonality in three stages. While the age-range 60–65 marks also here the bending point from an increase in seasonality to a constant pattern, the age when the slope becomes steeper again is shifted to the right. Seasonality for cardiovascular deaths shows a strong upward tendency after ages 90–95. This three-stage-process is also repeated for cerebrovascular diseases with only slightly changing ages as turning-points. I would like to stress that the puzzling pattern is not the outcome of our model. If we had chosen a polynomial for our estimation procedure those unwanted boundary effects could have been implicit in the model as mentioned briefly in the end of Section 4.4.2. Using the P-Spline approach, though, has the advantage that "[b]oundary effects do not occur if the domain of the data is properly specified" [87, p. 98]. Excluding, thus, data problems, we propose an interaction between "real" changes in susceptibility and compositional changes due to mortality selection. Following the mortality model proposed by Robine [310], increasing mortality reflects vanishing resistance towards environmental hazards. The same should hold for seasonality: with increasing age, seasonal fluctuations should become larger as the human body becomes more and more susceptible to the detrimental effects of winter. At the same time, we observe a selection effect in mortality: "All populations are heterogeneous. [...] Some individuals are frailer than others, innately or because of acquired weaknesses. The frail tend to suffer high mortality, leaving a select subset of survivors. [...] As a result of compositional change, death rates increase more slowly with age

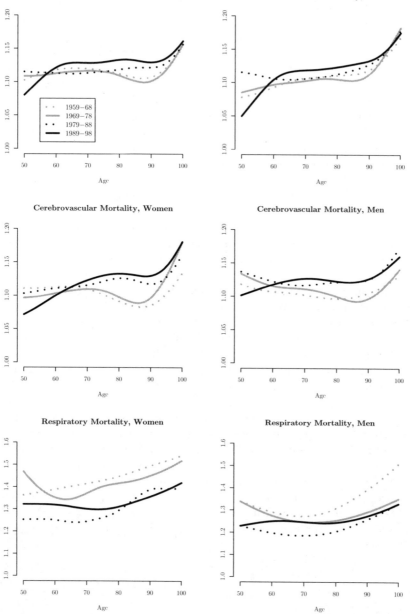

Fig. 4.12. Seasonality of Selected Causes of Death by Sex and 10-Year-Calendar Period

than they would in a homogeneous population." [384, p. 858]. This might also have a decreasing effect on the magnitude of seasonality in deaths. In our case we can argue that this selection effect is relatively weak before age 65, as not many people have died out of the population. At subsequent ages the push-factor for the seasonal amplitude (higher susceptibility) is balanced out by the pull-factor (mortality selection). This effect can be easily simulated following the concepts of Vaupel and Yashin [386]. Figure 4.13 shows one of the "ruses" selection effects can play: Our population consists simply of two sub-populations. The frail sub-population is getting seasonally more susceptible in a linear fashion (dotted, gray line). The more robust sub-population — as shown by the dashed, gray line — is relatively immune to stressful environmental conditions during winter into their late 80's. During the last few years of their lives, seasonality increases at a faster pace. We do not know who belongs to the robust group and who to the frail group. What we observe is the population level illustrated by the solid, black line.[16]

By this simple simulation with two subpopulations we can easily see that our observed outcome in Figures 4.11 and 4.12(upper 4 panels) could be generated by such a process. Further support can be drawn from these graphs by looking at the development over calendar time: the depressing impact of the selection effect is getting smaller over time. This could reflect the fact that in the past there were only relatively robust survivors in those higher age-groups, whereas nowadays people are reaching those ages who would not have been able to do so only 20 years earlier.

The lower two panels in Figure 4.12 show the change in seasonality with age for deaths from respiratory deaths. For this cause of death, we have not discovered a pattern as for the two previous causes. After a slight decrease for women as well as for men until age 65, seasonality increases steadily with age. The two panels also give support for the previous finding in Figure 4.10 (page 109): Over the course of the observation period, seasonal fluctuations have become smaller in more recent decades as indicated by the four plotted lines. Thus, improvements in general living conditions seemed to help in reducing the annual cold-related death toll due to infections of the respiratory tract — especially for the elderly. Our results indicate, for example, that seasonal fluctuations were smaller during the last observed time period (1989–1998) for female as well as for male nonagenarians than for anyone during the period 1959–1968.

---

[16] The data were simulated as follows: $N_{50}^{\text{frail}} = 5 \times N_{50}^{\text{robust}}$; $q_x^{\text{frail}} = 0.06 + 0.0008 \times \text{age}$,

$$q_x^{\text{robust}} = \begin{cases} 0.06 + 0.0002 \times \text{age} & \text{, if age} \leq 87.5 \\ (0.06 + 0.0002 \times 87.5) + 0.0018 \times \text{age} & \text{, else.} \end{cases}$$

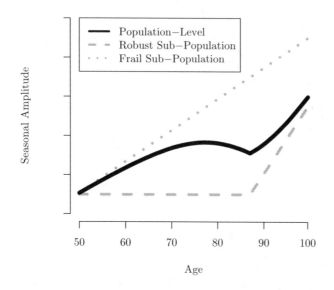

Fig. 4.13. Simulating the Impact of a Selection Effect on the Seasonal Amplitude

4.5.3 Seasonality by Region & Age

Figure 4.14 shows the development of seasonal mortality by age and region in the US for women and men for the last observed decade, 1989–1998. Because no reliable estimates turned out for Alaska and Hawaii, the two states have been omitted. No differences can actually be detected between the seven remaining regions. Also the possible mis-specification of some states from the group "Mountain" did not result in an estimation which differs from the other categories. One can see the aforementioned (cf. Figures 4.11 and 4.12) non-linear increase of seasonality with age. All regions follow this pattern rather closely. These results are unexpected: Previous studies usually indicated that regions with a warm or moderate climate (e.g. the UK, Ireland, Portugal, Spain, Greece) tend to have higher seasonal fluctuations in mortality and deaths than colder regions such as Russia, Canada or Scandinavian countries [97, 98, 135, 147, 252]. This has usually been attributed to the fact that people in colder regions have higher indoor temperatures and avoid exposure to outdoor cold. If those findings could have been converted to the United States, one would assume that the regions "South Atlantic" and "East/West South Central" should show higher seasonality than other regions. According to the "Köppen Climate Classification", all states covered in these two regions belong to the "Humid Subtropical Climate". Surprisingly, they do not deviate in

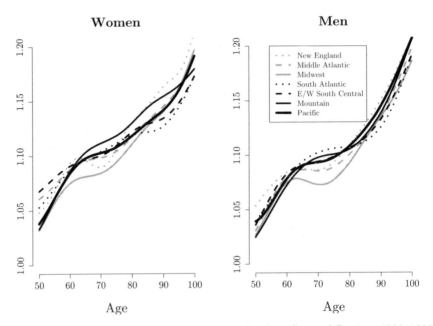

Fig. 4.14. Seasonality of All Cause Mortality by Age, Sex and Region, 1989–1998

any way from the other regions in the United States which are less humid and cooler. This underlines that social and cultural factors are important forces in shaping the seasonal pattern of deaths, as climate appears to be negligible. It has to be mentioned, though, that "region" in the United States is not only correlated with climate but also with socio-economic status and life expectancy. Residents in New England spent on average more time in school than women and men in the regions "South Atlantic" or "South Central".[17] At the same time, life expectancy is also lower in those regions [290]. This could suggest also an alternative explanation: there are two opposing forces which cancel each other out. On the one hand, the regional differences do exist as in Europe between warm and cold regions. That would imply that the southern states show higher seasonality than the states in the northeast. On the other hand, this differential is counteracted by a selection effect. Mortality is higher in the south of the United States. Due to these higher death rates, frail people tend to die at younger ages than in the North, which should have a rather depressing effect on seasonality. We consider the first explanation (no regional differences) to be more likely than the balanced outcome of two opposing forces. If the latter were true, it would require a social gradient by education: Due to a selection effect, people with low education should also

---

[17] Based on our own calculations using the number of years spent in school of deceased women and men. The results were similar for all ages above 50 as well as for people being 80 years old.

show lower amplitudes in their mortality fluctuations. As will be shown later in this chapter (page 118), a social gradient is observable — with the opposite direction, though: people with an academic degree have generally lower seasonality than people with only a few years spent in formal education.

4.5.4 Seasonality by Region & Period

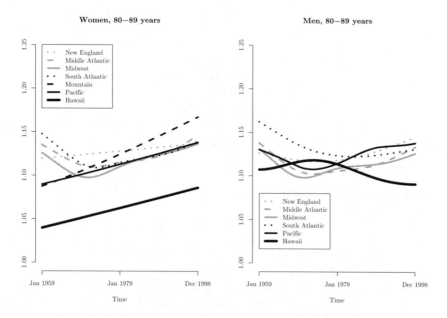

Fig. 4.15. Seasonality of All Cause Mortality by Region and Sex, 1959–1998

Figure 4.15 portrays how seasonal death fluctuations have changed over time in various regions of the United States. For reasons of clarity, only results for the age-group 80-89 years have been plotted. Due to numerical optimization problems,[18] it was possible to display only six regions for men (missing: "Alaska", "Mountain" and "East/West South Central") and seven for women (missing: "Alaska" and "East/West South Central"). Despite this unfortunate loss of information, several interesting features can be observed: The decrease in seasonality discovered in Figure 4.9 (page 108) did not occur in the US as a whole. Rather, three regions were responsible for this development for women and for men likewise: Middle Atlantic, South Atlantic and the Midwest. They

---

[18] While none of the λ-parameters reached one of their limits, no values for θ were possible to be input to lower the variance of the Pearson residuals anywhere close to 1.

showed decreasing seasonality for the first decade observed. All other regions already showed an increase during that period. With the exception of Hawaii (thick, solid, black line) trends have converged for the remaining regions since the late 1960s. This suggests that the existing climatic differences have become less and less relevant over time, as social circumstances and living conditions have become more alike in all regions. Hawaii represents an outlier — especially for women. One could either argue that seasonality in Hawaii is smaller than in other regions because of the predominant tropical climate. There, less precautions are required to avoid cold-related mortality during certain seasons as the temperature varies there less than in other (climatic) regions of the United States. It could also be, however, a statistical artifact due to the small number of deaths in Hawaii compared to the other analyzed regions. This latter hypothesis receives support from the study by Seto et al. [341] . They found differences of 22% between winter and summer mortality from coronary artery disease mortality . This shows that seasonal mortality in Hawaii does not differ from the United States as a whole, since we found roughly the same results in our description of winter/summer differences for cardiovascular diseases (Winter/Summer Ratio 1.206, cf. Table 4.2 on page 89).

4.5.5 Seasonality by Education & Age

Educational level serves as an indicator for socioeconomic status. How this variable affects seasonal fluctuations in deaths over age for women and men during the period 1989–98 is portrayed in Figure 4.16. For women and men alike, seasonal fluctuations are the highest for the category "not stated" given by the thin, dashed gray line. Apart from that residual category, a clear social gradient in seasonal mortality is observable until age 90. The biggest difference is to be seen between people who have earned a college degree or more (black solid line) and who have received no formal education at all (gray solid line). Persons who belong to the highest educational group have the lowest seasonal amplitude and vice versa. Again, it is remarkable how little women and men differ from each other in terms of seasonal fluctuations. The social gradient diminishes with age and vanishes completely for both sexes at about age 90. The path to convergence is interesting: People with highest completed education show a relatively steep slope whereas the pattern of people without any formal education is rather constant over time. One could therefore argue that people with relatively poor education face seasonal fluctuations in deaths throughout large parts of their adult lives which highly educated people only have to face at very advanced ages. Our estimates show that education does not matter for seasonal mortality when people are 90 years old. It is hard to make any inferences about the last years in our age span until the 100th birthday. It seems as if people with the least formal education ("elementary school or less" depicted in the gray , solid line) do not become more susceptible to stressful environmental living conditions. Whether a direct effect or an

indirect (compositional) effect, or both, cause this stationary pattern is hard
to answer. A direct effect would assume that people with low education are so
weak in general that they die regardless of the current season. Contrastingly,
a selection effect is also imaginable: As people with lower education tend to
die at younger ages [374], only a highly selected subgroup is still alive at ages
above 90. It is possible, that those people are especially strong in withstand-
ing environmental stress during winter. This latter hypothesis receives further
support when the development after age 90 is investigated for the other educational groups. A social gradient is still observable but the other way round.
However, the ones facing higher seasonal fluctuations are highly educated people, whereas people with less education display smaller seasonal amplitudes.
This pattern is possibly a reflection of a compositional effect as people with
higher education are less selected than people with lower education.

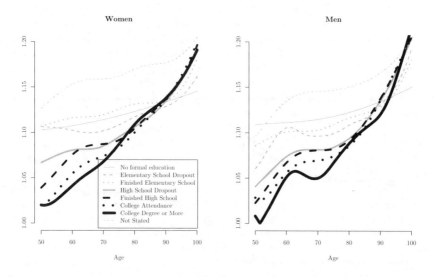

Fig. 4.16. Seasonality of All Cause Mortality by Age, Sex and Educational Status,
1989–1998

We investigated the influence of socio-economic status on seasonal mortality further by analyzing not only mortality from all causes but also from
selected causes. The results for cardiovascular mortality are shown in the upper two panels of Figure 4.17, respiratory mortality is plotted in the lower
two panels. Women's results are in the left column, men's seasonal fluctuations by age are displayed on the right. In all four panels we detect the
aforementioned (Fig. 4.16) social gradient: The more years spent in formal
education, the lower the seasonal fluctuations. One important difference is,
though, that the relative differences for respiratory diseases are smaller than
for cardiovascular diseases. Both causes of death are known to have a social

gradient [69, 210]. For mortality in general, however, the extent of the slope is larger for respiratory diseases than for cardiovascular diseases. This suggests that an inverse relationship of the social gradient exists across causes of death between general susceptibility and seasonal susceptibility.

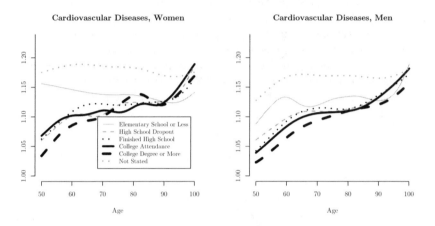

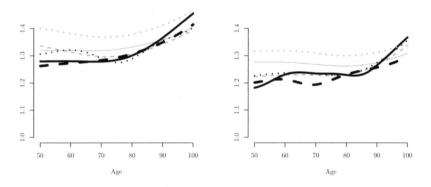

Fig. 4.17. Seasonality of Mortality from Cardiovascular and Respiratory Diseases by Sex and Educational Status, 1959–1998

4.5.6 Seasonality by Marital Status & Age

Seasonal differences in deaths by marital status are shown in Figure 4.18 by sex and age. Although the numbers of deaths by marital status vary considerably by marital status for women and men (cf. Table 4.4, page 92), the estimates for both sexes are again very similar. While the variable "education" provided a clearly visible social gradient, "marital status" does not show such a clear-cut picture. Nevertheless, married people appear to have lower amplitudes in seasonal mortality across their life-course than widowed or never married people. This supports the idea of a protective effect of marriage also for seasonal mortality. Two possible causal pathways are: Married people can share their financial resources and are therefore able to have higher quality in housing and access to better medical care. It could also be the presence of another person in the household who is able to provide help in an emergency (e.g. calling an ambulance in case of a possible stroke). The lack of these factors is possibly reflected in the higher seasonality of never married and widowed people. Most likely these people live alone and don't have access to two sources of income. From mortality research in general it is known that divorced people are showing higher death rates than married people. In the case of seasonality, however, they are rather indistinguishable from married women and men. One could hypothesize for the US, therefore, that the presence of a partner is less important than the access to economic resources: divorced people are also likely to live alone. If this were decisive they should show similar seasonality as never married and widowed people. What makes them different is that they don't lose their financial resources.

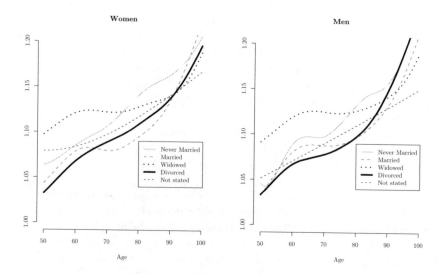

Fig. 4.18. Seasonality of All Cause Mortality by Age, Sex and Marital Status, 1989–1998

We note indications for a selection effect. At about age 90, the amplitudes in seasonality are converging among the analyzed marital status groups, suggesting even a crossover. This converging trend is also observed in studies on mortality in general [e.g. 125]. It can be argued that people who were never married have typically a higher mortality rate throughout their life. Consequently, only a selected subgroup survives to those high ages, while the married are still more heterogenous in their composition with respect to frailty.

4.6 Summary

Seasonal fluctuations in deaths in the United States between 1959 and 1998 have been analyzed in this chapter. While models using information on the actual events (=deaths) and on the exposed population are preferable, sometimes only data on deaths are available — without any information on the individuals at risk. This analysis represents such an approach relying only on death counts. These data are derived from annual Public-Use-Files from the Centers for Disease Control and Prevention (CDC) in the United States. The time span covers the period 1959–98. Although deaths at all ages are included, our analysis restricts itself to the age-range 50–99 years. Almost 80 Mio. individuals died during that period in the given ages. They formed the basis of our analysis.

We developed a new method specifically designed to meet our needs in the presence of overdispersed count data. This analysis represents the first extensive application of this new method. We used a log-linear model where additive terms for the trend (one term) and for the season (at least two terms) were related to the mean of the observed deaths at a certain time or age via a log-link. These components are allowed to vary smoothly over time (or age). We fit this varying-coefficient model by using P-Splines which are the well-known B-Splines with a penalty on their respective regression coefficients. Thus, we did not impose any parametric form on either the trend or on the seasonal component but rather estimated changes over time (or age) data-driven. It has been shown with simulated data, that our new approach fits data with the given structure very well and much better than the standard methods.

Our analysis over calendar-time resulted in a slightly upward moving trend since the early 1970s for seasonal mortality from all causes as well as from cardiovascular and cerebrovascular diseases. This could reflect on the one hand that the differences between summer and winter mortality have become bigger on the individual level. The introduction of air conditioning and the widespread usage of central heating can serve as an explanation. It would imply that the former decreased summer mortality faster than the latter shrunk cold-related mortality. On the other hand, one can argue that compositional changes caused this increase over time. Because of the progress made in survival in general, relatively frail people attain high ages who would have died in the past at younger ages. They are most likely the ones who are more susceptible. In the case of respiratory disease we observed a decrease over time which could be attributed to the spread of central heating.

Seasonality of deaths is increasing with age. This increase is, however, neither linear nor monotonous. We observed, rather, a development in three stages: After an initial increase between ages 50 to 60/65, seasonality remains relatively constant for about twenty years after which they start increasing again. This puzzling pattern — especially for cerebrovascular diseases — may hint at an interaction between "real" changes in susceptibility (=increasing trend) and compositional changes due to mortality selection (=depressing effect).

In European countries large variations in seasonality have been observed between countries with warm, moderate, and cold climate. This pattern has not been reflected in our regional analysis of the US. The examination by age showed the expected trajectory of an increase as people are getting older. Nevertheless, the slope does not differ if people are living in a rather warm or cold state. Our analysis over period shows a converging trend over time which is probably caused by a tendency towards similar social circumstances and living conditions in all regions of the United States.

Seasonality in deaths by educational status has not been investigated previously. Our decomposition approach resulted in a clear social gradient. The lower the educational status, the larger are the differences between winter and summer. This effect can be observed until about age 90 when all educational groups display more or less the same seasonality. Beyond age 90, we observed a crossover which might have been caused by a selection effect: while frail people with low education are most likely already dead, frail people with a college degree are still alive and are more likely to die in winter than the rather healthy, homogeneous group with lower education.

Our explorative approach into the question whether marital status is as important for seasonal mortality as for mortality in general was not as successful as the investigation into educational status. Married women and men appear to have lowest seasonal fluctuations over age, while never married and widowed people have higher seasonality. Unfortunately, the trajectories of the four analyzed marital status groups are partly overlapping. This implies that a straightforward distinction as for mortality in general is not possible.

This analysis of seasonality in deaths in the United States found support for the surprising finding of previous studies of increasing seasonality over time. Cardiovascular and cerebrovascular diseases follow this trend rather closely, whereas respiratory diseases showed a decreasing trend. Our "three-stage-increase" of seasonality with age showed that a statement like "seasonality increases with age" is too simple. The most important findings from our study are:

- We found no differences in seasonality by region — neither over time nor by age — as we could have expected from previous literature on Europe. This underlines the importance of social factors compared to climate.
- In a pilot approach of analyzing the importance of education on seasonal mortality, we detected a strong social gradient. The higher the educational

status, the lower is the seasonal fluctuation in death for most of the adult life.

- The most important finding is probably the lack of differences of seasonal fluctuations in seasonal mortality for women and men. While women face throughout their entire life course lower mortality than men, the relative differences between winter and summer seem to be negligible.

5

The Impact of Social Factors on Excess Winter Mortality in Denmark

5.1 Introduction

5.1.1 The Data of Denmark

This chapter analyzes the impact of social factors on seasonality in mortality in Denmark, focusing on winter excess mortality. Denmark has been chosen deliberately. No other country in the world has collected more data on its population [112]. Information on almost every aspect of life is computerized and stored in several hundred administrative, official statistical and in research registers. For example, these registers contain information on vital events as well as on tax records, medical records, etc. [7, 96]. These individual-level registers can be linked via a 10-digit unique person identifier [349]. This allows for reconstructing the life-course of every Danish individual for all registered events. The prime tool for demographers is the Danish Demographic Database [287] which already contains the most often used demographic variables such as birth date, sex, education, date of death, cause of death (if applicable), etc. This database starts on 01 January 1980 and is updated regularly.

5.1.2 (Seasonality in) Mortality in Denmark

Besides the unchallenged data-quality, Denmark is appealing to mortality researchers also because it does not follow the mortality patterns of its neighboring countries. The linear increase observed in record life expectancy throughout the world for women as well as for men suggests an annual increase of 0.246 (women) and 0.222 (men) years [279]. In Denmark, however, life expectancy at birth rose slower than in most other OECD countries since the 1970s [74]. Chenet et al. [46] calculated an increase for the 11 year-period between 1979 and 1980 of 0.9 years for men whereas 2.442 could have been expected from the study of Oeppel and Vaupel [279]. Sweden, which neighbors Denmark, exhibited an increase of 2.6 years. The lag in the development of female life expectancy is even more alarming: In contrast to the 2.673 years suggested by record life expectancy, Danish women could only expect to live 0.35 years longer in 1990 than in 1979 [46]. The causes of death contributing most to the differential development of life expectancy in Denmark and Sweden were malignant neoplasms — especially respiratory cancer — and cerebrovascular diseases [46]. This previous study which compared Denmark and Sweden suggested that "mortality rates are sensitive to even minor differences in social and cultural factors across countries". There has been much debate which "social and cultural" factors are to be blamed. As Jacobsen et al. [173] discovered, the observed decelerated mortality rates are explained better by cohort than period effects: women born between the two World Wars constitute the most unfortunate birth cohort. The lack of the same effect for men rejects the intuitive hypothesis that early life conditions are mainly responsible. The generally accepted explanation is the high smoking prevalence of women born during these years. In the beginning of the 1990s the proportion of smoking women was higher in Denmark than in any of the other 86 countries analyzed. Simultaneously, smoking-related causes of death increased since the 1950s, whereas the number of people dying from "non-smoking causes" steadily declined in Denmark during the same period [181].[1] Other factors such as the relatively high alcohol consumption can also play a major role in the lagging behind of survival improvements in Denmark [10].

Less is known about seasonal mortality and the impact of social factors. So far, only one study investigated seasonal mortality exclusively in Denmark [302]. There are, however, two major drawbacks: The analysis was based on a random sample of the Danish population. This shortcoming is relatively minor as the sample size of 46,293 individuals was still relatively large. The major problem was the lack of any variables apart from sex, age, and cohort. Three other studies examined seasonal mortality in Denmark briefly in conjunction with other European countries [62, 147, 252]. Compared to the UK, this number of publications is very small.

Overall, seasonal mortality in Denmark is on the European average. Nevertheless, differences between winter and summer mortality are higher there than in other Scandinavian countries or in neighboring Germany [147, 252]. The only study which investigated the impact of social factors on seasonal mortality so far which used Danish data is Healy's study [147]. Unfortunately, his analysis was not based on individual-level data but rather on cross-country comparisons using ecological data. Hence, his conclusions can only be applied in the form of "countries with high housing quality experience low excess winter mortality", not permitting statements on the influence of social factors within a country. This topic remains, thus, an uncharted territory for Denmark.

---

[1] It should be noted that the high smoking prevalence of Danish women has seriously been tried to be explained by the bad role model effect of the Danish queen — a well known smoker [193]. Others, however, have heavily criticized this suggestion on methodological grounds as well as on common sense [174, 236].

5.1.3 Research Questions

As a consequence of the lack of research on seasonal mortality in Denmark, we analyzed whether the findings from other countries can be applied to Denmark, too. In addition, we also tested hypotheses which have not been put forward previously in the field of seasonal mortality at all. Our research questions were:

- **Age.** As individuals grow older, their mortality increases. Various biological theories offer explanations ("error catastrophe", "Hayflick limit", "free radical damage" .... For an overview, please consult: [247, 398].) The result is a *shrinking* resistance against a *given* environment. The environment, however, is not constant. The seasonal mortality pattern with its peak during winter shows also that certain periods of the year are more stressful than others for the human body. If susceptibility of the individual is increasing *and* the adverse effects of the environment are also seasonally changing, we should anticipate an increase in seasonal mortality with age. This expectation has been met by most of the studies of seasonal mortality by age — starting with the pioneering analysis of Quetelet [300] for Belgium in 1838. However, the basis of the data in many previous studies was questionable in drawing conclusions on the relationship between seasonal mortality and age as shown by Rau and Doblhammer [302, p.199].[2]

- **Sex.** Sex, beside age, is the most important determinant in mortality differentials. At least since the middle of the 18th century [e.g. 66] it is well known that women live longer on average. The survival advantage of women is founded biologically as well as behaviorally [227, 229]. As environmental hazards are seasonally oscillating we can raise the conjecture that men face higher excess mortality in winter due to lower biological resistance to adverse effects of nature. In addition, their behavior such as a higher smoking rate at higher ages, for instance, increases their chances to die of typical seasonal illnesses like cardiovascular diseases, too [421]. Results of many previous studies were surprising: If a differentiation by sex has been performed in the analysis, typically no significant differences were found [98, 121, 262, 419]. Rau and Doblhammer [302] found slightly larger seasonal mortality fluctuations for men than for women. This tendency, however, was not statistically significant.

- **Wealth.** Income, education and occupational status are regarded as the most influential factors in determining socioeconomic mortality differentials [371]. In the present study "wealth" was used as an indicator for socioeconomic status. It is a composite index on the household level, taking any monetary transfer into account. As we analyzed almost exclusively only retired people (age 65+), wealth seems to be a good proxy for measuring income as well as occupational status. Since the classic study of Kitagawa and Hauser [195], an inverse relationship has been regularly found

---

[2] See also Section 4.5.2 on page 110.

between income and occupational class on the one hand, and mortality on the other hand [e.g. 210].[3] Higher socioeconomic status reduces the risk of many diseases via lower occupational risks, lower stress, better diets, more exercise as well as more information and better access to health care [314]. The literature is divided whether socioeconomic status matters with respect to seasonal mortality. Various studies found no support that lower socioeconomic groups face higher excess mortality during winter [121, 214, 215, 342]. Contradictory evidence has been discovered as well in several studies [79, 147, 251]. Donaldon and Keatinge [79], for example, point out that "[c]old related mortality in the retired (65–74) age group was generally higher in men of class 5 (unskilled) than class 1 (professional), or other classes, with little difference between men, and women or housewives" [79, p. 790].

Most of these findings can be criticized methodologically as their analyses are based on ecological data on the electoral ward level [e.g. 214, 342], or even on the national level [147]. Neglecting the cross-country comparison, the divergence of the outcomes is surprising as all of the studies were based on data from the UK. This chapter can thus expand the present knowledge in two ways: First, it is based on data from a whole population on the individual level; secondly, with the use of Danish data, a country is analyzed which has not been studied before.

- **Education.** Another indicator which is often used to measure socioeconomic differences in mortality is educational attainment [e.g. 103, 124, 195, 210, 219, 296, 374]. This variable has several desirable characteristics [cf. 374]. For example, education is better suited than occupation-related indicators as it stays constant even in retirement. Typically an inverse relationship is found: the lower the educational level, the higher are the mortality risks.

  Apart from the analysis in Chapter 4, studying the impact of education on seasonal mortality fluctuations represents a novel approach. We assume to find a similar finding as in the United States where people with a college degree showed lower excess winter mortality than people with relatively little formal education.

- **Housing Quality.** The quality of housing is closely related to socioeconomic status. Its pre-dominant position in the field of seasonal mortality does not allow it to be subsumed under this category, though. Marsh et al. [245] reviewed the impact of housing conditions on health. A shortened and slightly modified version of their overview is given in Table 5.1.

  It clearly shows that most housing problems increase mortality risks — especially for diseases which are highly seasonal such as respiratory diseases, ischaemic heart diseases and strokes. The most important factor is

---

[3] Following Rogers et al. [314], already Friedrich Engels observed in his publication "Die Lage der arbeitenden Klasse in England", written in 1844, that factory workers in Manchester had relatively high mortality.

Table 5.1. Housing Problems and their Health Consequences

Housing Deficiency	Health Consequence
Overcrowding	• increased risk of infectious disease
	• increased risk of respiratory disease
Damp and Mould	• respiratory problems
	• asthma
Indoor pollutants and infestation	• asthma
Cold	• diminished resistance to respiratory infection
	• hypothermia
	• bronchospasm
	• ischaemic heart disease, myocardial infarction and strokes

Source: Marsh et al. [245, p. 6], shortened and slightly modified

probably cold as "man is a tropical animal" [209, p. 338]: mortality is at a minimum between 18 and 20 °C [37, 79, 98]. Consequently it is not surprising that central heating is a focal point in avoiding cold-related mortality and that the decrease in seasonal mortality fluctuations over time is attributed to its widespread use [16, 54, 57, 76, 77, 81, 98, 147, 187, 220, 251, 252, 253, 280, 340, 404]. Only Kunst et al. [208] doubt whether the increasing use of central heating is that important. They assume that socioeconomic progress in general is responsible for the decrease in winter excess mortality.

• **Car Ownership.** Nevertheless, "Warm housing is not enough" [186]. Donaldson and Keatinge [78, p. 90] point out that "outdoor cold stress has been independently associated with high excess winter mortality." They argue that the best protection from indoor cold is useless if people face stress from cold outdoors. It is a recurrent finding that people in colder regions show less excess winter mortality [e.g. 135, 147, 252]. The larger proportion of people wearing several layers of clothes in conjunction with avoiding time spent outdoors in those countries explains a large proportion of this reduced cold-related death toll [81, 97, 98]. For example, in Yakutsk — the coldest city in the world with an average temperature of −26.6°C between October and March — people are not experiencing excess winter mortality, an outcome of wearing very warm clothing outdoors and spending as much time as possible indoors [76]. As suggested by Donaldson and Keatinge [77], increased car ownership in southeast England helped in reducing the number of excess winter deaths as people spent less time outdoors. Thus, we used the information, whether people own a car or not, as an indicator whether avoiding outdoor cold stress is of importance for seasonal mortality in Denmark.

- **Marital Status.** Marital status is another important factor in differential mortality research. Comparable to the results by age, sex, wealth, and housing quality, mortality differentials by marital status are known for more than 150 years with Farr's observations on the "Influence of Marriage on the Mortality of the French People" published in 1858 [125]. It is unanimously accepted that married people live longer than widowed, divorced or never married people [223]. The differences are much bigger for men than for women [129]. Among the three unmarried groups, divorced people face the highest mortality risks [163].

  Typically two potential causal pathways (being not exclusive of each other) are offered on how marital status affects mortality [see for an overview: 125, 223]: The first explains the lower death rates of married people by a *protection* effect. Married people are less prone for risky, unhealthy behavior; they suffer less from stress-related diseases and are helped by their respective partner when ill. From an economical perspective, marriage correlates with better general living conditions by pooling financial resources. The second explanation proposes a *selection* effect into marriage. In the words of Lillard and Panis [223, p. 314]: "The argument is straightforward: Persons with observably poor health, and those with chronic conditions or dangerous or unhealthy lifestyles [...], may find it more difficult to attract a spouse than do healthy, relatively settled individuals [...]. By a similar argument, those in good health may be better able to maintain a marital relationship and thus have lower dissolution rates."

  Despite this wealth of literature on the impact of marital status on mortality and its consistent findings, no study so far has addressed the question whether marital status also matters for annual fluctuations in mortality. Without predecessors, our study presents an exploratory first step. We hypothesize that married people show less vulnerability to cold stress. Two reasons can be given to support this idea: First, married people are more robust on average than others due to the selection effect into marriage. Secondly, the protective effects of marriage by avoiding unhealthy behaviors should give them a survival advantage during winter.

- **Living Alone.** There is evidence in the literature that people who are living alone tend to have higher mortality [201]. This variable is often treated as a sub-factor of marital status (usually it is assumed that married people are not living alone). Rogers et al. [314], for example, calculated that the mortality risk of US adults who are not married and are living alone is roughly 50% higher than for married people who live with their spouse and two children.[4] Also Rogers [313] discovered elevated mortality for people who live alone — regardless of whether they were previously married or not.

  In a society like the Danish, however, one can not generalize that being married automatically means not living alone and being not married means

---

[4] This study controlled, of course, for other factors such as sex, age, race, income.

living alone. As a consequence, we treated this binary variable extra and controlled simultaneously for marital status. Only one recent study exists which investigates the question whether people who are living alone have an excess risk of dying in winter as compared to people who share their household with at least one more person [405]. They were, however, not able to detect any significant differences.

5.1.4 Summary

Danish data provide a rich data-source for the analysis of mortality in general and of seasonal mortality in particular. Thanks to the availability of linkable person-registers, individual life-courses can be reconstructed on almost any relevant aspect of life with unmatched precision on the timing of the event as well as on the quality of the data.

Denmark shows different mortality patterns than most other Western European countries. Especially the slow increase of life expectancy during the last thirty years has been of concern for epidemiologists and politicians. The relatively high smoking prevalence among Danish women born between the two World Wars is quite likely the root cause. Not much is known on seasonal mortality in Denmark. Compared to other European countries, Danish seasonal mortality is "mid-table". It fares, however, worse than its neighboring countries. Not much is known so far about the impact of social factors on cold-related mortality.

Our study asks the following questions:

- How does seasonal mortality change with age?
- Can we find different susceptibility to cold stress for women and men?
- Can we shed more light on the ambiguously discussed topic of the impact of socioeconomic status on seasonal mortality? We use wealth (on the household level) and highest attained education (on the individual level) as indicators for socioeconomic status.
- Do people who own a car face less cold stress outdoors and have consequently lower seasonal mortality fluctuations?
- Are the typical mortality differentials by marital status also mirrored in the seasonal mortality pattern?
- Are individuals who are living alone more vulnerable to the environmental hazards during winter than people who share the household with at least one other person?

5.2 Data and Methods

5.2.1 Data Description

The base population are all people who were 65 years or older in Denmark between 01 January 1980 and 31 December 1998. If we bind the age-axis at a certain point, our base population is a rectangle in the Lexis diagram. There are three ways of entering our data-set:

- people were 65 years or older on 01 January 1980
- people become 65 years old between 02 January 1980 and 31 December 1980
- people immigrated into Denmark between 01 January 1980 and 31 December 1998 being 65 years or older

Likewise there were also three possibilities to exit the data-set:

- people who died between 01 January 1980 and 31 December 1998 being 65 years or older
- people who were 65 years or older and alive on 31 December 1998
- people who emigrated out of Denmark between 01 January 1980 and 31 December 1998 being 65 years or older

As already mentioned in the introduction of this chapter, Denmark's population registers are unique in the world concerning quantity and quality of the information provided. The focal point is a unique person-identifier called "CPR". In its original version it consists of a ten-digit number. The first six numbers indicate the birth date. The remaining four digits contain a serial number, sex of the individual ($\female$: even number; $\male$: odd number) and some controls [349]. While it is true that one CPR refers uniquely to one person, it is possible under rare circumstances that one person has more than one CPR [289]. As pointed out by Petersen [289], the person-number ("PNR") used in the Danish Demographic Database [288] eradicated this problem: one person corresponds to one person-number and exactly vice-versa.

Table 5.2. Population Registers used in Our Analysis

Register-Name	Time-Span Covered	Key-Variables
idperson	1980–98	birth data, sex
mortality	1980–98	date of death, cause of death
bil	1992–98	car ownership
dwelling	1991–98	housing information: installations size per person; age of house
education	1980–98	highest educational level attained
household	1980–98	number of people living in the same household
maristat	1980–98	marital status
wealth	1980–96	wealth quartile on family level based on all kinds of of income (pension, rent, ...)

Table 5.2 shows the population registers used in our analysis: The data-set
idperson consisting of 1,842,377 individuals serves as our base population.
Out of them 999,605 died during the observation period and are contained
in the data-set mortality. For 93% of them at least one cause of death was
available (931,526).[5] These mortality data reflect nicely the high-quality of the
population registers in Denmark: Only three individuals from this million had
values outside the possible range of 01 January 1980 – 31 December 1998. One
particular problem was the changing coding scheme for causes of death. Until
the end of 1993, Danish authorities used ICD-8 for coding causes of death.
Afterwards they switched directly to ICD-10. This step induced problems.
First, conversion tables are usually only available from one revision to the next.
Secondly, and more importantly, ICD-10 introduced an alphanumeric coding
scheme whereas previous revisions were purely numerical. The problematic
task of producing comparable time-series for causes of death was impeded
even further. Fortunately, it was possible to reconstruct comparable data for
the three causes which are high-risk diseases for seasonal mortality, and which
have been used in the most in-depth analysis of winter excess mortality so
far [98]: Ischaemic Heart Disease, Cerebrovascular Diseases and Respiratory
Diseases. The following table (Table 5.3) shows the coding for these three
causes by coding scheme (ICD-8 vs. ICD-10):

Table 5.3. Coding of Causes of Death in Denmark by Coding Scheme

Cause of Death	ICD-8	ICD-10
Ischaemic Heart Disease	410–410	I20–I25
Cerebrovascular Diseases	430–438	I60–I69
Respiratory Diseases	460–519	J00–J98

Starting in 1992, a car register (data-set bil) was installed. Each record
in this database gives information about the registration, the de-registration
(if applicable) the kind of car and the person who registers for every car in
Denmark. We simplified this data by ignoring changes from one vehicle to another one. We coded a dummy variable which only indicates whether a person
owns a car at a certain point of time or not. Out of the 1,8 Mio. people in the
base population, 502,455 individuals were coded to be car-owners following
this coding convention. Surprisingly, it happened that people were registered
for a car for some time after their deaths. Rather than excluding those illog-
ical cases from the analysis completely, we rather assumed that the relatives
de-registered the car simply awhile later.
The dwelling register (started in 1991) contains various information about
the size of the dwelling, its age and its installations. In contrast to most other

---

[5] The Danish Demographic Database contains information on primary, secondary,
and tertiary cause of death.

databases in the Danish registers, housing information is annually available, and not on a daily or monthly basis. As previous seasonal mortality literature is mainly concerned about the housing quality, we relied on the information given for installations. Denmark is a relatively homogeneous country with relatively similar living standards. Therefore we only made a distinction between people who have the maximum number of installations (toilet, central heating, bath) versus the rest (versus not stated). 91.92% of the apartments of the individuals had the maximum number of installations, 6.52% had less than the maximum and 1.56% were not possible to be assigned.

Education (data-set `education`) measures the highest educational level attained by any individual and is available for the whole time period (1980–1998). Education is coded using eight digits to reflect any possible combination of educational pathways. Coordinating with Jørn Korsbo Peterson — he is the maintainer of the Danish Demographic Database — this abundance of information[6] was grouped into three categories which is the typical approach taken by researchers using Danish register data.

Table 5.4. Educational Categories

Code	Danish Description	English Description	ISCED Code[†]	Share
1	Almenuddanelse	Lower Secondary Education or less	0–2	61.42%
2	Gymnasie og erhvervsgaglige uddannelser	(Upper) Secondary Education, post secondary non tertiary education, skilled manual worker	3–4	27.75%
3	Videregående og ph.d.	Tertiary education or higher	5–6	10.83%

† ISCED is the International Standard Classification of Education [370].

Table 5.4 describes which categories were used for the coding of education, how large their proportion is and to which ISCED categories [370] the present classification corresponds. People who attended primary school only or in conjunction with lower secondary school were assigned to category 1 ("lower education"). 61.42% of the people belonged to this group. Roughly 28% of the people have an intermediate level of education (Code 2, "middle"). They attended upper secondary education and/or are skilled manual workers. People with an academic degree, regardless of whether it a Bachelor, a Master or a Ph.D., are members of the highest educational group. About 11% of all individuals in the data-set are in this third category ("high").

The data-set `household`, which is updated annually, contains information on the number of people having the same household identification

---

[6] The actual number of possible education levels was 436.

number. This was used to assess how many people are living in the same
flat/apartment/house. Although the actual number of people is known, we
used a binary variable to indicate whether a person is living alone or not. At
the time of death (or censoring) 53.55% were living alone, for the remaining
46.45% at least one more person was living in the same household.

In the data-set `maristat`, the marital status of the population is recorded.
Every person at any point of time is assigned to exclusively one of the following categories: Married, divorced, widowed, unmarried, registered partnership,
revoked registered partnership and "longestliving of two partners". The last
three categories constitute combined less than 0.03% of all cases and have
been excluded from any further analysis.

The data-set `wealth` is a special measure of socioeconomic status. It includes not only the salary measured in income but also other kinds of revenue.
A typical example is receiving rent from a house one owns. Finally, the complete income is annually measured in Danish Krones. One important advantage of this variable is that it is measured on the family level. This implies,
for instance, that a woman who has no income of her own but is married to a
millionaire is not classified as poor. Wealth has already been transformed into
four categories by Statistics Denmark. Those four groups represent quartiles
of wealth (0–25%, 25–50%, 50–75%, 75–100%). This variable was available
only for the time period 1980 until 1996. Any analysis involving this variable
was, thus, restricted to the first 17 years of our observation period.

5.2.2 Method

Introduction: Why Logistic Regression?

Event-history analysis represents the appropriate framework to study the
time-to-failure distribution of events of individuals over their life course. In
demographic applications "Failure" can not only be death but also transition
to the first child, re-entry into the labor-market, etc. Traditional approaches
like the linear OLS model are not appropriate for these kind of data for several
reasons. For example, lifetimes are (necessarily) positive, the assumption of a
normal distribution for the error term in the OLS model does not hold because
the normal distribution is defined from $-\infty$ to ∞.[7] The problem of *censoring*
is more serious. This appears when the event of interest has not happened until
the last moment of observation (e.g. if a person survived until a certain point
of time which marks the end of the study period) [56]. Event-history models,
sometimes also coined survival models, are able to incorporate these special
data characteristics. While most event-history models are designed for continuous time, we have decided to employ a logistic regression model which can be
considered as a survival model for discrete time [cf. 85]. Various reasons can
be brought up to support such an approach [cf. 5, 6, 418]. The decisive ones

---

[7] This drawback could be mediated by taking the log of the lifetime.

for our analysis were: first, it allows to incorporate time-varying covariates easily. Secondly, an important "consideration concerns the number of *ties* in the data. Events are tied when two or more subjects in the sample have events at the same time" [418, p. 16]. In our application it is, of course, possible that individuals die during the same month at a certain age. "The presence of ties can lead to serious bias in parameter estimates when using Cox's method for proportional hazards models [...]. On the other hand, discrete-time models can handle ties without introducing bias in parameter estimates" [418, p. 16–17]. The third reason is especially important for our huge data set: The calculation takes considerably less time with logistic regression than with the Cox-Model which appears to be the default choice in most applications. In practice, the results between the methods differ only marginally. A comparison between a continuous and a discrete time model in the appendix of Rau and Doblhammer [302] shows almost indistinguishable regression coefficients for a seasonal mortality analysis. The major practical difference between the two approaches is found in modeling the duration dependency. For example in the common proportional hazards regression, a baseline hazard is estimated (non-parametrically in the case of a Cox-Model) and the effect of the covariates shifts this baseline duration dependency proportionally up or down.[8] In the case of logistic regression, this time dependency has to be entered as a covariate (or as covariates) into the model.

The Model

The logistic regression we used is outlined in Equation 5.1:

$$\log\left(\frac{P_{it}}{1-P_{it}}\right) = \alpha + \beta_{\text{Winter}}x_{1;ti} + \beta_{\text{Spring}}x_{2;ti} + \beta_{\text{Fall}}x_{3;ti} +$$
$$+ \sum_{\text{age}} \gamma_{\text{age}}x_{\text{age};ti} + \sum_{\text{period}} \delta_{\text{period}}x_{\text{period};ti} + \text{further covariates}$$

$$(5.1)$$

where:

$$x_1 = \begin{cases} 1 & \text{if current month is Dec, Jan or Feb} \\ 0 & \text{otherwise.} \end{cases}$$

$$x_2 = \begin{cases} 1 & \text{if current month is Mar, Apr or May} \\ 0 & \text{otherwise.} \end{cases}$$

---

[8] Also in the other common approach, the accelerated failure time models (AFT), a baseline hazard is estimated. The main difference to the proportional hazards model (PH) is the effect of the covariates which does not work on the hazard function but on the failure time [141].

$$x_3 = \begin{cases} 1 & \text{if current month is Sep, Oct or Nov} \\ 0 & \text{otherwise.} \end{cases}$$

The log of the odds-ratio (which is the probability that individual i experiences death at time t divided by one minus this probability) is related to an intercept denoted by α and a set of time-fixed and time-varying covariates.

The coefficients β_{Winter}, β_{Spring} and β_{Fall} are of primary interest in our analysis as they correspond to the influence of the covariates x_1, x_2, and x_3 which indicate as binary variables the seasons Winter, Spring, and Fall. The obtained estimates have to be interpreted therefore in relation to the reference group summer which has been left out.

The effect of age on mortality is captured in the set of regression coefficients denoted by γ_{age}. The age-groups corresponding to the set of dummy-variables $\sum_{\text{age}} x_{\text{age}}$ are (in years): 65–69 (Reference Group), 70–74, 75–79, 80–84, 85–89, 90–94, 95–99, 100 and older.

Possible period effects are accounted for by the set of dummy-variables δ_{period} which measure the influence of the period dummies denoted by $\sum_{\text{period}} x_{\text{period}}$.

The dummies for the periods were the following calendar years: 1980–84, 1985–90, 1991–93 (Reference Group), 1994–96, 1997–98.[9]

Controlling for other effects has been denoted in Equation 5.1 above by "further covariates". That means, for example, that in a model where the influence of living arrangements (living alone yes/no) has been investigated, we controlled for education, marital status and wealth in addition to season, age, and period. The actual variables belonging to "further covariates" are given in every estimated model presented in latter parts of this chapter.

Interpreting Results from the Applied Logistic Regression Model

- **Odds-Ratios vs. Relative Risks**

  Strictly speaking, the exponentiated regression coefficients (e.g. $e^{\beta_{\text{Winter}}}$) have to be interpreted as odds-ratios. If the probability of the event is rather small, however, these odds-ratios are close to the relative risks known from standard event-history models and can be interpreted as such [28, 159, 257, 414]. This approximate equality of odds-ratios and relative risks in the case of events which are relatively rare is explained in the following example.

  In our data we have roughly 1 Mio. deaths but more than 180. Mio person-months lived. This situation is shown in Table 5.5 in a simplified manner. With these data, we want to calculate the relative risk as well as the odds-ratio for death among women in relation to men.

---

[9] The unequally spaced distinction across the periods has been chosen as these years (apart from 1984/85) reflect changes in the availability of data (cf. Section 5.2.1 starting on page 131).

Table 5.5. Hypothetical Example: Survival Status by Sex

	Survived?		
	Yes	No	Σ
Women	100×10^6	0.5×10^6	100.5×10^6
Men	80×10^6	0.5×10^6	80.5×10^6
Σ	180×10^6	1.0×10^6	181.0×10^6

Following Woodward [414], a risk is defined by the number of cases who experienced a certain event divided by the number of cases at risk. The relative risk (RR) of death of women compared to men is therefore:

$$RR = \frac{\frac{0.5 \times 10^6}{100.5 \times 10^6}}{\frac{0.5 \times 10^6}{80.5 \times 10^6}} = \frac{0.004975}{0.006211} = 0.800998 \tag{5.2}$$

In contrast, the odds are defined as the number of cases who experienced a certain event divided by the number of cases who did not experience the event [414]. The odds-ratio (OR) is therefore:

$$OR = \frac{\frac{0.5 \times 10^6}{100 \times 10^6}}{\frac{0.5 \times 10^6}{80 \times 10^6}} = \frac{0.005}{0.00625} = 0.8 \tag{5.3}$$

The relative risk RR in this example is 0.800998. The odds-ratio OR is 0.8. We can therefore conclude for our application where events are relatively rare, that odds-ratios are approximating relative risks very closely.

- **Interpreting Our Models**

  The regression coefficient which is used mainly in our results is β_{Winter}. Due to the size of the data-set we estimated separate models for the different groups of interest. Therefore, the point and confidence estimates given (or plotted) have to be interpreted always in relation to the specific reference group which is summer. An example might clarify this: Given that we want to analyze the effect of education which is measured in three levels (low, middle, high), we estimated a separate model for each educational group. Let's assume we have a point estimate for people with high education of 0.2 and a standard error for this coefficient of 0.02. The 95% confidence interval for this coefficient is therefore: $0.2 \pm 1.96 \times 0.02 = 0.2 \pm 0.0392$. If we exponentiate these estimates, we obtain a point estimate for the odds-ratio/relative risk of $e^{0.2} = 1.2214$ and confidence estimate of $e^{0.2-0.0392}$; $e^{0.2+0.0392} = 1.1745; 1.27023$.

A valid interpretation is:
- For people with high education, the relative risk of dying in winter is significantly higher than during summer because the confidence interval does not include 0 (or 1 in the case of $e^{\beta_{\text{Winter}}}$).

- The regression results indicate a relative risk of dying which is 22% higher during winter than during summer for people with high education.

Given we have parameter estimates for people with middle education of 1.30 (lower 95% CI), 1.325 (point estimate), and 1.35 (upper 95% CI), we can not make any inferences whether the excess risk during winter is *significantly* higher for people with middle education than with high education. This drawback is less serious than it may appear at first sight: Because of the size of our data-set, it is quite likely that even the smallest differences between two parameters turn out to be significant. But even if a difference, for example, between 1.23 and 1.24 turns out to be significant, one has to question whether this significant difference is of actual practical relevance. Sachs [321] distinguishes, therefore, in his textbook between statistical significance and practical significance.[10]

5.2.3 Problems of the Data Analysis

Timevarying Covariates

It should be pointed out that age, period, and current month have been coded properly as time-varying covariates. Other covariates have been assumed to be time-constant despite their inherent time-varying nature. The main reasons are computational resources. In typical applications there is no problem to represent time-varying covariates adequately, as they change rarely and/or the number of individuals covered in the data-set is of manageable quantity. In our application however, every person-month lived is a new record. Our 1.8 million subjects in the base population survived roughly 100 months on average. Consequently, the data-set contains 180 million person-months lived and the same number of records.[11] To obtain a final data set with all the (time-varying) information, one needs to calculate data-sets with these 180 Mio. records for each variable separately, as they are all given in single data-sets linkable via the PNR. Even if the base population is broken down by sex and into 5 year birth cohorts, the data-sets are too large to be sorted and merged together.[12] The actual approach was to use time-constant covariates instead of time-varying covariates by taking the last observed realization of the covariate for each individual. The question is then, of course: How much does this simplification reduce the quality of the analysis? In most cases the loss of information is of minor importance for several reasons:

---

[10] "Weiter sei noch auf den zuweilen nicht beachteten **Unterschied zwischen statistischer Signifikanz und "praktischer" Signifikanz** hingewiesen: praktisch bedeutsame Unterschiede müssen schon mit nicht zu umfangreichen Stichproben erfaßt werden können" [321, p. 187; boldface in source document].

[11] There are precisely 186,271,440 person months lived. 106,322,677 person-months were lived by women and 79,948,763 by men.

[12] A trial dataset for one sex and five birth years resulted in a file, which was larger than 3GB.

- At advanced ages, variables like wealth (measured in quartiles on the family level), education, and housing quality are changing their values only very rarely. Thus, an approach where these variables are coded as time-constant on the one hand, and as time-varying on the other hand, should both give approximately the same results because neither the number of exposures nor the number of occurrences change.
- Some variables like housing quality or wealth are only available on an annual basis. Thus, in some cases it would not even be possible at all to code the change into the month when it actually happened.[13]
- The annually measured variables are only available if the person has survived until the end of the year. Consequently, nothing is known at the moment of death about those covariates. The closest information one could obtain is the one from the previous year which we used in our approach.
- For the variable of car ownership the validity can be doubted, as it measures only the registration of the car but not its use. In many cases the car got de-registered several months after the death of the person. While it is impossible for the deceased to use a car after her/his death, one can neither assume that the person used the car during the month(s) preceding death.

The two remaining variables which are intrinsically time-varying even at those advanced ages are "marital status" and "living alone yes/no". Our approach used the last information available, which means that the number of events is correct. The exposure time, however, is biased. For the variable "living alone yes/no", people who were alone at the end of their lives have probably not lived throughout the whole observation period alone. Thus, the exposure time for this category in our models is too large and regression estimates would result in even higher values for those people if the variable was coded as time-varying. Reciprocally, the exposure time for people who were not alone is too large which should result in lower mortality estimates if the variable was coded more precisely. Marital status is more problematic. The number of events in our models for each category is entered correctly. The exposure time is exact only for the group "never married / single". The categories "widowed" and "divorced" contain too many exposures, while "married" contains less exposure time (It is likely that the people who are widowed and/or divorced in our data have spent some time during the follow-up being married). As a consequence, the mortality estimates for the categories "divorced" and "widowed" should be higher than in our results and the ones for "married" should be lower.

Summing it up, using time-constant covariates instead of time-varying covariates, because of technical resource problems, appears less of a problem than it first suggests. Many variables are approximately time-constant anyway

---

[13] Typical approaches would assume that the changes take place either in the middle or in the end of the year. Those implementations are arbitrary and would influence our model estimates severely as we are interested in the actual month of death.

at ages over 65. The impact of variables like "marital status" and "living alone yes/no" is also manageable if the results are carefully interpreted. This view gains some support from a paper recently published in the British Medical Journal. In their study "Vulnerability to winter mortality in elderly people in Britain: population based study", Wilkinson et al. use exclusively time-fixed covariates — also for the question whether somebody was living alone or not [405].

Competing Risks

We analyzed mortality for various causes of death. It can be assumed that the risk of dying from one cause is not independent from the risk of dying from another cause in the case of human mortality [61]. Therefore it appears to be most natural to estimate a competing risks model. We are, however, faced with a dilemma: [196, p. 51–52, emphasis in source document]:

> "In competing-risks modeling we often need to make some assumptions about the dependence structure between the potential failure times. Given that we can only observe the failure time and cause and not the potential failure times these assumptions are not testable with only competing risks data. This is called the *identifiability dilemma*. [...] This means that given what we actually see, (T, δ), we can never distinguish a pair of dependent competing risks from a pair of independent competing risks." [14]

As pointed out by Allison [6], not much can be done about this dilemma. Although it is "possible to formulate models that incorporate dependence among event types but, for any such model, there's an independence model that does an equally good job of fitting the data" [6, p. 209].

If independence (or quasi-independence [cf. 61]) is assumed, one can follow either one of the following two approaches: either one is estimating a model with all causes *simultaneously*, or one is estimating a model for each cause of death *separately*. Both approaches are statistically equivalent. It has been shown, for example in Prentice et al. [293], Kalbfleisch and Prentice [183] and Allison [6], that the likelihood function for all causes together (i.e. simultaeously for j causes of death) can be factored into separate likelihood functions for each of the j causes of death. The only advantage of a simultaneous estimation therefore is "to reduce the number of statements needed to specify the models" [6, p. 188]. On the contrary, there are some advantages of estimating models separately: First, one does not have to specify the same functional form and not the same set of covariates for all causes of death. Secondly, "a further implication is that you don't need to estimate models

---

[14] In the quotation above, T indicates the duration (e.g. age); δ denotes the last observed status of the subject (e.g. alive/censored, death from cause a, death from cause b, ...).

for all event types unless you really want to. If you're only interested in the effects of covariates on deaths from heart disease, then just estimate a single model for heart disease, treating all other death types as censoring. Besides reducing the amount of computation, this fact also makes it unnecessary to do an exhaustive classification of death types. You only need to distinguish the event type of interest from all other types of events" [6, p. 188]. These advantages, in conjunction with the identifiability dilemma, let us choose to run models separately.

5.3 Results

5.3.1 Descriptive Results

The upper panel in Figure 5.1 gives an overview about the distribution of deaths during the observation period from 1980 until 1998 for both sexes. Each gray vertical bar represents the monthly number of deaths (adjusted to a standard length of 30 days) in Denmark at ages 65 and higher. Clearly, a distinct seasonal pattern can be observed. Each January is marked by a black triangle, whereas August is illustrated by a black square. With a few exceptions, these two months represent typically the maximum and the minimum in numbers of deaths in every year. With regard to the heavy media coverage after the summer of 2003 on heat-related mortality, it should be stressed that deaths during summer were always below the average number of deaths during the whole observation period of 19 years.

The seasonal pattern for the whole time period can be described by the "Winter / Summer-Ratio", which has been discussed in Chapter 3 as seasonality index φ_1 (see page 41). This index results in a value of 1.17, which means that 17% more people are dying during winter than during summer. In contrast to the initial description in Chapter 3, the months which served as nominator and as denominator have been slightly changed: December, January and February are the months with the highest numbers of death as shown in the two lower panels of Figure 5.1. To have a year whose seasons are divided into four consecutive parts of equal length, summer was defined for the months June, July, August.

The two lower panels in Figure 5.1 show the same data aggregated into one year, separated by sex and converted into monthly contributions given in percentages; women's seasonality of deaths is displayed in the lower left panel with a gray barplot, the lower right panel depicts the corresponding pattern for men in black. For clarification, in both panels a horizontal line has been drawn at 8.3% to indicate the value of a uniform distribution.

The differences in the Winter/Summer Ratio (φ_1) are relatively small among the two sexes. Women's seasonality measured by φ_1 is 1.18, men's $\varphi_1 = 1.17$. For both sexes the six months with the highest number of deaths is followed by the six months of lowest deaths. Consequently, Hewitt's test for seasonality

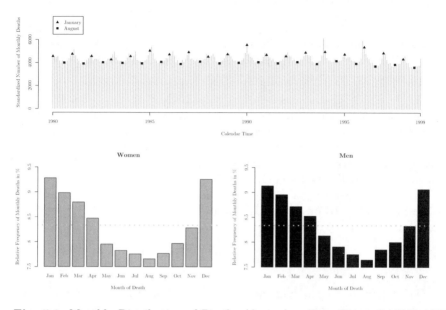

Fig. 5.1. Monthly Distribution of Deaths Above Age 65 in Denmark, 1980–1998 and Its Aggregation into Twelve Months by Sex (standardized for length of month)

resulted in a maximum rank sum of 57 which corresponds to significance on the $\rho = 0.013$ level which is the lowest possible value for this nonparametric test (cf. Chapter 3 (page 39), 150, 395).[15]

5.3.2 Absolute Level of Mortality

Using our discrete-time event-history approach, we are mainly presenting relative mortality risks.[16] To get an overview about the absolute differences between winter and summer mortality, a seasonal life-table has been calculated. To estimate a life-table, two inputs and one assumption are required:

Occurrences: The occurrences in our application are deaths at a certain (integer) age in a specific month for either women or men.

Exposures: In our case, the exposures are women and men who are at risk of dying during a certain (integer) age in a specific month.

---

[15] Also, any other test, which was presented in Chapter 3, resulted in highly significant values for these Danish data.

[16] To be precise, we will present odds-ratios. But as pointed out before and also shown, for example, by Woodward [414], odds-ratios are often a good approximation to the relative risk. Since the number of events in our application is relatively rare to the number of exposures, we can safely use this approximation.

Assumption: The function $a(x)$ usually specifies the "mean number of person-years lived in the interval by those dying in the interval" [297, p. 43]. In our case, we give a value of 0.5 as the mean number of person-months lived in the interval (a month) by those dying in the interval in an integer age. This value of 0.5 corresponds to the assumption that deaths occur in the middle of the month.

We picked the death rates — usually denoted by m_x — as our life table function of choice. These standard rates for mortality from all causes have been plotted by age in Figure 5.2 on page 146 in the upper left panel for women (gray) and men (black). The other three panels show the results from ischaemic heart disease (upper right), cerebrovascular diseases (lower left), and respiratory diseases (lower right). The death rates for these three causes have been estimated using a multiple decrement lifetable approach as outlined in Preston et al. [297] on pages 71ff. Accordingly, the rates $_m m_x^i$ at age x in month m for cause-of-death i are:

$$_m m_x^i = \frac{_m d_x^i}{_m L_x}. \tag{5.4}$$

The number of people dying at age x in month m from cause i is denoted by $_m d_x^i$. The people who are exposed to the risk of dying are denoted by $_m L_x$.

We plotted the resulting death rates $(m(x))$ by age in Figure 5.2 on page 146. The upper left panel shows results for mortality from all causes. The remaining three panels contain information on the seasonal pattern for the selected causes of death: ischaemic heart disease (upper right), cerebrovascular (lower left) diseases and respiratory diseases (lower right). Several interesting features can be discovered in the four panels:

- All four causes of death show a distinct difference between summer and winter mortality. Albeit on a lower overall level, these differences are larger for respiratory diseases than for ischaemic heart disease and cerebrovascular diseases.
- On the plotted log-scale, we observe for mortality from all causes, from ischaemic heart disease and from cerebrovascular diseases, a linear increase in mortality with age. This corresponds to an exponential increase in mortality.
- For all-cause-mortality, three reference lines have been plotted to give an impression on how much winter mortality is exceeding summer mortality. Winter mortality for women at age 80 can be seen at the intersection of the gray dashed vertical line and the gray dashed horizontal line. The equivalent for men is shown at the intersection of the gray dashed vertical line and the black dashed horizontal line. Following the horizontal reference lines to the right, we can see that summer mortality reaches the level of winter mortality two years later for women and three years later for men.
- At first glance it is surprising that the mortality curves for women and men are converging (all-cause-mortality, ischaemic heart disease) or even

are crossing over. This does not reflect what is observed in reality. It is an outcome of pooling data for the years 1980 to 1998. Since mortality is lower for females than for males, the average (calendar) time was earlier when women died at those high ages where converging mortality is displayed. Due to the progress in survival chances, men are catching up. In any graph which is aggregating mortality information over several units of time, the plotted gap between female and male mortality is therefore smaller than the one measured at one unit of time.

The following sections present the results of our discrete-time event-history analysis. To condense the information, the regression coefficients are given in a figure and in a table only for the first analysis. For the remaining analyzed variables, only the graphs are included in the main text. The corresponding tables can be obtained from the author.

5.3.3 Seasonal Mortality by Sex and Cause of Death

In a first step, seasonal mortality has been analyzed by sex and cause of death. Separate logistic regressions have been conducted for men and women for mortality from all causes, ischaemic heart disease mortality, cerebrovascular diseases and respiratory diseases.

The odds-ratios and the 95% confidence intervals for the parameter estimates from this discrete-time event-history analysis are shown in four panels in Figure 5.3. By looking at Figure 5.3 a), one can recognize that the differences between women and men for seasonal mortality from all causes are rather negligible. Although we can detect that the excess in mortality during winter is higher for women than for men, the differences are relatively small. Women's relative mortality risk (RMR) in winter is 18 percent higher than in summer. Men's excess is 16 percent. Excess mortality from Ischaemic Heart Disease (Figure 5.3 b) is slightly higher for both sexes than from all causes. Again, women's RMR is higher than men's ($e_{\female}^{\beta_{\text{Winter}}} : 1.235; e_{\male}^{\beta_{\text{Winter}}} : 1.204$). Male cold-related excess mortality surpasses women's only for cerebrovascular diseases in all seasons (Figure 5.3c). Similarly important for high winter excess mortality are respiratory diseases. Although the share of ischaemic heart disease combined with cerebrovascular diseases among all diseases is larger (IHD & Cerebrovascular Diseases: $\approx 40\%$; Respiratory Diseases: $\approx 7\%$), the excess from respiratory diseases is considerably higher (see Figure 5.3d). Men's risk of dying from respiratory diseases is 36.5% higher in winter than in summer. Women's risk is elevated by more than 55%. It should be emphasized, however, that we are using relative mortality measurements. Therefore it is not possible to filter out whether winter mortality is extremely high or summer mortality is extremely low.

Relatively similar results for winter excess mortality for both sexes with a slight "advantage" for women have been reported previously for all-cause

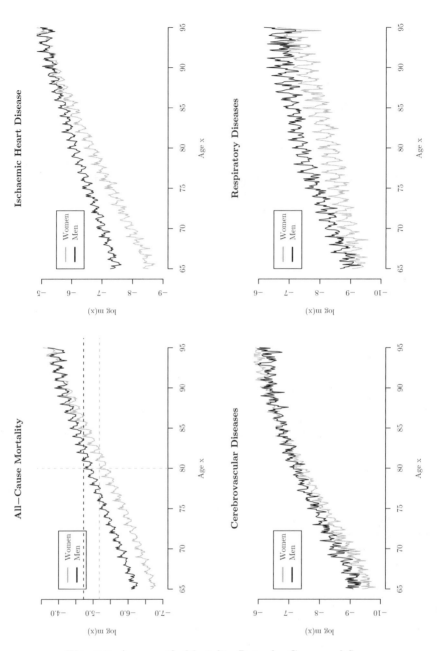

Fig. 5.2. Age-specific Mortality Rates by Cause and Sex

mortality [37, 98, 121, 419], as well as for heart diseases [246].[17] Our results are contradictory to findings from mortality research in general where women typically have lower mortality rates at all ages. These results should be interpreted with care for two reasons:

- If the analysis does not correct for age, those differentials might be the outcome of an age effect: due to higher life-expectancy of women, the mean age in a female population should be higher than in the corresponding male population. In conjunction with the increase of seasonality with age as previous articles stated [e.g. 102, 251, 300], women's seasonality could simply be larger because of their higher susceptibility to cold climate at advanced ages. Our analysis, however, controlled for possible confounding with age.

- A possible solution for this surprising finding might be the specific Danish situation: As already outlined in the introduction to this chapter, life expectancy in Denmark rose slower than anywhere else in comparable countries — especially for women. The main reason for the decelerated increase in life expectancy was the high smoking prevalence among females in Denmark. This reasoning might also apply to seasonal mortality in our analysis. When looking at the results from respiratory diseases (Fig. 5.3 d), it can be easily detected that women and men both display substantial excess mortality during winter. Women's relative risk of dying during the cold season is even higher than that of men. This might be traced back to the cohort of heavily smoking women who were born between the two World Wars and which is strongly represented in our data. But not only this compositional effect of a large proportion of smoking women in Denmark can be brought up to explain the higher excess mortality of women than of men in Denmark. There are also indications for a direct sex-effect of smoking between women and men. Although "it is too early to conclude that women may be more sensitive than men to some of the deleterious effects of smoking" [238, p. 787], several articles from Prescott et al. point into the direction that smoking has more severe effects on health for women than for men [e.g. 294, 295]. In one of her studies which is based on data from Denmark, Prescott et al. [295] show that this differential among women and men was visible in particular for the relevant seasonal diseases (cardiovascular, cerebrovascular and respiratory diseases) but not for cancer [295].

5.3.4 Winter Excess Mortality by Age, Sex, and Cause of Death

Age is the most important single determinant of mortality. Therefore, we calculated seasonal mortality for five-year age-groups in a second step. To fa-

---

[17] This finding of larger seasonal variations of coronary heart disease in New Zealand by Marshall et al. [246] only applied to the Non-Maori population.

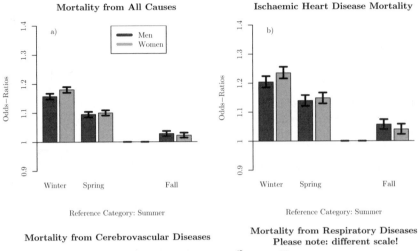

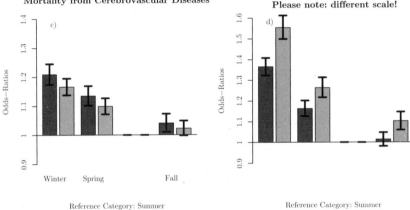

Fig. 5.3. Seasonal Mortality by Sex and Cause of Death (Odds-Ratios and 95% Confidence Intervals)

cilitate interpretation, only the estimated winter odds-ratios have been plotted in Figure 5.4. The results for winter excess mortality from all causes are shown in Fig. 5.4 a) for women and men. For women as well as for men, seasonal mortality increases with age. Between ages 65 and 69 the risk of dying in winter is about 10% higher for women as well as for men ($e_{\female}^{\beta \text{Winter}}$: 1.102; $e_{\male}^{\beta \text{Winter}}$: 1.095). Winter excess mortality is increasing with age. Danish people face excess winter mortality of about 15% in their mid 70s ($e_{\female}^{\beta \text{Winter}}$: 1.146; $e_{\male}^{\beta \text{Winter}}$: 1.149). When Danish people survive until 90 years of age, women's risk of dying is about 23% higher in winter than in summer; for men, the risks are slightly higher (90–94 years: 26.2% ; 95–99 years: 28.0%). Although the Danish data are of high quality, results for centenarians should

Table 5.6. Regression Results, Seasonal Mortality by Sex and All Cause Mortality

Women

Covariate		β	e^{β}	s.e.	ρ
Intercept (α)		-6.618		0.007	<.0001
Winter		0.165	1.180	0.004	<.0001
Spring		0.095	1.100	0.004	<.0001
Summer (RG)		-	-	-	-
Fall		0.022	1.022	0.004	<.0001
Age (in Years)	65-69 (RG)	-	-	-	-
	70-74	0.444	1.558	0.006	<.0001
	75-79	0.931	2.536	0.006	<.0001
	80-84	1.473	4.363	0.006	<.0001
	85-89	2.016	7.511	0.006	<.0001
	90-94	2.529	12.537	0.007	<.0001
	95-99	2.918	18.499	0.009	<.0001
	100+	2.815	16.695	0.021	<.0001
Period	1980-84	0.033	1.034	0.005	<.0001
	1985-90	-0.004	0.996	0.005	0.377
	1991-93 (RG)	-	-	-	-
	1994-96	-0.007	0.993	0.005	0.149
	1997-98	-0.066	0.936	0.006	<.0001

Men

Covariate		β	e^{β}	s.e.	ρ
Intercept (α)		-6.102		0.006	<.0001
Winter		0.146	1.157	0.004	<.0001
Spring		0.090	1.095	0.004	<.0001
Summer (RG)		-	-	-	-
Fall		0.027	1.028	0.005	<.0001
Age (in Years)	65-69 (RG)	-	-	-	-
	70-74	0.443	1.557	0.005	<.0001
	75-79	0.893	2.441	0.005	<.0001
	80-84	1.298	3.662	0.005	<.0001
	85-89	1.679	5.361	0.006	<.0001
	90-94	1.997	7.365	0.007	<.0001
	95-99	2.026	7.586	0.013	<.0001
	100+	1.004	2.729	0.036	<.0001
Period	1980-84	0.107	1.113	0.005	<.0001
	1985-90	0.041	1.042	0.005	<.0001
	1991-93 (RG)	-	-	-	-
	1994-96	-0.030	0.971	0.005	<.0001
	1997-98	-0.105	0.900	0.006	<.0001

Table 5.7. Regression Results, Seasonal Mortality by Sex and Ischaemic Heart Disease

Women

Covariate		β	e^{β}	s.e.	ρ
Intercept (α)		-8.448		0.014	<.0001
Winter		0.211	1.235	0.008	<.0001
Spring		0.138	1.148	0.008	<.0001
Summer (RG)		-	-	-	-
Fall		0.040	1.040	0.009	<.0001
Age (in Years) 65-69 (RG)		-	-	-	-
	70-74	0.647	1.910	0.014	<.0001
	75-79	1.285	3.615	0.013	<.0001
	80-84	1.927	6.870	0.013	<.0001
	85-89	2.522	12.458	0.013	<.0001
	90-94	3.068	21.492	0.014	<.0001
	95-99	3.466	31.992	0.018	<.0001
	100+	3.309	27.347	0.041	<.0001
Period	1980-84	0.299	1.348	0.009	<.0001
	1985-90	0.168	1.183	0.009	<.0001
	1991-93 (RG)	-	-	-	-
	1994-96	-0.200	0.819	0.011	<.0001
	1997-98	-0.382	0.682	0.013	<.0001

Men

Covariate		β	e^{β}	s.e.	ρ
Intercept (α)		-7.449		0.011	<.0001
Winter		0.186	1.204	0.008	<.0001
Spring		0.131	1.140	0.008	<.0001
Summer (RG)		-	-	-	-
Fall		0.056	1.057	0.008	<.0001
Age (in Years) 65-69 (RG)		-	-	-	-
	70-74	0.470	1.599	0.010	<.0001
	75-79	0.942	2.564	0.009	<.0001
	80-84	1.352	3.866	0.010	<.0001
	85-89	1.753	5.769	0.011	<.0001
	90-94	2.092	8.103	0.014	<.0001
	95-99	2.174	8.792	0.024	<.0001
	100+	1.116	3.052	0.069	<.0001
Period	1980-84	0.323	1.381	0.009	<.0001
	1985-90	0.171	1.186	0.009	<.0001
	1991-93 (RG)	-	-	-	-
	1994-96	-0.214	0.807	0.011	<.0001
	1997-98	-0.392	0.676	0.013	<.0001

Table 5.8. Regression Results, Seasonal Mortality by Sex and Cerebrovascular Diseases

Women

Covariate		β	e^{β}	s.e.	ρ
Intercept (α)		-9.346		0.023	<.0001
Winter		0.154	1.166	0.013	<.0001
Spring		0.095	1.099	0.013	<.0001
Summer (RG)		-	-	-	-
Fall		0.023	1.023	0.013	0.077
Age (in Years)	65-69 (RG)	-	-	-	-
	70-74	0.766	2.152	0.024	<.0001
	75-79	1.506	4.507	0.022	<.0001
	80-84	2.226	9.261	0.021	<.0001
	85-89	2.800	16.438	0.021	<.0001
	90-94	3.220	25.023	0.023	<.0001
	95-99	3.385	29.518	0.031	<.0001
	100+	2.998	20.053	0.078	<.0001
Period	1980-84	0.090	1.094	0.014	<.0001
	1985-90	-0.004	0.996	0.013	0.776
	1991-93 (RG)	-	-	-	-
	1994-96	-0.167	0.846	0.015	<.0001
	1997-98	-0.306	0.736	0.018	<.0001

Men

Covariate		β	e^{β}	s.e.	ρ
Intercept (α)		-8.945		0.023	<.0001
Winter		0.190	1.209	0.015	<.0001
Spring		0.127	1.135	0.015	<.0001
Summer (RG)		-	-	-	-
Fall		0.040	1.041	0.016	0.010
Age (in Years)	65-69 (RG)	-	-	-	-
	70-74	0.679	1.973	0.021	<.0001
	75-79	1.352	3.866	0.020	<.0001
	80-84	1.896	6.662	0.020	<.0001
	85-89	2.293	9.903	0.021	<.0001
	90-94	2.562	12.960	0.026	<.0001
	95-99	2.440	11.471	0.046	<.0001
	100+	1.157	3.181	0.147	<.0001
Period	1980-84	0.134	1.144	0.016	<.0001
	1985-90	-0.001	0.999	0.016	0.946
	1991-93 (RG)	-	-	-	-
	1994-96	-0.236	0.790	0.019	<.0001
	1997-98	-3868.000	0.000	0.022	<.0001

Table 5.9. Regression Results, Seasonal Mortality by Sex and Respiratory Diseases

Women

Covariate		β	e^β	s.e.	ρ
Intercept (α)		-9.077		0.025	<.0001
Winter		0.441	1.554	0.019	<.0001
Spring		0.234	1.264	0.020	<.0001
Summer (RG)		-	-	-	-
Fall		0.098	1.103	0.020	
Age (in Years)	65-69 (RG)	-	-	-	-
	70-74	0.355	1.426	0.023	<.0001
	75-79	0.633	1.882	0.023	<.0001
	80-84	0.953	2.595	0.023	<.0001
	85-89	1.310	3.706	0.024	<.0001
	90-94	1.750	5.755	0.028	<.0001
	95-99	2.188	8.920	0.042	<.0001
	100+	2.014	7.495	0.106	<.0001
Period	1980-84	-0.443	0.642	0.021	<.0001
	1985-90	-0.244	0.784	0.019	< .0001
	1991-93 (RG)	-	-	-	-
	1994-96	-0.222	0.801	0.021	<.0001
	1997-98	-0.081	0.922	0.023	0.000

Men

Covariate		β	e^β	s.e.	ρ
Intercept (α)		-8.750			<.0001
Winter		0.311	1.365	0.016	<.0001
Spring		0.151	1.163	0.017	<.0001
Summer (RG)		-	-	-	-
Fall		0.014		0.017	0.413
Age (in Years)	65-69 (RG)	-	-	-	-
	70-74	0.548	1.730	0.020	<.0001
	75-79	1.077	2.936	0.019	<.0001
	80-84	1.431	4.183	0.020	<.0001
	85-89	1.729	5.632	0.022	<.0001
	90-94	1.941	6.969	0.029	<.0001
	95-99	1.854	6.383	0.054	<.0001
	100+	0.979	2.661	0.139	<.0001
Period	1980-84	-0.096	0.909	0.018	<.0001
	1985-90	-0.023	0.977	0.017	0.163
	1991-93 (RG)	-	-	-	-
	1994-96	-0.220	0.803	0.020	<.0001
	1997-98	-0.137	0.872	0.022	<.0001

be interpreted with great care: As indicated by the large confidence intervals, not many people belong to this category. Consequently, just a few erroneous cases of people who died after their 100th birthday, may have a large impact on the estimated regression coefficients.

Further insights can be gained by investigating the patterns for the three selected causes of death: ischaemic heart disease, cerebrovascular diseases and respiratory diseases (Fig. 5.4 b,c,d). The relatively close resemblance of mortality from ischaemic heart disease with mortality from all causes should not be surprising as this cause of death alone contributes about 30% to all deaths. Also cerebrovascular diseases which contribute about 10% display an increase with age, albeit the slope is less smooth than for Figures 5.4 a) and b). While the relative risks of dying from ischaemic heart disease during winter is higher for women, men's relative risks are higher for cerebrovascular diseases. This is in contrast with the susceptibility to these diseases for mortality in general: Men's mortality rate from ischaemic heart disease is typically higher than women's, whereas the chance of dying from stroke (cerebrovascular disease) is greater for women.[18]

Winter excess mortality caused by respiratory diseases (cf. Fig. 5.4 d) does also increase with age for women. The development for men does not show any clear trend. Although the relative risk of dying from respiratory diseases is higher for men when they are 85–89 years old than for men 65–69 years ($e^{\beta_{\text{Winter}}}_{\sigma'65-69y}$: 1.283; $e^{\beta_{\text{Winter}}}_{\sigma'85-89y}$: 1.504;), the odds-ratio decreases for men in their late 90s $e^{\beta_{\text{Winter}}}_{\sigma'85-89y}$: 1.263;). Due to the large 95% confidence interval for this estimate, one should be careful with its interpretation.

Generally speaking, our analysis supports the results from previous research. We obtained a general trend which has been observed by Quetelet from as early as 1838 [300]: the seasonal amplitudes in mortality are increasing with age. This has been also regularly found in former studies [eg. 102, 121, 251, 268, 302]. One could argue that with increasing age, the susceptibility towards adverse environmental conditions gains in relevance. Public health policies aiming to reduce the annual number of cold-related deaths should therefore be aimed at the most vulnerable group: the very old. The general advice to keep a warm indoor climate, avoid exposure to cold outdoors, ... is particularly important to people at advanced ages.

Our analysis can not answer the question conclusively whether the previously discovered higher excess winter mortality for women than for men (cf. Fig. 5.3) can be generalized. The differential age-composition of women and men in the population can not be the reason as shown in Fig. 5.4 a). In most age-groups women and men differ only marginally in the extent of winter excess mortality. It can be assumed that female excess winter mortality is caused by factors which are specific for Denmark. Respiratory diseases con-

---

[18] Information about mortality in general has been derived from own calculations based on the WHO database located at http://www.who.int/whosis. Data were taken for Denmark for the year 1998.

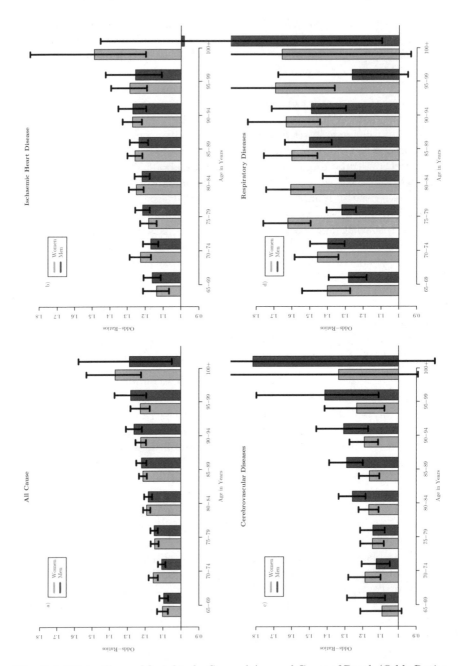

Fig. 5.4. Winter Excess Mortality by Sex and Age and Cause of Death (Odds-Ratios and 95% Confidence Intervals)

tribute only about 6–7% to all deaths. Nevertheless the differences between women and men with respect to winter excess mortality is especially large for that cause of death. The high smoking prevalence among Danish women in general can be offered as an explanation. This line of argumentation wins further support when one considers that the only significant differences in winter excess mortality from all causes is among people between 70 and 74 years of age. This is also the age-group with the largest differences between women and men in any age-group for ischaemic heart disease, and the only age-group where women exceed men in winter excess mortality from cerebrovascular diseases. Both causes of death are associated with smoking [3, 248, 294]. It has been analyzed previously that women born between the two World Wars show a high mortality most likely caused by a high smoking prevalence [173]. It can be therefore assumed that we observe rather a cohort effect than an age effect because these women constitute an important part in our data-set.

5.3.5 Seasonal Mortality by Sex, Wealth and Cause of Death

Socio-economic factors, besides age and sex, are important determinants of mortality differentials. The first indicator we analyzed was wealth which was measured on the household level and categorized into quartiles. In our model we controlled for age and period, marital status, education and the question whether somebody was living alone or with at least one more person. The coding was performed as outlined in section 5.2.1 starting on page 131.[19] The estimates for winter excess mortality for this variable are plotted in Figure 5.5 with summer serving as reference category. The four panels show the results for all-cause mortality (upper left panel), ischaemic heart disease (upper right panel), cerebrovascular diseases (lower left panel), and respiratory diseases (lower right panel) for women (left side in each panel) and men (right side in each panel). The poorest people are plotted in dark gray, people richer than 25% but poorer than 50% of the population are indicated by shaded bars in dark gray. The wealth quartile 50% –75% is shown in light gray and the richest 25% are in shaded light gray. Results for the poorest people should be interpreted with great care. Not many old people belong to this category (∼3.4%), hence the relatively large confidence intervals.

The general finding is that a social gradient is not observable. It is hard to track down visually any differences among the four social groups, for example, for winter excess mortality for female all-cause mortality (Figure 5.5a)) shows that the point estimates differ only marginally with a range from 1.181 (Quartile 1) to 1.202 (Quartile 4). Unfortunately, the statistical software used for the analysis (SAS) had problems with the estimation of seasonal mortality from all causes for men (Figure 5.5b). The results should therefore be

---

[19] The reference groups for the respective covariate-groups were: 65–69 Years (Age); 1991–93 (Period); Married (Marital Status); Alone (Living Alone Yes/No); Medium Education (Education).

interpreted with care. Nevertheless, the same tendency can be observed as for women: differences in excess winter mortality between the richest and the poorest people are rather negligible ($e_{Q1}^{\beta_{Winter}}$: 1.171; $e_{Q4}^{\beta_{Winter}}$: 1.187).

For the remainder of this section, results for the poorest quartile are not taken into account anymore as the number of deaths from ischaemic heart disease, cerebrovascular diseases and respiratory diseases in that social group is relatively small.

Figure 5.5 c) and d) portrays the seasonal nature of ischaemic heart disease for women (left) and men (right). Basically one can observe the same pattern as for all-cause-mortality: the risk of dying in winter is elevated by roughly the same amount across the three wealth quartiles. Men's risk of dying in winter rather than in summer is 27% higher in Quartile 25%–50% and 26% higher among the wealthiest. Women show a slight trend with an unexpected gradient where the richest face a relative risk of 28% in winter and women belonging to Quartile 25%–50% only of 21%. This tendency is, however, not statistically significant as the 95% confidence intervals overlap.

Results for the analysis of winter excess mortality for cerebrovascular diseases are displayed in Figure 5.5 e) and f). Not surprisingly, deaths from cerebrovascular diseases show a very similar pattern to deaths from ischaemic heart disease: Again, no significant (95%-level) differences have been estimated. From an overall perspective, the estimated values are somewhat smaller for cerebrovascular diseases than for ischaemic heart disease. While the relative risk of dying was 25.9% higher for the latter cause of death among men in the richest wealth quartile, it was only elevated 23.3% for the cerebrovascular diseases. It is interesting to note that the ordering of the wealth quartiles by winter excess mortality is the same for both causes of death: If we can speak of any social gradient for women at all, the slope is in the opposite direction than what would be expected. The wealthiest women face again a higher relative risk than women from poorer social strata.

The results for deaths from respiratory diseases are illustrated in Figure 5.5 g) and h). The first impression reiterates the finding from Figure 5.3d. Women's excess winter mortality is considerably higher than men's. But again there is no social gradient present.

Socio-economic factors have been established as an important determinant in mortality differentials [195, 210, 314]. Indeed, in many countries those differences are even increasing over time [e.g. 29, 71, 243, 284] — also in Denmark [233]. The lack of an effect of wealth on seasonal mortality is not surprising, though. It is rather a common finding that there is "no clear evidence of a relationship between socioeconomic status and seasonal mortality" [121, p. 274]. Several of those studies are, however, based on ecological data on the ward level [cf. 214]. This lack of correlation on the aggregated level must not necessarily correspond to a lack of correlation on the individual level

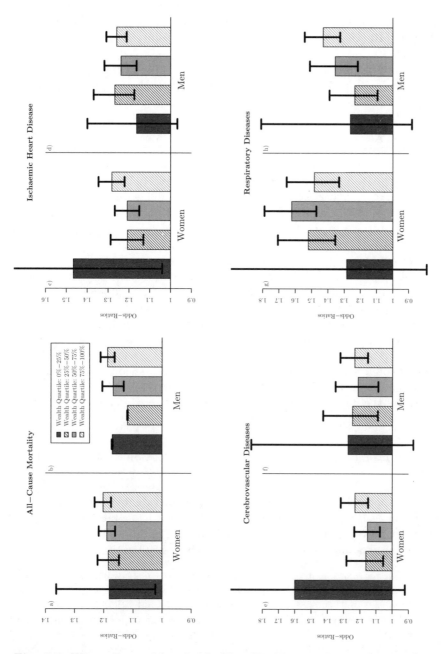

Fig. 5.5. Winter Excess Mortality by Sex, Wealth, and Cause of Death (Odds-Ratios and 95% Confidence Intervals)

[311].[20] If studied with individual level data, there are some first indications that socio-economic status does actually matter for seasonal mortality. Donaldson and Keatinge found that "cold related mortality in the retired (65–74) age group was generally higher in men of class 5 (unskilled) than class 1 (professional), or other classes, with little differences between men, and women or housewives" [79, p. 790]. The question which arises then is: why did we not find any impact of wealth in Denmark despite the high-quality of the Danish data on the individual level?

It is likely that the lack of any evidence is associated with the specific situation of Denmark. For example, the health system is tax-financed and open to everyone for free [171, 336].[21] Consequently, access to health care is independent of income and wealth which might be particularly important in the case of seasonal mortality. Despite the aspect of access to health care via economic resources, there is also a behavioral aspect for the relation between socio-economic status and mortality: "poor people behave poorly" [230, p. 809] with higher rates of smoking, less physical activity, poorer nutritional habits .... The amount of poor people in Denmark is, however, lower than anywhere else in Europe. Only 3.9% of the people in Denmark earn less than half of the mean income [162].[22] This implies that the absolute differences between the four wealth quartiles in Denmark are relatively small. Consequently, the socio-economic differences measured by wealth in the population which could be important for cold-related mortality [cf. 79] are rather negligible in the Danish context. Wealth (or income) is, however, only one approach to measure socio-economic status. Since we have shown in the previous chapter that an educational gradient exists in seasonal mortality in the United States, we will investigate the impact of formal school education on winter excess mortality in Denmark in the following section.

5.3.6 Winter Excess Mortality by Sex, Education and Cause of Death

Another approach to measure socio-economic status is by education. While weakening health can influence the income and wealth of a person, the highest educational level achieved remains unaffected. In addition, it is almost constant in the age-range analyzed here and it is better suited than measurements

---

[20] It should be mentioned that not all recent studies which discovered no impact of socio-economic factors on seasonal mortality used aggregate level data. For example, the analysis of van Rossum et al. [376] used individual level data. Their analysis was however aimed at a relatively homogeneous population: male civil servants.

[21] As pointed out by the Danish "Indenrigs- og Sundhedsministeriet" [171], this is not perfectly correct. Private expenditures for health care have to be given for some medicinal products, dentistry, and physiotherapy.

[22] Other European countries show much larger values. E.g. Portugal 24.5% , France 14.7%, UK 14.8%.

derived from occupational status, as the study population is 65 years or older and therefore most of them are no longer actively working anymore and are retired [374]. In addition, education is less related to *financial aspects* (like wealth), yet it is rather linked to behavioral aspects of health.

Figure 5.6 shows the results from the logistic regression analyzing the impact of education on winter excess mortality from all causes. The estimated odds-ratios for women are displayed on the left side (Fig. 5.6 a), winter excess mortality for men on the right side (Fig. 5.6 b). The results by cause of death are plotted in the Appendix in Figure D.1 on page 185. In this approach we controlled for age, period, marital status and wealth (we used the highest wealth quartile as the reference group).

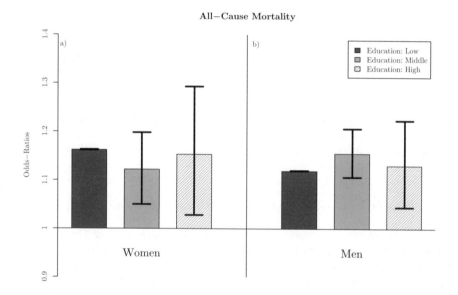

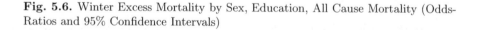

Fig. 5.6. Winter Excess Mortality by Sex, Education, All Cause Mortality (Odds-Ratios and 95% Confidence Intervals)

The results for winter excess mortality by educational attainment iterate the findings from the analysis of socio-economic status measured via wealth: no clear social gradient is observable neither for women nor for men. The relative risk of dying during winter is elevated by about 16% for females of the lowest educational group and roughly 15% for females of the highest educational group. This lack of a tendency can be also observed for men with slightly lower values (low: 1.120, high: 1.130). Although the problems of the software to estimate standard errors for women and men with the lowest education should lead to careful interpretations, the results for causes of death such as ischaemic heart disease and respiratory diseases (Fig. D.1, 185) support the view of a lack of a social gradient.

No previous literature exists so far which analyzed the impact of educational level on seasonal mortality. Only the analysis in the previous chapter (Chapter 4, page 83) touched this subject. In the analysis in the previous chapter using data from the United States, we have found an apparent social gradient: Generally speaking, people with higher education showed lower seasonal fluctuations in mortality. A lack of a differential of mortality in general by educational group can not be offered as an explanation. Actually, educational differentials in adult mortality do not only persist but even increase in both countries [103, 233, 296]. Errors in the coding of education in the data-set should not be the explanation either, Typically, an educational gradient was found when controlling for education in other analyses. For example, the regression model which resulted in Figure 5.5 a) for the richest women (shaded, light gray bar) controlled for age, period, marital status, living alone yes/no and education. Intermediate level of education served as reference category. People with lower education showed higher mortality (odds-ratio: 1.117) and vice versa (odds-ratio: 0.900). One can therefore conclude that education is not well-suited as a good proxy variable in a homogeneous country to determine seasonal mortality differences. This implies that behavior which is known to increase the risk of dying (for example, wearing not appropriate clothes outdoors) [80] is in Denmark independent from the knowledge people have acquired in school.

5.3.7 Winter Excess by Cause of Death and Housing Conditions

Housing conditions are closely related to socio-economic status. Omitting an analysis by housing quality after not finding any results for wealth and education would not be appropriate because of the crucial role housing conditions play. Poor housing conditions are a major health risk [245] — especially for typical seasonal diseases such as cardiovascular, cerebrovascular, and respiratory diseases [54, 121, 404]. Therefore a separate analysis has been conducted which examined whether housing conditions are of major relevance also in Denmark.

The results for winter excess mortality from all causes, ischaemic heart disease, respiratory diseases, and from cerebrovascular diseases, are plotted clockwise in Figure 5.7 starting in the upper left panel. In each panel, the left side shows the estimated odds-ratios for women, the right side for men. The dark gray color indicates bad housing conditions and barplots in light gray good housing conditions. We controlled for age, period, marital status, living alone and education. The influence of wealth has not been included because the data on housing conditions started only in 1991 and the availability of information on wealth finished in 1996.

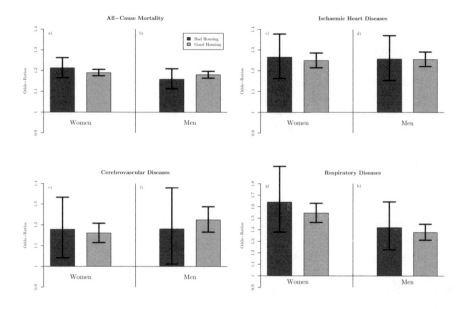

Fig. 5.7. Winter Excess by Sex, Cause of Death and Housing Conditions (Odds-Ratios and 95% Confidence Intervals)

The differences in winter excess mortality from all causes are rather small between people living in good housing conditions on the one hand and people living in less favorable houses and apartments on the other hand. The risk of dying during winter is elevated by 21% in poor housing conditions for females. Women who live in better houses and apartments have a lower relative risk; the differential is, nevertheless, relatively small (19%). A difference of two percentage points is also observed among men. Surprisingly, the direction is in the opposite direction: While men in poor housing face a relative risk of 16%, people in better housing show slightly higher odds-ratios (1.18). These differences are, however, not statistically significant on a 95% level. Cerebrovascular diseases show the same tendency, whereas the differences for ischaemic heart disease are even more minor: the odds-ratios are 1.266 for women during winter in poor housing and 1.250 in good housing conditions. For men, the corresponding values are 1.258 and 1.256. Albeit not statistically significant either, the only cause of death where good housing conditions appear to favor both sexes are respiratory diseases. The relative risk of dying for women during winter is 64% higher during winter than during summer if they live in relatively poor housing. In good housing conditions, the risk is only elevated by about 55%.

Although "warm housing is not enough" [186], it has often been singled out as a major determinant to avoid winter excess mortality [e.g. 16, 54].

It is therefore surprising that we did not find conclusive evidence for such a housing effect on winter excess mortality in Denmark. The key to answer this question lies probably again in the remarkable homogeneity of the Danish population on a high absolute level. "97–99 percent of those aged 70+ who live in ordinary housing are in houses with kitchen, toilets, central heating, and hot water " [128, p. 26]. Almost no apartments exist in Denmark without central heating, whose absence has often been described as the main factor triggering cold-related mortality [e.g. 16, 75, 77, 188, 251, 324, 325, 340]. Contrastingly, elderly people in the United Kingdom, the country in which most of these previous studies have been conducted, face severe housing problems [47]. For example, the 2001 census showed that more than 10% of all households in England still do not have central heating.[23] We can therefore not conclude that housing conditions are of minor importance for winter excess mortality. If the population is, however, rather homogeneous and on a high level in housing terms like in Denmark, the amount of excess mortality attributable to poor standards in houses and apartments is rather negligible.

5.3.8 Winter Excess Mortality by Cause of Death and Car Ownership

Whether one owns a car can be interpreted as another measurement of socio-economic status. We employ this indicator in our analysis following the suggestion of Donaldson and Keatinge [77]. They argue that increased car ownership reduced the annual amplitude in mortality by exposing less and less people to the cold outdoors. Consequently, one should assume that people with a car should show less winter excess mortality than the ones without.

The results for women and men are shown in Figure 5.8 for all-cause mortality as well as for ischaemic heart disease, cerebrovascular diseases and respiratory diseases. We controlled for age, period, marital status, living alone and education.[24]

For mortality from all causes, risks are elevated by 20% during winter for women if they did not own a car. In case of a car the risk was 22%. Men showed a similar value in the absence of a car (20%); their risk decreased if they owned a car. The same pattern can be observed for both sexes for cerebrovascular diseases: an increase for women and a decrease for men in the presence of a car. For ischaemic heart disease, almost no change was detectable (odds-ratio for women without car: 1.268, with car: 1.254; odds-ratio for men without car: 1.267, with car: 1.243). Respiratory diseases showed even a slight increase in winter excess mortality if a car was present. But none of these results was significant.

---

[23] Result based on own calculation derived from data available online at the Statistical Office of the United Kingdom [265]

[24] Like in the analysis for housing conditions, we excluded the variable wealth from our analysis for similar reasons: the car register provided data starting in 1992 and wealth was only available until 1996.

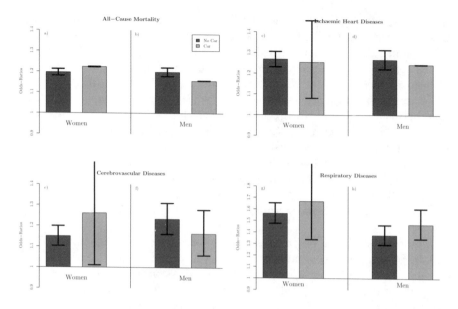

Fig. 5.8. Winter Excess Mortality by Sex, Cause of Death and Car Ownership (Odds-Ratios and 95% Confidence Intervals)

The suggestion whether increased car ownership decreased the amount of cold-related deaths during winter has never been analyzed so far in an empirical investigation. Our results indicate that the question whether one owns a car or not is rather irrelevant for the relative risks of dying in winter in Denmark. This could either mean that the availability of a car is of minor importance for excess winter mortality or another explanation could be that the system of public transportation in Denmark is of high quality. Buses operating on a regular basis and windproof bus shelters, as suggested by Keatinge and Donaldson [186], help in reducing exposure to outdoor cold. Consequently, being owner of a car or not is less important for seasonal mortality.

5.3.9 Winter Excess Mortality by Sex, Marital Status and Cause of Death

The impact of marital status on seasonal mortality is examined in Figure 5.9. The four panels show the results for all-cause mortality (upper left), ischaemic heart disease (upper right), cerebrovascular diseases (lower left), and respiratory diseases (lower right). Each of the four panels is divided into a left part for women and into a right part for men. In these subpanels the exponentiated regression coefficients are plotted for widowed (dark gray), divorced (dark gray, shaded), married (light gray), never married / single (light gray, shaded) people. The respective reference season in each case is summer. In this analysis we controlled for age, period, being alone, education, and wealth.

At a first glance no consistent pattern giving a straightforward interpretation is present. None of the four presented marital statuses shows consistently higher or lower values of winter excess mortality than the other ones. For "All-Cause Mortality" the odds-ratios for winter excess mortality for women vary between 1.157 for "divorced" and 1.205 for "widowed". The estimates for men are in a similar range (divorced: 1.127; never married: 1.203). Almost non-observable differences exist for mortality from ischaemic heart disease for women and especially for men (odds-ratios for women: widowed 1.243, divorced 1.210, married 1.226, never married 1.245; odds-ratios for men: widowed 1.243, divorced 1.260, married 1.257, never married 1.257). Larger differences do exist for cerebrovascular diseases and in particular for respiratory diseases.

Marital status is a well established factor to determine mortality differentials. International comparisons [e.g. 163] have shown that married women and men have lowest age-specific mortality rates compared to people in any other marital status. Typically divorced people face the highest mortality risks. It is a common finding that men benefit more from being married than women [129]. Two strains of causal explanation are usually given: selection effects and protection effects. A selection effect postulates that mentally and physically healthier persons are more likely to marry. Among other factors, a protection effect hypothesizes that married people have more emotional and social support, have better access to medical information and health services due to a higher income per person and it also reduces risk taking behavior, encouraging healthier lifestyles. [124].

Our study could not detect any advantage for married women and men in terms of winter excess mortality. While it is usually not the category showing highest winter excess mortality, it is neither displaying consistently lower cold-related mortality. We should be, however, careful with the interpretation of these variables as there is a bias towards not enough exposure time for married people and too many exposures for widowed and divorced people. If our results were true, an explanation could be that better access to medical care via a higher income per head is irrelevant in Denmark where medical services are open for everyone. Another reason could be that in this analysis by marital status we controlled — among other factors such as age, period, wealth, and education — also for the question whether somebody was living alone or not. If marital status operated for excess winter mortality via emotional and social support and fast help in case of an emergency, it was unlikely that this analysis yielded any significant results. Therefore we analyzed in a final step the question whether living arrangements matter for cold-related mortality.

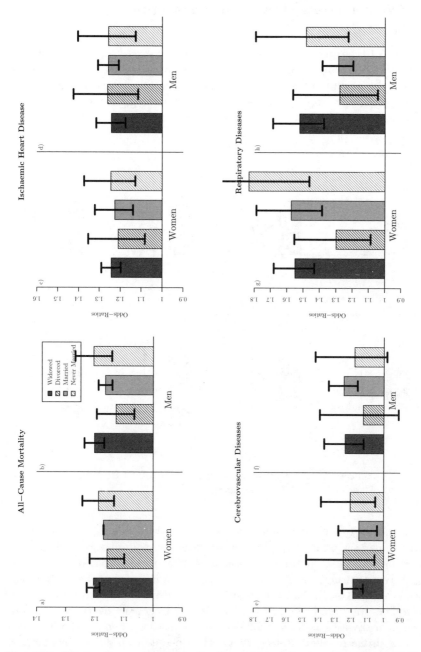

Fig. 5.9. Winter Excess Mortality by Sex, Marital Status, and Cause of Death (Odds-Ratios and 95% Confidence Intervals)

5.3.10 Winter Excess Mortality by Cause of Death and Living Alone

In Figure 5.10 the odds-ratios are plotted for winter excess mortality for people who either lived alone or not. Starting in the upper left panel in a clockwise direction the results are shown for mortality from all causes, ischaemic heart disease, respiratory diseases and cerebrovascular diseases. We controlled for age, period, marital status, wealth and education.

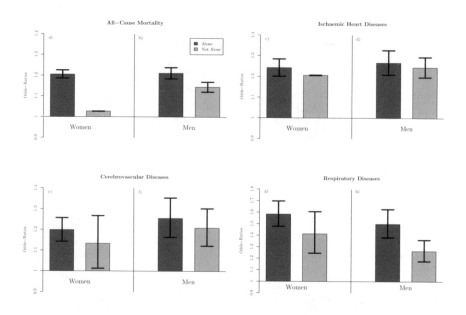

Fig. 5.10. Winter Excess Mortality by Sex, Cause of Death and Living Alone (Odds-Ratios and 95% Confidence Intervals)

For mortality from all causes, the relative risk of dying is 21% higher in winter than in summer for women as well as for men who are living alone. If men had at least one more person present in the household, the relative risk of dying during winter is 14.5% which is significantly lower (95% confidence level).[25] Also the differences are not significant for the selected causes of death. The same tendency can be detected for ischaemic heart disease, cerebrovascular diseases as well as for respiratory diseases: People who live alone are more prone to dying during winter than people who do not live alone.[26]

---

[25] The results for women should be interpreted with care as the software had problems with convergence. The value of 1.027 is probably too low.

[26] It should be noted that the smaller differences for ischaemic heart disease than for cerebrovascular diseases reflect the fact that in case of stroke it is much more

Respiratory diseases display the largest slope of all of these causes. If women live alone their relative risk of dying during winter is 58.4% higher than during summer; in presence of a partner, the risk was only 41.4% higher than during summer. For men, the differences in the odds-ratios is even larger (odds-ratio alone: 1.499; odds-ratio not alone: 1.265).

The empirical evidence in the literature suggests that there is a strong positive effect on mortality if people live alone rather than with a partner [15, 23, 123, 180, 226]. In the case of seasonal mortality, two studies exist measuring the impact on seasonal mortality. The one which investigated the effect on winter excess mortality could not detect any significant differences [405]. One study analyzed the question for heat-related mortality during extreme heat waves [267]. Their paper reflected also our finding: If people are living alone during periods of adverse environmental conditions, it is better not to live alone but together with a partner to avoid mortality. The possible linkage is probably via emotional and social support. Also the possibility that somebody is present in the case of an emergency to provide first aid and call for an ambulance can have a considerable influence.

5.4 Summary

The aim of this chapter was to analyze the determinants of excess winter mortality in Denmark. Denmark was chosen mainly because of its data. No other country in the world has as much information available about the whole population in a longitudinal dimension as Denmark. These population register data have been analyzed using a discrete time event-history approach. In our analysis several findings from the literature were tested for the first time in a longitudinal perspective for an entire population on the individual level. As the data were available as individual life course histories, we used a discrete-time event-history model for our analysis.

Denmark follows the typical pattern of developed countries in the Northern hemisphere with the highest annual numbers of death in December and a minimum in August. Winter deaths exceed summer deaths by about 17%. We have shown that winter excess mortality becomes more pronounced with increasing age. The oldest people tend to be the most vulnerable group not only in terms of overall mortality but also in their amount of cold-related deaths. Women seem to have higher fluctuations between winter- and summer-mortality than men. Previous literature suggested that there are no sex-related differences in excess winter mortality. Our finding could be caused by the specific situation in Denmark with a relatively high prevalence of smoking among women which has an impact on typical seasonal diseases. Especially for respiratory diseases we detected considerably higher winter excess mortality for women than for

---

important to have quick help available than in the case of myocardial infarction [347].

men.

The lack of impact of socio-economic status on cold-related mortality has been reported previously in the literature. Neither wealth nor education seems to be correlated with excess winter mortality. Again, this could be caused by the homogeneity of the Danish population where the differences between relatively poor and relatively rich people are smaller in absolute terms than in other countries. Also housing conditions are less problematic for an increased risk of dying during the cold season in Denmark than in the UK, which was most often the country of analysis in previous studies. In socio-economic terms, Denmark is not only homogeneous. This homogeneity is, in addition, also at a very high level. Really poor housing conditions are hard to find; more than 90% of all households have the maximum number of installations which are recorded in the housing.

We did not find any association between car ownership and excess winter mortality. This means that car ownership is either not a good proxy to measure exposure to outdoor cold during winter or that there are only marginal differences in time spent outdoors for old people who own a car and who don't (maybe due to high standard of public transportation). Despite its importance for mortality analysis in general, we could not find any effect of marital status on excess winter mortality. More crucial are the living arrangements: If somebody is living alone, the relative risk of dying during winter is much higher for him or her than people who share the apartment with at least one more person.

Many studies as well as our results point in the direction that socio-economic conditions do not have an impact of excess winter mortality. This does not imply that they do not differ in general. Many previous studies used aggregate level data which do not allow to make inferences on the individual level. And, indeed, when looking at the individual level, it has been observed that people of lower socio-economic status face higher mortality risks during winter than in summer compared to people from higher social strata (cf. Chapter 4, page 83 or Donaldson and Keatinge [79]). The lack of findings for Denmark for socio-economic status can probably be attributed to the homogeneous character of the country at a relatively high level. Or as Peter Høeg observed in his novel: "Seen from my perspective, Denmark's entire population is middle-class. The truly poor and the truly rich are so few as to be almost exotic" [151, p. 25].

6

Outlook: The Impact of Reducing Cold-Related Mortality

6.1 Introduction

While the previous two chapters dealt with factors which influence the extent of seasonal mortality fluctuations, this small chapter wants to answer the question: If we are able to eliminate or at least diminish the seasonal fluctuations in mortality, what is the public health benefit? We answer this question by investigating how much life expectancy would increase if people did not have to face the adverse environmental conditions during winter, but were actually exposed to summer conditions for their whole life. Thus, we compare "real" mortality conditions and the corresponding remaining life expectancy with "summer" mortality conditions.

6.2 Data, Methods, and Results

Our aim is to calculate a seasonal life-table. To obtain it, we extend the standard construction of the life-table. Two data sets are usually required — the number of people alive in a certain age and the number of people who have died at that age. Our approach is similar, but we use more information for a given calendar year.

- The number of people alive in a certain month at a certain (integer) age.
- The number of people who died during a certain month at a certain (integer) age.

  These data are provided in two data-sources.

- Monthly death counts by age were obtained from the Multiple Cause of Death Public Use Files as described in Chapter 4. The year 1998, the last year which was analyzed in the chapter on US death counts, was chosen for the current analysis.

- Monthly population counts for the year 1998 by sex were obtained from the US Bureau of the Census [373].

One additional item of information is needed, usually denoted as $a(x)$ in life-table notation: the mean number of person-years (or in our application: person-months) lived in the interval by those dying in the interval. We assumed that people die on average in the middle of each month, thus assigning the value 0.5 to all ages. In our analysis, we restricted ourselves to a range from 50 to 100 years of age.

Using this information we were able to calculate all life-table functions. To ascertain that our approach worked, we compared remaining life expectancy at age 50 from our calculations with life-table calculations from the Human Life Table Database (HLD) [167]. The HLD calculations resulted in values of e_{50} of 31.63 years for women and 27.29 years for men. We considered our approach satisfactory, as these "official" results correspond closely to our estimations for age 50 in April for women (our result: 31.629 years) and for age 50 between June and July for men (June: 27.339, July: 27.269).

We estimated "summer" mortality by fitting a straight line to the natural logarithm of the yearly minimum probabilities of dying (q_x-values). This approach is shown in Figure 6.1. The solid lines represent the observed, real, age-specific probabilities of dying on a log-scale in light gray for women and in dark gray for men. The dotted lines show our fitted values from linear regression. The legend in the lower right corner of the figure shows that this linear approach fitted our data remarkably well. We obtained adjusted values for r^2 of 0.997 for women and 0.999 for men.

Table 6.1 shows the results from the comparison of real mortality with summer mortality. For that purpose we calculated remaining life expectancy in both ways for every five years starting from age 50 until age 95 for women as well as for men. We can see that remaining life expectancy at age 50 could be increased by 0.83 years for women and by 1.08 years for men if summer mortality conditions prevailed for the rest of their lives rather than the observed mortality conditions. The absolute gain in years decreases at more advanced ages. The proportional benefit, however, increases. At age 90, remaining life expectancy of women as well as of men could be increased by 13% (women: 12.95%; men: 13.43%).

6.3 Discussion

Our analysis has shown that the differences between the observable remaining life expectancy at age 50 is increased by 0.83 years for women and 1.08 years for men. It should be pointed out that these gains at a particular age do not apply only to the "rescued" people, but to *all* women and *all* men. Although such an increase in life expectancy seems to be only moderate, an economic

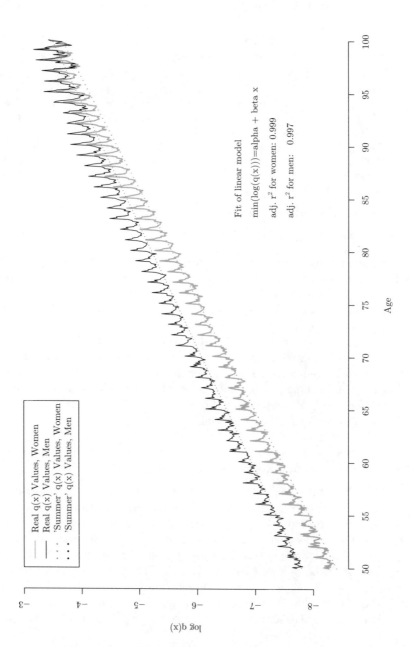

Fig. 6.1. Real and "Summer" Probabilities of Dying and Fit of the Linear Model

Table 6.1. Gains in Life Expectancy from Reducing Annual Cold-Related Mortality

Age x	Women				Men			
	e_x^{real}	e_x^{Summer}	Gains in e_x	$\frac{Gain}{e_x^{real}}\%$	e_x^{real}	e_x^{Summer}	Gains in e_x	$\frac{Gain}{e_x^{real}}\%$
50.00	31.85	32.68	0.83	2.59	27.70	28.77	1.08	3.90
55.00	27.42	28.20	0.78	2.86	23.51	24.59	1.08	4.60
60.00	23.19	23.91	0.72	3.13	19.59	20.66	1.07	5.45
65.00	19.22	19.87	0.65	3.38	16.01	17.02	1.01	6.33
70.00	15.52	16.13	0.61	3.90	12.77	13.72	0.95	7.46
75.00	12.16	12.75	0.59	4.82	9.93	10.80	0.87	8.76
80.00	9.12	9.78	0.66	7.22	7.44	8.28	0.84	11.31
85.00	6.53	7.22	0.69	10.53	5.42	6.16	0.74	13.66
90.00	4.47	5.05	0.58	12.95	3.87	4.39	0.52	13.43
95.00	2.73	3.06	0.33	12.00	2.54	2.77	0.23	8.98

perspective could emphasize the relevance of this additional life year won. Recent studies conducted at the University of Chicago and at Yale estimated the impact of health and life expectancy improvements on national wealth [261, 274]. Murphy and Topel estimate "that improvements in life expectancy alone added approximately $ 2.8 trillion *per year* (in constant 1992 dollars) to national wealth between 1970 and 1990" [261, p. 2–3]. During those two decades remaining life expectancy at age 50 rose a bit more than five years for women as well as for men. The potential gain from reducing cold-related mortality is, in comparison, relatively small (0.8 years for women and about 1 year for men). Nevertheless, national wealth could benefit from such a reduction in considerable sums as well.

It should be stressed, however, that these gains outlined in Table 6.1 present a *theoretical maximum* for several reasons. For example:

- Period life-tables do not describe the mortality experience of a real cohort but of a synthetic cohort. This applies even more to the case of a seasonal lifetable. The results are only correct if the current rates would prevail.[1]
- If a life has been saved in winter, it does not imply that the "rescued" person has the same probabilities of dying for her/his remaining life as the rest of the cohort. Typically, people who would have died without the saving are frailer and, thus, more susceptible to death than their peers [385, 387]. "More generally, individuals of the same age may differ from differ from each other in their 'frailty' or relative risk of death" [377, p. 154].

---

[1] Life expectancy at current *rates* is different from life expectancy at current *conditions* as shown by Vaupel [380].

7

Concluding Chapter: Summary of Findings

The impact of seasonal effects on diseases and mortality has been known for more than 2000 years. Surprisingly little is, however, known about its determinants. To understand and tackle a phenomenon, it is of importance to have the current state of knowledge about it. The literature review presented in Chapter 2 showed that biomedical approaches could explain the basic annual pattern observed in seasonal mortality with a peak in winter and a trough in summer, but not the "seasonality paradox": Cold regions show consistently smaller differences between summer and winter mortality than countries where a warm or moderate climate prevails. Thus, social and cultural influences play an integral part in mediating seasonal fluctuations in mortality and, consequently, also in reducing the annual number of cold-related deaths. The historical literature review has shown the importance of those non-biological factors already in the past. The literature claims that, nowadays, avoiding indoor as well as outdoor cold by having a warm indoor climate, and reduced time spent outdoors during cold spells, plays a crucial role for minimizing the risk of dying during winter.

Chapter 3 reviewed indices, tests, and time-series methods for seasonality to indicate which methods are suited best to analyze seasonal data. For "normal" applications with a smooth annual pattern with one peak and one trough, Hewitt's test [150] is suited best to test for seasonality. This test should be used in conjunction with a descriptive index like the "Winter/Summer-Ratio" to have also a measurement of the extent of differences between winter and summer since Hewitt's test is a nonparametric test based on ranks. None of the standard methods we analyzed for seasonal time-series fulfilled our requirements. It can be generally stated that the methods X-12, SABL, STL, TRAMO/SEATS and BV4 performed well on relatively simple data patterns. For situations with a variable trend, a changing seasonal component and overdispersion, a situation which is rather common in real data, all of these approaches fail to produce satisfactory results as we have shown in simulation studies.

For our analysis of seasonality in US death counts between 1959 and 1998 (Chapter 4, page 83), we developed a new method which returned a correct estimation of the trend and the seasonal component for the same models for which the standard methods (X12, BV4, ...) failed in Chapter 3. In our model, we allowed the trend and the seasonal component to vary smoothly over time (or age). We estimated these models in a data-driven approach (thus, we did not impose any parametric form on these components) by fitting a varying-coefficients model using P-Splines.

Our most important findings from the analysis were: cold-related mortality increases with age which supports previous findings in the literature. Seasonal mortality over time increased slightly since the 1970. This reflects probably the widespread introduction of air conditioning which makes summer mortality decrease at a faster pace than mortality is decreasing during any other season of the year.

We discovered that women and men do not differ considerably with respect to seasonal fluctuations in mortality. This has been found in previous analyses. Nevertheless, the question remains how it is possible that women face lower mortality risks than men throughout their life course — which corresponds to lower susceptibility to adverse environmental conditions — but show the same relative response to seasonal effects as men do.

It should have been assumed from comparative European studies that warmer regions in the US show larger fluctuations in seasonality than colder regions. We found, however, no differences. Especially the trend over time shows a slightly converging pattern which could reflect a tendency towards similar living conditions in all regions of the United States.

Our investigation pursued a novel approach by analyzing the effect of education as a proxy for socio-economic status and marital status on seasonal mortality. Both constitute important determinants for differential mortality in the United States and elsewhere. We did not find support that marital status has an important influence on seasonal mortality. We discovered, however, a social gradient by education in seasonal mortality. The less years spent in formal education, the higher are the annual fluctuations in mortality. This is an effect which has not been discovered elsewhere.

Besides the analysis of death *counts* in the US American data over time and age, we investigated the determinants of excess winter mortality in Denmark using an event-history approach. This country represents the "El Dorado" of all countries with respect to the quality and wealth of data: Denmark's person registers allow to follow life courses on the individual level in a longitudinal perspective on almost any phenomenon of interest. Similar to the case of the analysis of US death counts, we found an increase with age for all-cause mortality as well as for ischaemic heart disease, cerebrovascular diseases and respiratory diseases.

While many studies as well as our analysis of deaths in the United States (Chapter 4) found no differences between seasonal mortality of women and men, we discovered that women's excess mortality surpasses the one of men in Denmark. Most likely the explanation is specific for Denmark: Women have a higher smoking prevalence there than in most other countries. This behavioral characteristic affects typical seasonal diseases like cardiovascular and cerebrovascular diseases but in particular respiratory diseases. Women with the highest smoking prevalence in Denmark were born between the two World Wars and constitute a major part of the female population in our data. Despite our findings for the United States, we could not detect any effect of socio-economic status on seasonal mortality in Denmark. This could be explained by the homogeneity of the Danish population being on a relatively high level rather than by a general absence of an effect of socio-economic conditions on seasonal mortality. More importantly, concerning the amount of excess winter mortality in Denmark is the question whether somebody is living alone or not, rather than socioeconomic status or marital status. If people are living alone they have higher relative mortality risks in winter than women and men who share an apartment with at least one more person.

Our analysis has shown that the most vulnerable groups are old people, people who are living alone and people of lower socio-economic status. Public health policies which aim to reduce the annual number of cold-related deaths in a country should therefore focus on these groups. In Chapter 6 we used US data for the year 1998 to estimate the maximum theoretical gains in life expectancy if those public policies were successful. We calculated that at age 50 about 0.8 years of life years could be won for women and about 1 year of life for men. Although these gains sound only moderate in size, they may have a huge economic impact on national wealth in absolute numbers.

A

Appendix for Literature Review

A.1 Methodological Aspects of the Literature Review

In 1994, the British Medical Journal published an article named "The scandal of poor medical research: Sloppy use of literature often to blame" [179]. In the case of seasonal mortality, there is a considerable risk for "sloppy use" as scientists from various disciplines are working on that subject. Consequently, it is likely that researchers from one discipline are not aware of important findings from another area. An exhaustive search for literature is therefore indispensable. For this purpose, bibliographic reference indices (e.g. OVID, Population Index) have been searched as well as databases which give online access to articles (e.g. JSTOR, ScienceDirect). Relying only on databases for literature reviews may include various problems such as incompleteness [59]. However, querying several databases in conjunction with the archives of journals and using cross-references, it is fairly certain that no seminal paper on seasonal mortality has been left out. More details on the indices, databases, and journals searched are given in Table A.1.

Table A.1. Databases Used for Literature Search

- Population Index
- JSTOR
- OVID
- British Medical Journal (BMJ)
- The Lancet
- Journal of Epidemiology
  and Community Health (JECH)

- ScienceDirect
- Springer LINK Search
- EBSCO
- Ingenta
- New England Journal
  of Medicine (NEJM)

One possible shortcoming has to be pointed out anyway: There might be a "Tower of Babel Bias" in this review [134]. This phenomenon refers to the problem that the inclusion of English as the only language in literature searches may lead to different findings than in multilingual approaches. Including studies in German and French besides English moderates the possibility of a "Tower of Babel—Bias", however, this drawback can not be completely eradicated.

Population Index. The *Population Index* is the main database for demographic and population literature published between 1986 and 2000. Its range of about 400 journals covers not only demography but also biology, economics, geography, and sociology. While the emphasis is on European languages, relevant literature in Asian languages is also included.

The site is available online at: `http://popindex.princeton.edu`

JSTOR. JSTOR is an online article archive of the most prominent journals in almost every academic discipline. Articles are usually provided starting with Volume 1 of each journal. That implies to have a vast resource available — especially for historical articles which would be very hard to obtain otherwise.

The site is available online at: `http://www.jstor.org`

OVID. OVID is probably the largest of the databases presented here. It is a reference database run by the Max Planck Society. With the various databases it covers such as *Medline, Sociofile, EconLit, Dissertation Abstracts, etc.* and its broad temporal perspective (while most databases start in the 1960s, the collection for data from *PSYCINFO* began in 1887) the primary literature on seasonal mortality should be identifiable.

The site is available online at: `http://http://ovid.gwdg.de`

ScienceDirect, Springer LINK Search, EBSCO, Ingenta ScienceDirect, Springer LINK Search, EBSCO, and Ingenta are bibliographic databases. The majority of the articles are available online, otherwise the bibliographic information is given for ordering. The URLs for their homepages and the number of available online journals according to themselves is given here:

Database	Journals	Homepage
ScienceDirect	1800+	`http://www.sciencedirect.com`
Springer LINK	500+	`http://link.springer.de`
EBSCO	"thousands"	`http://www.ebsco.com`
Ingenta	6000+	`http://www.ingenta.com`

BMJ, NEJM, The Lancet, JECH. Medicine and Epidemiology are the disciplines which publish most of the research on seasonal mortality. The choice for these four journals was made because they are leading in their field and, especially the British Medical Journal and the Journal of Epidemiology and Community Health, have published findings on winter excess deaths regularly.

A.2 Appendix for Literature Review

A.2.1 Studies on Seasonal Mortality of Cardiovascular, Cerebrovascular and Respiratory Disease

Cardiovascular Diseases

- **In General:** [18] [19] [82] [91] [208] [235] [411]
- **(Acute) Myocardial Infarction:** [36] [37] [138] [199] [345] [356]
- **Coronary Thrombosis:** [187]
- **Coronary Heart Disease:** [246] [340]
- **Coronary Artery Disease:** [341]
- **Arterial Thrombosis:** [97] [188]
- **Ischaemic Heart Disease** [58] [76] [77] [81] [98] [176] [253] [269] [317] [322] [355] [376]
- **Heart Attack** [57]
- **Hypertension** [58]

Cerebrovascular Diseases

- **In General:** [19] [58] [76] [77] [81] [82] [98] [253] [376]
- **Stroke:** [37] [57] [269] [345]
- **Cerebral Infarction:** [36]
- **Cerebral Thrombosis:** [187]

Respiratory Diseases

- **In General:** [18] [19] [36] [58] [76] [77] [81] [82] [98] [97] [187] [188] [208] [235] [246] [269] [319] [376]
- **Pneumonia:** [37] [319]
- **Influenza:** [63] [319]
- **Bronchitis:** [319]

B

Appendix for Measuring Seasonality

B.1 Empirical Distributions for Hewitt's & Rogerson's Tests

The articles for Hewitt's test [150] and its generalization by Rogerson [315] for peak period of 3,4, and 5 months printed significance values for the respective distributions of their test statistics based on Monte-Carlo simulations. Exact significance levels have only been calculated for Hewitt's test by Walter [395]. In the original contributions, the distributions have been determined by Monte-Carlo simulations. In my opinion, the number of runs (Hewitt's Test: 5000; Rogerson's Extension: 20,000 for each peak period) is relatively small. Therefore I programmed functions which allow you to make your own Monte-Carlo simulations. Table B.1 shows for peak periods of 6 (Hewitt), 5, 4, and 3 months (Rogerson) the significance values from the original papers (column: "Orig. Values") and also the exact values for Hewitt's test (column: "Exact Values"). The last seven columns are taken from my own simulations where I generated between 10^1 and 10^7 random sequences of ranks from 1 to 12.[1] For Hewitt's test we can see that our simulated results are converging towards the exact values. The orignal (simulated) values give the correct results for two decimals. If further exactness is required I recommend to take the orignal values. As no exact values are given for Rogerson's test, I suggest to use my results from 10,000,000 randomly generated sequences. I have basically used the same algorithm for Rogerson's tests as for Hewitt's test. Thus, we can expect that our results are converging towards the exact values also for the tests for a peak period of 3, 4, and 5 months. The code to simulate the four distribution functions is given below.

---

[1] A sample of size taken 12 was taken from the twelve integers $1, 2, \ldots, 12$ without replacement.

Table B.1. Comparison of Significance Values for Hewitt's Test and Rogerson's Extensions: Orignal Simulations vs. Own Simulations

Length of Peak	Rank Sum	Orig. Values[†]	Exact Values[‡]	Values of Own Simulations (by number of randomly generated sequences)						
				10^1	10^2	10^3	10^4	10^5	10^6	10^7
Hewitt										
6	57	0.0134	0.0130	0.0	0.02	0.009	0.1110	0.01206	0.012922	0.0129574
	56	0.0248	0.0253	0.0	0.02	0.017	0.0226	0.2410	0.025032	0.0251664
	55	0.0464	0.0483	0.0	0.04	0.033	0.0439	0.04770	0.047849	0.0482275
	54	0.0766	0.0805	0.0	0.09	0.067	0.0794	0.07919	0.079921	0.0804839
	53	0.1260	0.1299	0.1	0.19	0.139	0.1262	0.12687	0.129554	0.1298305
Rogerson										
5	50	0.0152	-	0.0	0.00	0.014	0.0165	0.01528	0.014965	0.0150873
	49	0.0294	-	0.0	0.01	0.024	0.0282	0.02949	0.029402	0.0293668
	48	0.0573	-	0.0	0.04	0.051	0.0561	0.05719	0.056105	0.0561672
	47	0.0949	-	0.2	0.11	0.086	0.0924	0.09360	0.093477	0.0934898
	46	0.1499	-	0.3	0.18	0.152	0.1474	0.14992	0.150608	0.1505676
4	42	0.0267	-	0.0	0.03	0.021	0.0234	0.02392	0.024418	0.0241888
	41	0.0509	-	0.0	0.04	0.052	0.0469	0.04677	0.047279	0.0469308
	40	0.0927	-	0.0	0.10	0.095	0.0914	0.08954	0.089382	0.0891868
	39	0.1540	-	0.2	0.14	0.153	0.1549	0.14844	0.147507	0.1475288
	38	0.2398	-	0.3	0.22	0.247	0.2409	0.23686	0.235546	0.2356594
3	33	0.0543	-	0.2	0.05	0.047	0.0552	0.05399	0.054786	0.0546313
	32	0.1056	-	0.3	0.10	0.084	0.1055	0.10441	0.105131	0.1052277
	31	0.1975	-	0.3	0.17	0.194	0.1994	0.19716	0.197245	0.1977746
	30	0.3220	-	0.4	0.34	0.347	0.3234	0.32170	0.322490	0.3223236
	29	0.4711	-	0.5	0.43	0.482	0.4717	0.46931	0.469512	0.4696976

[†] Sources: Hewitt et al. [150] and Rogerson [315]

[‡] Source: Walter [395]

C

Problems of Gaussian Densities to Smooth a Straight Line

As described in Section 4.4.2 (page 97ff), B-Splines are similar to Gaussian densities without the problematic characteristics of the latter. For example, with Gaussian densities, it is not possible to fit a straight line properly, because of its defintion from $[-\infty; \infty]$. Figure C.1 shows the typical result from such an approach: the so-called "Gaussian ripple" [86]).

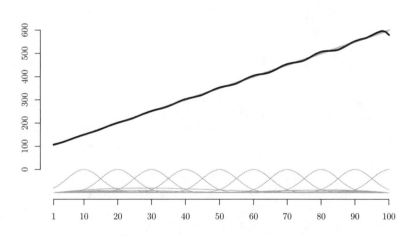

Fig. C.1. "Gaussian Ripple": The Problem of Normal ("Gaussian") Densities to Smooth a Straight Line

D

Appendix for Danish Register Analysis

D.1 Seasonal Mortality by Sex, Education and Cause of Death

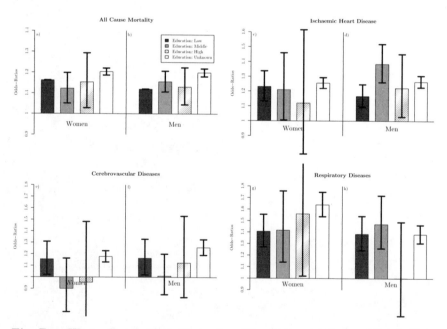

Fig. D.1. Winter Excess Mortality by Sex, Education, and Cause of Death (Odds-Ratios and 95% Confidence Intervals)

References

[1] Lars A. Akslen and Flora Hartveit. Seasonal Variation in Melanoma Deaths and the Pattern of Disease Process. A Preliminary Analysis. *Chronobiologia*, 15:257–263, 1988.

[2] M.R. Alderson. Season and mortality. *Health Trends*, 17:87–96, 1985.

[3] Munther I. Aldoori and Sakhawat H. Rahman. Smoking and stroke: a causative role (Editorial). *British Medical Journal*, 317:961–962, 1998.

[4] Paul D. Allison. Measures of Inequality. *American Sociological Review*, 43:865–880, 1978.

[5] Paul D. Allison. Discrete-time methods for the analysis of event histories. *Sociological Methodology*, 13:61–98, 1982.

[6] Paul D. Allison. *Survival Analysis Using the SAS System*. SAS Institute Inc, Cary, NC, 1995.

[7] Otto Andersen. Register data for research. Presentation given at the course "The data of Denmark", Odense, DK, 30 April 2001, 2001.

[8] H. Ross Anderson, Antonio Ponce de Leon, J. Martin Bland, Jonathan S. Bower, and David P. Strachan. Air pollution and daily mortality in London: 1987–92. *British Medical Journal*, 312:665–669, 1996.

[9] Gunnar Andersson and Henriette Engelhardt. Zensus. In Günter Endruweit and Gisela Trommsdorff, editors, *Wörterbuch der Soziologie*. Lucius & Lucius, Stuttgart, D, 2002.

[10] Kirill F. Andreev. *Evolution of the Danish Population from 1835 to 2000*. Odense Monographs on Population Aging 9. University Press of Southern Denmark, Odense, DK, 2002.

[11] John Angus. Old and New Bills of Mortality; Movement of the Population; Deaths and Fatal Diseases in London During the Last Fourteen Years. *Journal of the Statistical Society of London*, 17:117–142, 1854.

[12] Andrew B. Appleby. The Disappearance of Plague: A Continuing Puzzle. *The Economic History Review*, 33:161–173, 1980.

[13] Maurice Aubenque, Paul Damiani, and Hélène Massé. Variations saisonnières et séries chronologiques des causes de décès en France de 1900

à 1972. *Cahiers de Sociologie et de Démographie Médicales*, 19:17–22, 1979.

[14] Robert D: Auerbach and Jack L. Rutner. The Misspecification of a Nonseasonal Cycle as a Seasonal by the X-11 Seasonal Adjustment Program. *The Review of Economics and Statistics*, 60:601–603, 1978.

[15] Kirsten Avlund, Mogens Trab Damsgaard, and Bjørn E. Holstein. Social Relations and Mortality. An Eleven Year Follow-Up Study of 70-Year-Old Men and Women in Denmark. *Social Science and Medicine*, 47:635–643, 1998.

[16] Paul Aylin, Sara Morris, Jon Wakefield, Ana Grossinho, Lars Jarup, and Paul Elliott. Temperature, housing, deprivation and their relationship to excess winter mortality in Great Britain, 1986–1996. *International Journal of Epidemiology*, 30:1100–1108, 2001.

[17] A. Bailo, L. Palacios-Araus, A. Diaz, D. I. Toja, and J. Bertranpetit. Natality and mortality seasonality in the Spanish Central Pyrenees. *Antropologia portuguesa (1986–1987)*, 4–5:125–133, 1986.

[18] F. Ballester, P. Michelozzi, and C. Iñiguez. Weather, climate, and public health (Editorial). *Journal of Epidemiology and Community Health*, 57:759–760, 2003.

[19] Ferran Ballester, Dolores Corella, Santiago Pérez-Hoyos, Marc Sáez, and Ana Hervás. Mortality as a Function of Temperature. A Study in Valencia, Spain, 1991–1993. *International Journal of Epidemiology*, 26:551–561, 1997.

[20] G.A. Barnard. Introduction to Pearson (1900) On the Criterion that a Given System of Deviations from the Probable in the Case of a Correlated System of Variables is Such that it Can be Reasonably Supposed to have Arisen from Random Sampling. London, Edinburgh and Dublin Philosophical Magazine and Journal of Science, vol. 50, 5th series, pp. 157–175. In Samuel Kotz and Norman L. Johnson, editors, *Breakthroughs in Statistics. Volume II. Methodology and Distribution*, pages 1–10. Springer, Heidelberg, Germany, 1992.

[21] Richard E. Barrett. Seasonality in vital processes in a traditional Chinese population. *Modern China*, 16:190–225, 1990.

[22] David N. Barron. The Analysis of Count Data: Overdispersion and Autocorrelation. *Sociological Methodology*, 22:179–220, 1992.

[23] A. Baumann, B. Filipiak, J. Stieber, and H. Löwel. Familienstand und soziale Integration als Prädiktoren der Mortalität: eine 5-Jahres-Follow-up-Studie an 55- bis 74jährigen Männern und Frauen in der Region Augsburg. *Zeitschrift für Gerontologie und Geriatrie*, 31:184–192, 1998.

[24] Nina Baym. Thoreau's View of Science. *Journal of the History of Ideas*, 26:221–234, 1965.

[25] BBC. Cold kills 'thousands' in a week. Available online at: http://news.bbc.co.uk/, 2003.

[26] Alain Bideau, Jacques Dupâquier, and Jean-Noël Birabenë. La mortalité de 1800 à 1914. In Jacques Dupâquier, editor, *Histoire de la population*

française 3. De 1789 à 1914. Presses Universitaires de France, Paris, F, 1988.

[27] Alain Bideau, Jacques Dupâquier, and Hector Gutierrez. La mort quantififée. In Jacques Dupâquier, editor, *Histoire de la population française 2. De la renaissance à 1789*. Presses Universitaires de France, Paris, F, 1988.

[28] Francesco C. Billari. Introduction to Event History Analysis. Course given at the Max Planck Research School for Demography, Rostock, Germany, 2001.

[29] C. Borrell, A. Plasencia, I. Pasarin, and V. Ortun. Widening social inequalities in mortality: the case of Barcelona, a southern European city. *Journal of Epidemiology and Community Health*, 51:659–667, 1997.

[30] Fabrice Boulay, Frédéric Berthier, Colette Dahan, and Albert Tran. Seasonal Variations in Vericeal Bleeding Mortality and Hospitalization in France. *The American Journal of Gastroenterology*, 96:1881–1887, 2001.

[31] Menno Jan Bouma and Mercedes Pascual. Seasonal and internannual cycles of endemic cholera in Bengal 1891–1940 in relation to climate and geography. *Hydrobiologica*, 460:147–156, 2001.

[32] George E.P. Box, Gwilym M. Jenkins, and Gregory C. Reinsel. *Time Series Analysis. Forecasting and Control*. Prentice Hall, Englewood Cliffs, NJ, 3rd edition, 1994.

[33] S.A. Bremner, H.R. Anderson, R.W. Atkinson, A.J. McMichael, Strachan D.P., J.M. Bland, and J.S. Bower. Short term associations between outdoor air pollution and mortality in London 1992–4. *Occupational and Environmental Medicine*, 56:237–244, 1999.

[34] Peter J. Brockwell and Richard A. Davis. *Introduction to Time Series and Forecasting*. Springer, New York, NY, 1996.

[35] Andrew G. Bruce and Simon R. Jurke. Non-Gaussian Seasonal Adjustment: X-12 ARIMA Versus Robust Structural Models. SRD Report Series 92/14, Bureau of the Census, Statistical Research Division, Washington, D.C., 1992.

[36] G.M. Bull. Meteorological correlates with myocardial and cerebral infarction and respiratory disease. *British Journal of Preventive Social Medicine*, 27:108–113, 1973.

[37] G.M. Bull and Joan Morton. Environment, Temperature and Death Rates. *Age and Ageing*, 7:210–224, 1978.

[38] Statistisches Bundesamt. Benutzerhandbuch zu BV4.1, RC 1 (deutschsprachige Programmversion). Technical report, Statistisches Bundesamt, Gruppe Mathematisch-Statistische Methoden, Wiesbaden D, 2003.

[39] J.P. Burman. Seasonal Adjustment by Signal Extraction. *Journal of the Royal Statistical Society. Series A (General)*, 143:321–337, 1980.

[40] B. Cadet, J.M. Robine, and D. Leibovici. Dynamique de la mortalité asthmatique en france: fluctuations saisonnières et crise de mortalité en 1985–87. *Rev. Epidém. et Santé Pub*, 42:103–118, 1994.

[41] A. Colin Cameron and Pravin K. Trivedi. *Regression Analysis of Count Data*. Cambridge University Press, Cambridge, UK, 1998.

[42] MJ Campbell and Tobías Aurelio. Causality and temporality in the study of short-term effects of air pollution on health. *International Journal of Epidemiology*, 29:271–273, 2000.

[43] Ann G. Carmichael. Infection, Hidden Hunger, and History. *Journal of Interdisciplinary History*, 14:249–264, 1983.

[44] D.R. Cave and L.S. Freedman. Seasonal variations in the clinical presentation of crohn's disease and ulcerative colitis. *International Journal of Epidemiology*, 4:317–320, 1975.

[45] Hubert Charbonneau, Bertrand Desjardins, Jacques Légaré, and Hubert Denis. The Population of St. Lawrence valley, 1608–1760. In Michael R. Haines and Richard H. Steckel, editors, *A Population History of North America*, pages 99–142. Cambridge University Press, Cambridge, UK, 2000.

[46] Laurent Chenet, Merete Osler, Martin McKee, and Allan Krasnik. Changing life expectancy in the 1980s: why was Denmark different from Sweden? *Journal of Epidemiology and Community Health*, 50:404–407, 1996.

[47] David Clapham. Housing Frailer Elders in Great Britain. In Jon Pynoos and Phoebe S. Liebig, editors, *Housing Frail Elders. International Policies, Perspectives, and Prospects*, chapter 4, pages 68–88. The Johns Hopkins University Press, Baltimore, MD, 1995.

[48] Robert B. Cleveland, William S. Cleveland, Jean E. McRae, and Irma Terpenning. STL: A Seasonal-Trend Decomposition Procedure Based on Loess. *Journal of Official Statistics*, 6:3–73, 1990.

[49] William S. Cleveland. *The Elements of Graphing Data*. AT&T Bell Laboratories, Murray Hill, New Jersey, 1994.

[50] William S. Cleveland, Susan J. Devlin, and Irma J. Terpenning. The details of the SABL transformation, decomposition and calendar methods. Technical report, Computing Information Library, Bell Labs, Murray Hill, NJ, 1981.

[51] William S. Cleveland, Susan J. Devlin, and Irma J. Terpenning. The SABL statistical and graphical methods. Technical report, Computing Information Library, Bell Labs, Murray Hill, NJ, 1981.

[52] William S. Cleveland and Irma J. Terpenning. Graphical Methods for Seasonal Adjustment. *Journal of the American Statistical Association*, 77:52–62, 1982.

[53] W.P. Cleveland and G.C. Tiao. Decomposition of a Seasonal Time Series: A Model for the Census X-11 Program. *Journal of the American Statistical Association*, 71:581–587, 1976.

[54] J. Peter Clinch and John D. Healy. Housing standards and excess winter mortality. *Journal of Epidemiology and Community Health*, 54:719–720, 2000.

[55] CNN. Heat deaths: Chirac pledges action. Available online at:
http://www.cnn.com, 2003.

[56] D. Collett. *Modelling Survival Data in Medical Research.* Texts in Statistical Science. Chapman & Hall, London, UK, 1994.

[57] K.J. Collins. Low indoor temperatures and morbidity in the elderly. *Age and Ageing*, 15:212–220, 1986.

[58] Elvira Cordioli, Carmine Pizzi, and Marcello Martinelli. Winter mortality in Emilia-Romagna, Italy. *International Journal of Circumpolar Health*, 59(3–4):164–169, 2000.

[59] Carl Counsell and Hazel Fraser. Identifying relevant studies for systematic reviews (Letters). *British Medical Journal*, 310:126, 1995.

[60] Brian D. Cox, Margaret J. Whichelow, and A. Toby Prevost. Seasonal consumption of salad vegetables and fresh fruit in relation to the development of cardiovascular disease and cancer. *Public Health Nutrition*, 3:19–29, 2000.

[61] D.R. Cox and D. Oakes. *Analysis of Survival Data.* Chapman & Hall, London, UK, 1984.

[62] D.L. Crombie, D.M. Fleming, K.W. Cross, and R.J. Lancashire. Concurrence of monthly variation of mortality related to underlying cause in Europe. *Journal of Epidemiology and Community Health*, 49:373–378, 1995.

[63] Michael Curwen and Tim Devis. Winter mortality, temperature and influenza: has the relationship changed in recent years? *Population Trends*, 54:17–20, 1988.

[64] H.A. David and D.J. Newell. The identification of annual peak periods for a disease. *Biometrics*, 21:645–650, 1965.

[65] Lloyd Demetrius. Demographic Parameters and Natural Selection. *Proceedings of the National Academy of Sciences of the United States of America*, 71:4645–4647, 1974.

[66] Antoine Deparcieux. *Essai sur les probabilités de la durée de la vie humaine.* INED (reprint 2003), Paris, F, 1746.

[67] Paul Dierckx. *Curve and Surface Fitting with Splines.* Monographs on Numerical Analysis. Clarendon Press, Oxford, UK, 1995.

[68] Carolyn Diguiseppi. Why everyone over 65 deserves influenza vaccine (Editorial). *British Medical Journal*, 313:1162, 1996.

[69] Gabriele Doblhammer. *Socioeconomic Differentials in Austrian Adult Mortality.* PhD thesis, Sozial- und Wirtschaftswissenschaftliche Fakultät, Universität Wien, Wien, A, 1997.

[70] Gabriele Doblhammer. *The Late Life Legacy of Very Early Life.* Demographic Research Monographs. Springer, Heidelberg, Germany, 2004.

[71] Gabriele Doblhammer, Roland Rau, and Josef Kytir. Trends in educational and occupational differentials in all-cause mortality in Austria between 1981/82 and 1991/92. *Wiener Klinische Wochenschrift*, 117(13–15):468–479, 2005.

[72] Gabriele Doblhammer and James W. Vaupel. Lifespan depends on month of birth. *Proceedings of the National Academy of Sciences*, 98:2934–2939, 2001.

[73] Mary J. Dobson. *Contours of death and disease in early modern England*. Cambridge University Press, Cambridge, UK, 1997.

[74] M. Dolley. Denmark tries to raise life expectancy. *British Medical Journal*, 308:737–738, 1994.

[75] Gavin Donaldson. Trends in excess winter mortality, by age and sex. Presentation given at the workshop "Seasonality in Mortality", Duke University, NC, 07–08 March 2002, 2002.

[76] G.C. Donaldson, S.P. Ermakov, Y.M. Komarov, and W.R. Keatinge. Cold related mortalities and protection against cold in Yakutsk, eastern Siberia: observation and interview study. *British Medical Journal*, 317:978–982, 1998.

[77] G.C. Donaldson and W.R. Keatinge. Mortality related to cold weather in elderly people in southeast England, 1979-94. *British Medical Journal*, 315:1055–1056, 1997.

[78] G.C. Donaldson and W.R. Keatinge. Excess winter mortality: influenza or cold stress? Observational study. *British Medical Journal*, 324:89–90, 2002.

[79] G.C. Donaldson and W.R. Keatinge. Cold related mortality in England and Wales; influence of social class in working and retired are groups. *Journal of Epidemiology and Community Health*, 57:790–791, 2003.

[80] G.C. Donaldson, H. Rintamäki, and S Näyhä. Outdoor clothing: its relationship to geography, climate, behaviour and cold-related mortality in Europe. *International Journal of Biometeorology*, 45:45–51, 2001.

[81] G.C. Donaldson, V.E. Tchernjavskii, S.P. Ermakov, K. Bucher, and W.R. Keatinge. Winter mortality and cold stress in Yekaterinburg, Russia: interview study. *British Medical Journal*, 316:514–518, 1998.

[82] A.S. Douglas, T.M. Allan, and J.M. Rawles. Composition of Seasonality of Disease. *Scottish Medical Journal*, 36:76–82, 1991.

[83] C.J. Duncan, S.R. Duncan, and Susan Scott. Whooping Cough Epidemics in London, 1701–1812: Infection Dynamics, Seasonal Forcing and the Effects of Malnutrition. *Proceedings of the Royal Society of London: Biological Sciences*, 263:445–450, 1996.

[84] J. H. Edwards. The recognition and estimation of cyclic trends. *Annals of Human Genetics*, 25:83–86, 1961.

[85] Bradley Efron. Logistic Regression, Survival Analysis, and the Kaplan-Meier Curve. *Journal of the American Statistical Association*, 83:414–425, 1988.

[86] Paul Eilers and Brian D. Marx. Smoothing for Smarties. Course Material for ENAR Biometrics Meeting, Tampa, Florida, March 30, 2003, 2003.

[87] Paul H. C. Eilers and Brian D. Marx. Flexible Smoothing with B-splines and Penalties. *Statistical Science*, 11:89–102, 1996.

[88] Paul H. C. Eilers and Brian D. Marx. Flexible Smoothing with B-splines and Penalties: Rejoinder. *Statistical Science*, 11:115–121, 1996.

[89] Paul H. C. Eilers and Brian D. Marx. Generalized linear additive smooth structures. *Journal of Computational and Graphical Statistics*, 11:758–783, 2002.

[90] J. Harold Elwood and J. Mark Elwood. Seasonal Variation in the Prevalence at Birth of Anencephalus. In T. Miura, editor, *Seasonal effects on reproduction, infection and psychoses (Progress in Biometeorology, Vol. 5)*, pages 111–122. The Hague: SPB Academic Publishing, 1987.

[91] H. Eng and James B. Mercer. Mortality from cardiovascular disease in Ireland and Norway and its relationship to air temperature and wind chill. *Journal of Cardiovascular Risk*, 7:369–375, 2000.

[92] Environmental Protection Agency. NO_x. *How nitrogen oxides affect the way we live and breath*, volume EPA-456/F-98-005. United States Environmental Protection Agency. Office of Air Quality Planning and Standards, Research Triangle Park, NC, 1998.

[93] Environmental Protection Agency. Health and Environmental Impacts of PM. Available online at http://www.epa.gov/air/urbanair/so2/hlth1.html, 2004.

[94] Environmental Protection Agency. Health and Environmental Impacts of SO_2. Available online at http://www.epa.gov/air/urbanair/so2/hlth1.html, 2004.

[95] Marco Ercolani. Introduction to Time Series Analysis. Notes for Course at the Essex Summer School, University of Essex, Essex, UK, 2002.

[96] Eurostat. Statistics on Persons in Denmark. a register-based statistical system. Technical report, Office for Official Publications of the European Communities, Luxembourg, LUX, 2001.

[97] Eurowinter Group. Winter mortality in relation to climate. *International Journal of Circumpolar Health*, 59:154–159, 2000.

[98] Eurowinter Group. Cold exposure and winter mortality from ischaemic heart disease, cerebrovascular disease, respiratory disease, and all causes in warm and cold regions of Europe. *Lancet*, 349:1341–1346, 1997.

[99] Günter Ewert, Hildegard Marcusson, Wilhelm Oehmisch, Gerd E. Wiesner, Ingeborg Engelmann, and Christa Ladewig. *Sterblichkeit und Lebenserwartung. Analyse zum Gesundheitszustand der Bevölkerung im europäischen Vergleich der Deutschen Demokratischen Republik*. VEB Verlag Volk und Gesundheit, Berlin, D, 1981.

[100] Alexander Fabig. Personal Communications, 2002.

[101] Philippe Fargues and Ouaidou Nassour. Seasonal Variation in Urban Mortality: The Case of Bamako, 1974 to 1985. In Etienne Van de Walle, Gilles Pison, and Mpembele Sala-Diakanda, editors, *Mortality and society in Sub-Saharan Africa*, pages 99–122. Clarendon Press, Oxford, UK, 1992.

[102] Craig A. Feinstein. Seasonality of deaths in the U.S. by age and cause. *Demographic Research*, 6:469–486, 2002.

[103] J. Feldman, Jacob, Diane M. Makuc, Kleinman Joel C., and Joan Cornoni-Huntley. National trends in educational differentials in mortality. *American Journal of Epidemiology*, 129:919–933, 1989.

[104] Yuanhua Feng. Eine robuste, datengesteuerte Version des Berliner Verfahrens. *Wirtschaft und Statistik*, (10):786–795, 2000.

[105] Yuanhua Feng and Siegfried Heiler. A robust data-driven version of the Berlin Method. CoFE Diskussionspapiere 2000 No. 15, Center of Finance and Econometrics, University of Konstanz, Konstanz, D, 2002.

[106] G. Fichter and P. Volk. The Eastern Orientation of Merovingian Graves and the Seasonal Distribution of Morbidity and Mortality (using the Sasbach-Behans and Bischoffingen-Bigärten Cemeteries as Examples). *Journal of Human Evolution*, 9:49–59, 1980.

[107] R.A.P. Finlay. The Accuracy of the London Parish Registers, 1580–1653. *Population Studies*, 32:95–112, 1978.

[108] Björn Fischer. Decompositions of Time Series. Comparing Different Methods in Theory and Practice. Available online at: http://europa.eu.int/en/comm/eurostat/research/noris4/ documents/decomp.%pdf, Eurostat - VIROS (Virtual Institute for Research in Official Statistics), Luxembourg, 1995.

[109] Michael W. Flinn. *The European Demographic System, 1500–1820*. The Johns Hopkins University Press, Baltimore, MD, 1981.

[110] A.J. Flisher, C.D.H. Parry, D. Bradshaw, and J.M. Juritz. Seasonal variation of suicide in South Africa. *Biological Psychiatry*, 39:522–523, 1996.

[111] Robert Fogel. *Public Use Tape on the Aging of Veterans of the Union Army: Military, Pension, and Medical Records, 1860-1940*. Center for Population Economics, University of Chicago Graduate School of Business, and Department of Economics, Brigham Young University, Chicago, IL, 2000.

[112] Lone Frank. When an entire country is a cohort. *Science*, 287:2398–2399, 2000.

[113] L.S. Freedman. The use of a Kolmogorov-Smirnov type statistic in testing hypotheses about seasonal variation. *Journal of Epidemiology and Community Health*, 33:223–228, 1979.

[114] Wade Hampton Frost. The Age Selection of Mortality from Tuberculosis in Sucessive Decades (first published: 1939). *American Journal of Epidemiology*, 141:4–9, 1995.

[115] Timothy B. Gage. The Decline of Mortality in England and Wales 1861 to 1964: Decomposition by Cause of Death and Component of Mortality. *Population Studies*, 47:47–66., 1993.

[116] Patrick R. Galloway. Basic Patterns in Annual Variations in Fertility, Nuptiality, Mortality, and Prices in Pre-industrial Europe. *Population Studies*, 42:275–302, 1988.

[117] Jutta Gampe and Roland Rau. Trends in saisonalen Mortalitätsschwankungen — eine Analyse mittels *P*-splines. Presentation given

at the "Deutsche Statistische Woche", Potsdam, Germany, 22 August 2003, 2003.

[118] Jutta Gampe and Roland Rau. Seasonal Variation in Death Counts: P-Spline Smoothing in the Presence of Overdispersion. Poster presented at the 19th International Workshop on Statistical Modelling. Florence, Italy, 04 July 2004, 2004.

[119] Karla Gärtner. Zeitreihenanalyse der natürlichen Bevölkerungsbewegung 1957–1986. Darstellung der Entwicklung und methodische Anmerkungen. *Zeitschrift für Bevölkerungswissenschaft*, 14:161–186, 1988.

[120] Islay Gemmell, Philip McLoone, Andrew Boddy, Graham Watt, and Gordon Dickinson. Seasonal variation in mortality and morbidity in Scotland 1981–93. Technical report, University of Glasgow, Public Health Research Unit, 1999.

[121] Islay Gemmell, Philip McLoone, F.A. Boddy, Gordon J. Dickinson, and G.C.M. Watt. Seasonal variation in mortality in Scotland. *International Journal of Epidemiology*, 29:274–279, 2000.

[122] Eric Ghysels and Denise R. Osborn. *The Econometric Analysis of Seasonal Time Series*. Cambridge University Press, Cambridge, UK, 2001.

[123] M.D. Gliksman, R. Lazarus, Wilson A., and S.R. Leeder. Social support, marital status and living arrangement correlates of cardiovascular risk factors in the elderly. *Social Science and Medicine*, 40:811–814, 1995.

[124] N. Goldman. Mortality Differentials: Selection and Causation. In Neil J. Smelser and Paul B. Baltes, editors, *International Encyclopedia of the Social & Behavioral Sciences*, pages 10068–10070. Elsevier, Amsterdam, NL, 2001.

[125] Noreen Goldman. Marriage Selection and Mortality Patterns: Inferences and Fallacies. *Demography*, 30:189–208, 1993.

[126] Dianne G. Goodwin and James W. Vaupel. Concentration Curves and Have-Statistics for Ecological Analysis of Diversity: Part III: Comparison of Measures of Diversity. Working Paper WP-85-91, International Institute for Applied Systems Analysis, Laxenburg, Austria, December 1985.

[127] J. Goodwin, R.S. Taylor, V.R. Pearce, and K.L.Q. Read. Seasonal cold, excursional behavior, clothing protection and physical activity in young and old subjects. *International Journal of Circumpolar Health*, 59:195–203, 2000.

[128] Georg Gottschalk. Housing and Supportive Services for Frail Elders in Denmark. In Jon Pynoos and Phoebe S. Liebig, editors, *Housing Frail Elders. International Policies, Perspectives, and Prospects*, chapter 2, pages 19–44. The Johns Hopkins University Press, Baltimore, MD, 1995.

[129] Walter R. Gove. Sex, Marital Status, and Mortality. *The American Journal of Sociology*, 79:45–67, 1973.

[130] John Graunt. Natural and Political Observations Made Upon the Bills of Mortality. In *Reprinted in: John Graunt and Gregory King: The Earliest Classics (1973)*. Gregg International Publishers, 1662.

[131] V. Grech, O. Aquilina, and J. Pace. Gender differences in seasonality of acute myocardial infarction admissions and mortality in a population-based study. *Journal of Epidemiology and Community Health*, 55:147–148, 2001.

[132] P.J. Green and B.W. Silvermann. *Nonparametric Regression and Generalized Linear Models. A roughness penality approach*. Monographs on Statistics and Applied Probability 58. Chapman & Hall, Boca Raton, FL, 2000.

[133] Major Greenwood and G. Udny Yule. An Inquiry into the Nature of Frequency Distributions Representative of Multiple Happenings with Particular Reference to the Occurrence of Multiple Attacks of Disease or of Repeated Accidents. *Journal of the Royal Statistical Society*, 83:255–279, 1920.

[134] Geneviève Grégoire, François Derderian, and Jacques Le Lorier. Selecting the Language of the Publications Included in a Meta-analysis: Is There a Tower of Babel bias? *Journal of Clinical Epidemiology*, 48:159–163, 1995.

[135] Mikael Grut. Cold-related death in some developed countries. *The Lancet*, (8526):212, 1987. 24 January 1987.

[136] William Augustus Guy and M.B. Cantab. An Attempt to Determine the Influence of the Seasons and Weather on Sickness and Mortality. *Journal of the Statistical Society of London*, 6:133–150, 1843.

[137] R. Charon Gwynn, Richard T. Burnett, and George D. Thurston. A Time-Series Analysis of Acidic Particulate Matter and Daily Mortality and Morbidity in the Buffalo, New York, Region. *Environmental Health Perspectives*, 108:125–133, 2000.

[138] Staffan Gyllerup. Cold climate and coronary mortality in Sweden. *International Journal of Circumpolar Health*, 59(3–4):160–163, 2000.

[139] Helinä Hakko. *Seasonal Variation of Suicides and Homicides in Finland. With special attention to statistical techniques used in seasonality studies*. PhD thesis, Faculty of Medicine, University of Oulu, FIN, 2000.

[140] Stephen K. Happel and Timothy D. Hogan. Counting snowbirds: The importance and the problems with estimating seasonal populations. *Population Research and Policy Review*, 21:227–240, 2002.

[141] Frank E. Harrell Jr. *Regression Modeling Strategies. With Applications to Linear Models, Logistic Regression, and Survival Analysis*. Springer Series in Statistics. Springer, New York, NY, 2001.

[142] Joachim Hartung. *Statistik. Lehr- und Handbuch der angewandten Statistik*. R. Oldenbourg Verlag, München, D, 1999.

[143] Barbara Harvey. *Living and Dying in England, 1100-1540. The Monastic Experience*. Clarendon Press, Oxford, UK, 1993.

[144] Barbara Harvey and Jim Oeppen. Patterns of morbidity in late medieval England: a sample from Westmister Abbey. *The Economic History Review*, 54:215–239, 2001.

[145] Trevor Hastie and Robert Tibshirani. Varying-Coefficient Models. *Journal of the Royal Statistical Society. Series B (Methodological)*, 55:757–796, 1993.

[146] John Hatcher. Mortality in the Fifteenth century: Some new evidence. *Economic History Review, 2nd Ser.*, 39:19–38, 1986.

[147] J.D. Healy. Excess winter mortality in Europe: a cross country analysis identifying key risk factors. *Journal of Epidemiology and Community Health*, 57:784–789, 2003.

[148] M. Hernández and C. García-Moro. Seasonal distribution of mortality in Barcelona (1983–1985). *Antropologia portuguesa*, 4–5:211–223, 1986–1987.

[149] D. Ann Herring and Robert D. Hoppa. Changing Patterns of Mortality Seasonality Among the Western James Bay Cree. *International Journal of Circumpolar Health*, 56:121–133, 1997.

[150] David Hewitt, Jean Milner, Adele Csima, and Andrew Pakula. On Edwards' criterion of seasonality and a non-parametric alternative. *British Journal of Preventive Social Medicine*, 25:174–176, 1971.

[151] Peter Høeg. *Miss Smilla's Feeling for Snow*. The Harvill Press, London, UK, 1997.

[152] W.W. Holland, A.E. Bennett, I.R. Cameron, C. du V. Florey, S.R. Leeder, R.S.F. Schilling, A.V. Swan, and R.E. Waller. Health effetcs of particulate pollution: reappraising the evidence. *American Journal of Epidemiology*, 110:527–659, 1979.

[153] Mary F. Hollingsworth and T.H. Hollingsworth. Plague Mortality Rates by Age and Sex in the Parish of St. Botolph's without Bishopsgate, London, 1603. *Population Studies*, 25:131–146, 1971.

[154] T.H. Hollingsworth. *Historical Demography*. Cornell University Press, Ithaca, NY, 1969.

[155] Robert D. Hoppa. *R*. PhD thesis.

[156] Peter Höppe. Aspects of human biometeorology in past, present and future. *International Journal of Biometeorology*, 40:19–23, 1997.

[157] Benoît Hopquin. «Plusieurs centaines à plusieurs milliers de morts» dues à la pollution. Available online at: http://www.cnn.com, 2003.

[158] Susan Dadakis Horn. Goodness-of-fit tests for discrete data: A review and an application to a health impairment scale. *Biometrics*, 33:237–247, 1977.

[159] David W. Hosmer and Stanley Lemeshow. *Applied Logistic Regression*. Wiley Series in Probability and Mathematical Statistics. Applied probability and statistics section. John Wiley & Sons, New York, NY, 1989.

[160] Philip Hougaard, Mei-Ling Ting Lee, and G.A. Whitmore. Analysis of Overdispersed Count Data by Mixtures of Poisson Variables and Poisson Processes. *Biometrics*, 53:1225–1238, 1997.

[161] R.A. Houston. *The population history of Britain and Ireland, 1550-1750*. Cambridge University Press, Cambridge, UK, 1992.

198   References

[162] Stefan Hradil. Soziale Ungleichheiten, Milieus und Lebensstile in den Ländern der Europäischen Union. In Stefan Hradil and Stefan Immerfall, editors, *Die westeuropäischen Gesellschaften im Vergleich*, chapter 5, pages 475–519. Leske und Budrich, Opladen, D, 1997.

[163] Yuanreng Hu and Noreen Goldman. Mortality differentials by marital status: An international comparison. *Demography*, 27:233–250, 1990.

[164] Human Life-Table Database. Data by country: Denmark. Contributions from Väinö Kannisto and Danmarks Statistik, accessible online at: http://www.lifetable.de, April 2003.

[165] Human Life-Table Database. Data by country. Accessible online at: http://www.lifetable.de, July 2004.

[166] Human Life-Table Database. Data by Country: United States of America. Felicitie C. Bell and Michael L. Miller. Life Tables for the United States Social Security Area 1900-2100. Actuarial Study No. 116, accessible online at: http://www.lifetable.de, February 2004.

[167] Human Life-Table Database. Data by Country: United States of America. Accessible online at: http://www.lifetable.de, August 2004.

[168] Robert A. Hummer, Richard G. Rogers, and Isaac W. Eberstein. Sociodemographic Differentials in Adult Mortality: A Review of Analytic Approaches. *Population and Development Review*, 24:553–578, 1998.

[169] Maud M.T.E. Huynen, Pim Martens, Dieneke Schram, Matty P. Weijenberg, and Anton E. Kunst. The impact of heat waves and cold spells on mortality rates in the Dutch population. *Environmental Health Perspectives*, 109:463–470, 2001.

[170] Ross Ihaka and Robert Gentleman. R: A language for data analysis and graphics. *Journal of Computational and Graphical Statistics*, 5(3):299–314, 1996.

[171] Indenrigs- og Sundhedsministeriet. Health care in denmark. Available online at: http://www.im.dk/publikationer/healthcare_in_dk/all.htm (accessed 17 August, 2004), 2002.

[172] Kim Iskyan. The killer season. this summer was deadly, but winter could be even worse. Available online at: http://slate.msn.com, 2004.

[173] R. Jacobsen, N. Keiding, and E. Lynge. Long term mortality trends behind low life expectancy of Danish women. *Journal of Epidemiology and Community Health*, 56:205–208, 2002.

[174] Rune Jacobsen, Allan Jensen, Niels Keiding, and Elsebeth Lynge. Queen Margrethe II and mortality in Danish women. *The Lancet*, 358:75, 2001.

[175] Jitka Jelinková and Martin Braniš. Mortality during winter smog episodes 1982, 1985, 1987 and 1993 in the Czech Republic. *Int Arch Occup Environ Health*, 74:565–573, 2001.

[176] Bengt Johansson. Cold and ischaemic heart disease. *International Journal of Circumpolar Health*, 59(3–4):188–191, 2000.

[177] Vincenz John. *Geschichte der Statistik: ein quellenmässiges Handbuch für den akademischen Gebrauch wie für den Selbstunterricht. Erster*

Teil: Von dem Ursprung der Statistik bis auf Quetelet (1835). Verlag von Ferdinand Enke, Stuttgart, D, 1884.

[178] Judy Jones. UK seeks to prevent 50 000 winter deaths from "fuel poverty". *British Medical Journal*, 322:510, 2001.

[179] R. Jones, J. Scouller, F. Grainer, M. Lachlan, S Evans, and N Torrance. The scandal of poor medical research: Sloppy use of literature often to blame (Letters). *British Medical Journal*, 308:591, 1994.

[180] I.M. Joung, H. van de Mheen, K. Stronks, F.W. van Poppel, and Mackenbach J.P. Differences in self-reported morbidity by marital status and by living arrangment. *International Journal of Epidemiology*, 23:91–97, 1994.

[181] Knud Juel. Increased mortality among Danish women: population based register study. *British Medical Journal*, 321:349–350, 2000.

[182] E. Jutikkala and M. Kauppinen. The Structure of Mortality during Catastrophic Years in a Pre-Industrial society. *Population Studies*, 25:283–285, 1971.

[183] J.D. Kalbfleisch and R.L. Prentice. *The Statistical Analysis of Failure Time Data*. John Wiley & Sons, New York, N.Y., 1980.

[184] H. Kanai and I. Nakamura. Congenital Malformations by Month of Birth. In T. Miura, editor, *Seasonal effects on reproduction, infection and psychoses (Progress in Biometeorology, Vol. 6)*, pages 123–130. The Hague: SPB Academic Publishing, 1987.

[185] William Keatinge. Effects of temperature on health. Presentation given at the workshop "Seasonality in Mortality", Duke University, NC, 07–08 March 2002, 2002.

[186] William Keatinge and Gavin Donaldson. Winter deaths: warm housing is not enough (Letters). *British Medical Journal*, 323:166, 2001.

[187] W.R. Keatinge. Seasonal mortality among elderly people with unrestricted home heating. *British Medical Journal*, 293:732–733, 1986.

[188] W.R. Keatinge, S.R.K. Coleshaw, and J. Holmes. Changes in seasonal mortalities with improvement in home heating in England and Wales from 1964 to 1984. *International Journal of Biometeorology*, 33:71–76, 1989.

[189] W.R. Keatinge and G.C. Donaldson. Mortality related to cold and air pollution in London after allowance for effects of associated weather patterns. *Environmental Research*, 86:209–216, 2001.

[190] W.R. Keatinge, G.C. Donaldson, Elvira Cordioli, M. Martinelli, A.E. Kunst, Mackenbach J.P., S. Näyhä, and I. Vuori. Heat related mortality in warm and cold regions of Europe: observational study. *British Medical Journal*, 321:670–673, 2000.

[191] Julia A. Kelsall, Scott L. Zeger, and Jonathan M. Samet. Frequency domain log-linear models; air pollution and mortality. *Applied Statistics*, 48:331–344, 1999.

[192] Maurice G. Kendall and Alan Stuart. *The Avanced Theory of Statistics.*, volume 1, Distribution Theory. Hafner Publishing Company, New York, NY, third edition, 1969.

[193] Hugo Kesteloot. Queen Margrethe II and mortality in Danish women. *The Lancet*, 357:871–872, 2001.

[194] Kay-Tee Khaw and Peter Woodhouse. Interrelation of vitamin C, infection, haemostatic factors, and cardiovascular disease. *British Medical Journal*, 310:1559–1563, 1995.

[195] Evelyn M. Kitagawa and Philip M. Hauser. *Differential mortality in the United States: A Study in Socioeconomic Epidemiology.* Harvard University Press, Cambridge, MA, 1973.

[196] John P. Klein and Melvin L. Moeschberger. *Survival Analysis : Techniques for Censored and Truncated Data.* Statistics for Biology and Health. Springer, New York, NY, 2003.

[197] Susan E. Klepp. Seasoning and Society: Racial Differences in Mortality in Eighteenth-Century Philadelphia. *William and Mary Quarterly*, 51:473–506, 1994.

[198] G.A. Klevezal and N.I. Shishlina. Assessment of the Season of Death of Ancient Human from Cementum Annual Layers. *Journal of Archaelogical Science*, 28:481–486, 2001.

[199] Robert A. Kloner, Kenneth Poole, and Rebecca L. Perritt. When Throughout the Year is Coronary Death Most Likely to Occur? A 12-Year Population-Based Analysis of More Than 220 000 Cases. *Circulation*, 100:1630–1634, 1999.

[200] Donald Ervin Knuth. *Digital Typography.* CSLI Lecture Notes, no. 78. University of Chicago Press, Stanford, CA, 1999.

[201] Frances E. Kobrin and Gerry E. Hendershot. Do Family Ties Reduce Mortality? Evidence from the United States, 1966–1968. *Journal of Marriage and the Family*, 39:737–745, 1977.

[202] Hans-Peter Kohler and James Vaupel. Demography and its Relation to Other Disciplines. In Zdeněk Pavlík, editor, *Position of Demography Among Other Disciplines*, pages 19–26. Department of Demography and Geodemography, Charles University in Prague, Faculty of Science, Prague, CZ, 2000.

[203] A. Kolmogoroff. Sulla determinatione empirica di una legge di distributione. *Giornale dell'Istituto Italiano degli Attuari*, 4:83–91, 1933.

[204] A. Kolmogoroff. Confidence limits for an unknown distribution function. *Annals of Mathematical Statistics*, 12:416–463, 1941.

[205] N.D. Kondratieff. Die langen Wellen der Konjunktur. *Archiv für Sozialwissenschaft und Sozialpolitik*, 56:573–609 (reprinted in: The Review of Economic Statistics, Vol. 17, pp. 105–115), 1926.

[206] F. Kotěšovec, J. Skorkovský, Brynda J., Peters A., and Heinrich J. Daily mortality and air pollution in Northern Bohemia: different effects for men and women. *Cent. Eur. J. Publ. Health*, 8:120–127, 2000.

[207] Hermann Kühn, Hans-Peter Haack, and Thomas Jähnichen. Pneumonie und Jahreszeit. *Zeitschrift für die gesamte innere Medizin und ihre Grenzgebiete*, 26:617–621, 1971.

[208] A.E. Kunst, C.W.N. Looman, and J.P. Mackenbach. The Decline in Winter Excess Mortality in the Netherlands. *International Journal of Epidemiology*, 20:971–977, 1990.

[209] A.E. Kunst, C.W.N. Looman, and J.P. Mackenbach. Outdoor Air-Temperature and Mortality in the Netherlands — A Time-Series Analysis. *American Journal of Epidemiology*, 137:331–341, 1993.

[210] Anton Kunst. *Cross-national comparisons of socio-economic differences in mortality*. PhD thesis, Department of Public Health, Erasmus University Rotterdam, Rotterdam, NL, 1997.

[211] John Landers. *Death and the metropolis. Studies in the demographic history of London 1670–1830*. Cambridge University Press, Cambridge, UK, 1993.

[212] Peter Laslett. Introduction. In *The Earliest Classics*. Gregg International Publishers, 1973.

[213] D.A. Lawlor. Deprivation and excess winter mortality. *Journal of Epidemiology and Community Health*, 53:807–808, 1999.

[214] D.A. Lawlor, R Maxwell, and B.W. Wheeler. Rurality, deprivation, and excess winter mortality: an ecological study. *Journal of Epidemiology and Community Health*, 56:373–374, 2002.

[215] Deborah A. Lawlor, Daniel Harvey, and Howard G. Dews. Investigation of the association between excess winter mortality and socio-economic deprivation. *Journal of Public Health Medicine*, 22:176–181, 2000.

[216] Hervé Le Bras and Dominique Dinet. Mortalité des laïcs et mortalité des religieux: les bénédictins de St-Maur aux XVIIe and XVIIIe siècle. *Population*, pages 347–384, 1980.

[217] Jong-Tae Lee, Ho Kim, Yun-Chul Hong, Ho-Jang Kwon, Joel Schwartz, and David C. Christiani. Air Pollution and Daily Mortality in Seven Major Cities of Korea, 1991–1997. *Environmental Research (Section A)*, 84:247–254, 2000.

[218] Ronald Lee. Short-term variation: vital rates, prices, and weather. In E.A. Wrigley and R.S. Schofield, editors, *The Population History of England, 1541–1871*, chapter 9, pages 356–401. Cambridge University Press, Cambridge, UK, 1989.

[219] Mall Leinsalu, Vågerö, and Kunst Anton E. Estonia 1989–2000: enormous increase in mortality differentials by education. *International Journal of Epidemiology*, 32:1081–1087, 2003.

[220] Alexander Lerchl. Changes in the seasonality of mortality in Germany from 1946 to 1995: the role of temperature. *International Journal of Biometeorology*, 42:84–88, 1998.

[221] J.W.C. Lever. On the Sickness and Mortality Among the Troops in the United Kingdom. Abstract of the Statistical Report of Major Tulloch. *Journal of the Statistical Society of London*, 2:250–260, 1839.

[222] Daniel E. Lieberman. The Biological Basis for Seasonal Increments in Dental Cementum and Their Application to Archaeological Research. *Journal of Archaelogical Science*, 21:525–539, 1994.

[223] Lee A. Lillard and Constantijn W.A. Panis. Marital Status and Mortality: The Role of Health. *Demography*, 33:313–327, 1996.

[224] Wilfried Linke and Udo W. Kroschewski. Zeitreihenanalyse der natürlichen Bevölkerungsbewegung 1950 bis 1977. *Zeitschrift für Bevölkerungswissenschaft*, 5:215–234, 1979.

[225] Massimo Livi-Bacci. *Population and Nutrition. An Essay on European Demographic History*. Cambridge Studies in Population, Economy and Society in Past Time 14. Cambridge University Press, Cambridge, UK, 1991.

[226] Rikke Lund, Pernille Due, Bjørn Evald Modvig, Jens Holstein, Mogens Trab Damsgaard, and Per Kragh Andersen. Cohabitation and marital status as predictors of mortality — an eight year follow-up study. *Social Science and Medicine*, 55:673–679, 2002.

[227] Marc Luy. Die geschlechtsspezifischen Sterblichkeitsunterschiede — Zeit für eine Zwischenbilanz. *Zeitschrift für Gerontologie und Geriatrie*, 35:412–429, 2002.

[228] Marc Luy. *Warum Frauen länger leben. Antworten durch einen Vergleich von Kloster- und Allgemeinbevölkerung*. Materialien zur Bevölkerungswissenschaft, Bd. 106. Bundesinstitut für Bevölkerungsforschung, Wiesbaden, D, 2002.

[229] Marc Luy. Causes of Male Excess Mortality: Insights from a Cloistered Population. *Population and Development Review*, 29:647–676, 2003.

[230] J.W. Lynch, G.A. Kaplan, and J.T. Salonen. Why do poor people behave poorly? Variation in adult health behaviors and psychosocial characteristics by stages of the socioeconomic lifecourse. *Social Science and Medicine*, 44:809–819, 1997.

[231] W.R. Lyster. The altered seasons of death in America. *Journal of Biosocial Science*, 4:145–151, 1972.

[232] Johan P. Mackenbach, Vincent Borst, and Jos M.G.A. Schols. Heat-related mortality among nursing-home patients. *The Lancet*, 349:1297–1298, 1997.

[233] Johan P. Mackenbach, Vivian Bos, Otto Andersen, Mario Cardano, Guiseppe Costa, Seeromanie Harding, Alison Reid, Örjan Hemström, Tapani Valkonen, and Anton E. Kunst. Widening socioeconomic inequalities in mortality in six Western European countries. *International Journal of Epidemiology*, 32:830–837, 2003.

[234] Johan P. Mackenbach, Anton E. Kunst, Feikje Groenhof, Jens-Kristian Borgan, Giuseppe Costa, Fabrizio Faggiano, Józan, Mall Leinsalu, Pekka Martikainen, Jitka Rychtarikova, and Tapani Valkonen. Socioeconomic Inequalities in Mortality Among Women and Among Men: An International Study. *American Journal of Public Health*, 89:1800–1806, 1999.

[235] J.P. Mackenbach, A.E. Kunst, and C.W.N. Looman. Seasonal variation in mortality in the Netherlands. *Journal of Epidemiology and Community Health*, 46:261–265, 1992.

[236] Sten Madsen. Queen Margrethe II and mortality in Danish women. *The Lancet*, 358:75, 2001.

[237] Andres Magnusson. Historical excerpts. In Timo Partonen and Andres Magnusson, editors, *Seasonal Affective Disorder. Practice and Research*, chapter 1, pages 3–8. Oxford University Press, 2001.

[238] Perla J. Marang-van de Mheen, George Davey Smith, Carole L. Hart, and David J. Hole. Are women more sensitive to smoking than men? Findings from the Renfrew and Paisley study. *International of Epidemiology*, 30:787–792, 2001.

[239] Agustín Maravall. Brief Description of the Programs. Available online at: http://www.bde.es/servicio/software/tramo/summprogs.pdf, 2002.

[240] Lucien March. Some researches concerning the factors of mortality. *Journal of the Royal Statistical Society*, 75:505–538, 1912.

[241] G. Marcuzzi and M. Tasso. Mortality of the German linguistic isolates of the Western Italian Alps (Walser). *Antropologia portuguesa*, 52:239–259, 1994.

[242] Giorgio Marcuzzi and Miro Tasso. Seasonality of Death in the Period 1889–1988 in the Val di Scalve (Bergamo Pre-Alps, Lombardia, Italy). *Human Biology*, 64:215–222, 1992.

[243] M.G. Marmot and M.E. McDowall. Mortality Decline and Widening Social Inequalities. *The Lancet*, 8501:274–276, 1986.

[244] Osvaldo Marrero. The performance of several statistical tests for seasonality in monthly data. *Journal of Computational Statistics and Simulation*, 17:275–296, 1983.

[245] Alex Marsh, David Gordon, Christina Pantazis, and Pauline Heslop. *Home Sweet Home? The impact of poor housing on health.* Policy Press, Bristol, UK, 1999.

[246] Roger J. Marshall, Robert Scragg, and Paul Bourke. An Analysis of the Seasonal Variation of Coronary Heart Disease and Respiratory Disease Mortality in New Zealand. *International Journal of Epidemiology*, 17:325–331, 1988.

[247] Edward J. Masoro and Steven N. Austad, editors. *Handbook of the Biology of Aging.* Academic Press, San Diego, CA, 5 edition, 2001.

[248] Patrick E. McBride. The Health Consequences of Smoking. Cardiovascular Diseases. *Medical Clinics of North America*, 76:333–353, 1992.

[249] P. McCullagh and J.A. Nelder. *Generalized linear models.* Chapman and Hall, London, UK, 1989.

[250] John M. McCullough. Application of the Kolmogorov-Smirnov Test to Seasonal Phenomena May Be Inappropriate. *American Journal of Physical Anthropology*, 68:393–394, 1985.

[251] Michael McDowall. Long term trends in seasonal mortality. *Population Trends*, 26:16–19, 1981.

[252] C.M. McKee. Deaths in Winter: Can Britain learn from Europe? *European Journal of Epidemiology*, 5(2):178–82, 1989.

[253] Martin McKee, Colin Sanderson, Laurent Chenet, Sergei Vassin, and Vladimir Shkolnikov. Seasonal variation in mortality in Moscow. *Journal of Public Health Medicine*, 20:268–274, 1998.

[254] Thomas McKeown. Food, Infection, and Population. *Journal of Interdisciplinary History*, 14:227–247, 1983.

[255] Thomas McKeown and R. G. Record. Reasons for the Decline of Mortality in England and Wales during the Nineteenth Century. *Population Studies*, 16:94–122, 1962.

[256] C.E. McLaren, J.M. Legler, and G.M. Brittenham. The generalized χ^2-goodness-of-fit test. *The Statistician*, 43:247–258, 1994.

[257] Don McNeil. *Epidemiological Research Methods*. John Wiley & Sons, New York, NY, 1996.

[258] James Mercer and Sigurd Sparr. Preface. *International Journal of Circumpolar Health*, 59(3–4):152–153, 2000.

[259] France Meslé and Jacques Vallin. Reconstructing Long-Term Series of Causes of Death. *Historical Methods*, 29:72–87, 1996.

[260] Masako S. Momiyama. Changes in seasonality of human deaths from infectious diseases. In T. Miura, editor, *Seasonal effects on reproduction, infection and psychoses (Progress in Biometeorology, Vol. 5)*, pages 159–169. The Hague: SPB Academic Publishing, 1987.

[261] Kevin M. Murphy and Robert Topel. The Economic Value of Medical Research. Available online at: `http://gsbwww.uchicago.edu/fac/kevin.murphy/research/murphy&topel.pdf`. Forthcoming in: Kevin M. Murphy and Robert H. Topel (Eds.) Exceptional Returns (2003). Chicago, IL: Chicago University Press, 1999.

[262] Seiichi Nakai, Toshiyuki Itoh, and Taketoshi Morimoto. Deaths from heat-stroke in Japan: 1968–1994. *International Journal of Biometeorology*, 43:124–127, 1999.

[263] Jun-mo Nam. Interval estimation and significance testing for cyclic trends in seasonality studies. *Biometrics*, 51:1411–1417, 1995.

[264] National Center for Health Statistics. Table 1. Deaths, percent of total deaths, and death rates for the 10 leading causes of death in selected age groups, by race and sex: United States, 2000. *National Vital Statistics Report*, 50(16):13–48, September 2002. Available online at: `http://www.cdc.gov/nchs/fastats/pdf/nvsr50_16t1.pdf`.

[265] National Statistics Online. Census 2001. Housing. Available online at: `http://www.statistics.gov.uk/census2001/profiles/rank/rank_housing.asp`, 2004.

[266] National Statistics Online. Excess winter mortality. Available online at: `http://www.statistics.gov.uk/`, 2004.

[267] Mary P. Naughton, Alden Henderson, Maria C. Mirabelli, Reinhard Kaiser, John L. Wilhelm, Stephanie M. Kieszak, CArol H. Rubin, and Michael McGeehin. Heat-Related Mortality During a 1999 Heat Wave in Chicago. *American Journal of Preventive Medicine*, 22:221–227, 2002.

[268] Simo Näyhä. *Short and medium term variations in mortality in Finland.* PhD thesis, Department of Public Health Service, University of Oulu, Finland, 1980.

[269] Simo Näyhä. Seasonal variation of deaths in Finland: is it still diminishing? *International Journal of Circumpolar Health*, 59(3–4):182–187, 2000.

[270] NBER. Seasonal Adjustments in the NBER Macrohistory Data. Downloadable at: http://nber.org/databases/macrohistory/contents/sa.html, 2003.

[271] E.P. Neale. A New Zealand Study in Seasonal Fluctuations of External Migration, with Special Reference to the Computation of Mean Annual Populations. *Journal of the Royal Statistical Society*, 86:226–241, 1923.

[272] Andrew R. Ness and John W. Powles. Fruit and Vegetables, and Cardiovascular Disease: A Review. *International Journal of Epidemiology*, 26:1–13, 1997.

[273] Kristin L. Nichol, James Nordin, John Mullooly, Richard Lask, Kelly Fillbrandt, and Marika Iwane. Influenza Vaccination and Reduction in Hospitalization for Cardiac Disease and Stroke among the Elderly. *The New England Journal of Medicine*, 348:1322–1332, 2003.

[274] William D. Nordhaus. The Health of Nations. The Contribution of Improved Health to Living Standards. NBER Working Paper 8818, National Bureau of Economic Research, Cambridge, MA, March 2002.

[275] Martin Nourney. Methode der Zeitreihenanalyse. *Wirtschaft und Statistik*, pages 11–17, 1973.

[276] Martin Nourney. Weiterentwicklung des Verfahrens der Zeitreihenanalyse. *Wirtschaft und Statistik*, pages 96–101, 1975.

[277] Martin Nourney. Umstellung der Zeitreihenanalyse. *Wirtschaft und Statistik*, (Available online at: http://www.destatis.de), 1983.

[278] Kevin F. O'Brien and Donald Holbert. Note on the choice for statistic for testing hypotheses regarding seasonality. *American Journal of Physical Anthropology*, 72:523–524, 1987.

[279] Jim Oeppen and James W. Vaupel. Broken Limits to Life Expectancy. *Science*, 296:1029–1031, 2002.

[280] Noel D.L. Olsen. Prescribing warmer, healthier homes (Editorial). *British Medical Journal*, 322:748–749, 2001.

[281] Abdel R. Omran. The Epidemiologic Transition : A Theory of the Epidemiology of Population Change. *Milbank Memorial Fund Quarterly*, 49:509–538, 1971.

[282] Bart Ostro. Fine Particulate Air Pollution and Mortality in Two Southern California Counties. *Environmental Research*, 70:98–104, 1995.

[283] Finbarr O'Sullivan. A Statistical Perspective on Ill-Posed Inverse Problems. *Statistical Science*, 1:502–518, 1986.

[284] Gregory Pappas, Susan Queen, Wilbur Hadden, and Gail Fisher. The Increasing Disparity in Mortality between Socioeconomic Groups in the United States, 1960 and 1986. *The New England Journal of Medicine*, 329:103–109, 1993.

[285] Len Paulozzi. The seasonality of mortality in alaska. *Social Science and Medicine*, 15:335–339, 1981.

[286] Karl Pearson. On the Criterion that a Given System of Deviations from the Probable in the Case of a Correlated System of Variables is Such that it Can be Reasonably Supposed to have Arisen from Random Sampling. London, Edinburgh and Dublin: Philosophical Magazine and Journal of Science, Vol. 50, 5th Series, pp. 157–175. In Samuel Kotz and Norman L. Johnson, editors, *Breakthroughs in Statistics. Volume II. Methodology and Distribution (1992)*, pages 11–28. Springer, Heidelberg, Germany, 1900.

[287] Jørn Korsbo Petersen. The Danish Demographic Database - longitudinal data for advanced demographic methods. Research Report 15, Danish Center for Demographic Research. SDU - Odense University, Odense, DK, 2000.

[288] Jørn Korsbo Petersen. *The Danish Demographic Database - longitudinal data for advanced demographic methods*. Danish Center for Demographic Research, Odense, DK, research report 15 edition, 2000.

[289] Jørn Korsbo Petersen. Personal Communications, 2003.

[290] Linda Williams Pickle, Michael Mungiole, Gretchen K. Jones, and Andrew A. White. Atlas of United States Mortality. Technical report, National Center for Health Statistics, Hyattsville, MD, 1996.

[291] S.J. Pocock. Harmonic analysis applied to seasonal variations in sickness absence. *Applied Statistics*, 23:103–120, 1974.

[292] K. Poortema. On modelling overdispersion of counts. *Statistica Neerlandica*, 53:5–20, 1999.

[293] R.L. Prentice, J.D. Kalbfleisch, A.V. Peterson Jr., N. Flournoy, V.T. Farewell, and N.E. Breslow. The Analysis of Failure Times in the Presence of Competing Risks. *Biometrics*, 34:541–554, 1978.

[294] Eva Prescott, Merete Hippe, Peter Schnohr, Hans Ole Hein, and Jørgen Vestbo. Smoking and risk of myocardial infarction in women and men: longitudinal population study. *British Medical Journal*, 316:1043–1047, 1998.

[295] Eva Prescott, Merete Osler, Per Kragh Andersen, Hans Ole Hein, Knut Borch-Johnsen, Peter Lange, Peter Schnohr, and Jørgen Vestbo. Mortality in women and men in relation to smoking. *International Journal of Epidemiology*, 27:27–32, 1998.

[296] Samuel E. Preston and Irma T. Elo. Are Educational Differentials in Adult Mortality Increasing in the United States? *Journal of Aging and Health*, 7:476–496, 1995.

[297] Samuel H. Preston, Patrick Heuveline, and Michel Guillot. *Demography. Measuring and Modeling Population Processes*. Blackwell Publishers, Oxford, UK, 2001.

[298] Raimo Pullat. Die Struktur und die saisonmäßige Verteilung der Sterblichkeit der Talinner Bevölkerung im 18. Jahrhundert basierend auf Kirchenbüchern der Heiligengeistkirche. *Zeitschrift für Bevölkerungswissenschaft*, 11:401–412, 1985.

[299] Quantitative Micro Software. *EViews 4 User Guide*. Quantitative Micro Software, LLC, Irvine, CA, 2000.

[300] Adolphe Quetelet. *De l'influence des saisons sur la mortalité aux différens ages dans la Belgique*. M. Hayez, Bruxelles, B, 1838.

[301] R Development Core Team. *R: A language and environment for statistical computing*. R Foundation for Statistical Computing, Vienna, Austria, 2003. ISBN 3-900051-00-3.

[302] Roland Rau and Gabriele Doblhammer. Seasonal mortality in Denmark. The role of sex and age. *Demographic Research*, 9:197–222, 2003.

[303] Adi Raveh. Comments on Some Properties of X-11. *The Review of Economics and Statistics*, 66:343–348, 1984.

[304] Barry Reay. *Microhistories: demography, society and culture in rural England, 1800–1930*. Cambridge University Press, Cambridge, UK, 1996.

[305] Sijmen A. Reijneveld. The choice of a statistic for testing hypotheses regarding seasonality. *American Journal of Physical Anthropology*, 83:181–184, 1990.

[306] Christian H. Reinsch. Smoothing by Spline Functions. *Numerische Mathematik*, 10:177–183, 1967.

[307] Toni Richards. Weather, nutrition, and the economy: Short-run fluctuations in births, deaths, and marriages, france 1740–1909. *Demography*, 20:197–212, 1983.

[308] Zoltán Rihmer, Wolfgang Rutz, Hans Pihlgren, and Péter Pestiality. Decreasing tendeny of seasonality in suicide may indicate lowering rate of depressive suicides in the population. *Psychiatry Research*, 81:233–240, 1998.

[309] J.-M. Robine and J.W. Vaupel. Supercentenarians: slower ageing individuals or senile elderly? *Experimental Gerontology*, 36:915–930, 2001.

[310] Jean-Marie Robine. A new biodemographic model to explain the trajectory of mortality. *Experimental Gerontology*, 36:899–914, 2001.

[311] W.S. Robinson. Ecological correlations and the behavior of individuals. *American Sociological Review*, 15:351–357, 1950.

[312] J.H. Roger. A significance test for cyclic trends in incidence data. *Biometrika*, 64:152–155, 1977.

[313] Richard G. Rogers. The Effects of Family Composition, Health, and Social Support Linkages on Mortality. *Journal of Health and Social Behavior*, 37:326–338, 1996.

[314] Richard G. Rogers, Robert A. Hummer, and Charles B. Nam. *Living and Dying in the USA. Behavioral, Health and Social Differentials of Adult Mortality.* Academic Press, San Diege, CA, 1995.

[315] Peter A. Rogerson. A Generalization of Hewitt's Test for Seasonality. *International Journal of Epidemiology*, 25:644–648, 1996.

[316] Eugene Rogot, Richard Fabsitz, and Manning Feinlein. Daily variation in USA mortality. *American journal of epidemiology*, 103:565–575, 1976.

[317] Geoffrey Rose. Cold Weather and Ischaemic Heart Disease. *British Journal of preventive social Medicine*, 20:97–100, 1966.

[318] Paul-Andre Rosenthal. Thirteen Years of Debate: From Population History to French Historical Demography (1945–1958). *Population: an English Selection*, 9:215–241, 1997.

[319] Ira Rosenwaike. Seasonal variation of deaths in the United States, 1951–1960. *Journal of the American Statistical Association*, 61:706–719, 1966.

[320] Steven Ruggles. The limitations of English family reconstitution: English population history from family reconstitution 1580–1837. *Continuity and Change*, 14:105–130, 1999.

[321] Lothar Sachs. *Angewandte Statistik. Anwendung statistischer Methoden. Neunte, überarbeitete Auflage.* Springer, Berlin, Germany, 1999.

[322] Marc Saez, Jordi Sunyer, Aureli Tobias, Ferran Ballester, and Joesp Maria Antó. Ischaemic heart disease mortality and weather temperature in Barcelona, Spain. *European Journal of Public Health Medicine*, 10:58–63, 2000.

[323] Osamu Saito. Historical Demography: Achievements and Prospects. *Population Studies*, 50:537–553, 1996.

[324] Masako Sakamoto-Momiyama. *Seasonality in Human Mortality. A Medico-Geographical Study.* University of Tokyo Press, Tokyo, JP, 1977.

[325] Masako Sakamoto-Momiyama. Changes in the Seasonality of Human Mortality: A Medico-Geographical Study. *Social Science and Medicine*, 12:29–42, 1978.

[326] Robert Sallares. The emergence of falciparum malaria as a new disease in Roman Italy. Presented at the conference "Environmental Catastrophes and Recoveries in the Holocene", August 29 – September 2, 2002. Abstract available online at: http://atlas-conferences.com/cgi-bin/abstract/caji-10 (abstract accessed January 6, 2003), 2002.

[327] Jonathan Samet, Scott Zeger, Julia Kelsall, Jing Xu, and Laurence Kalkstein. Does weather confound or modify the association of particulate air pollution with mortality. *Environmental Research Section, Section A*, 77:9–19, 1998.

[328] Jonathan M. Samet, Francesca Dominici, Frank C. Curriero, Ivan Coursac, and Scott Zeger. Fine particulate air pollution and mortality in 20. U.S. cities. *The New England Journal of Medicine*, 343:1742–1749, 2000.

[329] Francis Sartor, René Snacken, Claude Demuth, and Denise Walckiers. Temperature, Ambient Ozone Levels, and Mortality during Summer, 1994, in Belgium. *Environmental Research*, 70:105–113, 1995.

[330] Walter Scheidel. Libitina's Bitter Gains: Seasonal Mortality and Endemic Disease in the Ancient City of Rome. *Ancient Society*, 25:151–175, 1994.

[331] Walter Scheidel. Measuring Sex, Age and Death in the Roman Empire. *Journal of Roman Archaeology*, Supplementary Series Number 21:1–184, 1996.

[332] Walter Scheidel. The meaning of dates on mummy labels: seasonal mortality and mortuary practice in Roman Egypt. *Jounal of Roman Archaeology*, 11:285–292, 1998.

[333] Walter Scheidel. Progress and Problems in Roman Demograpgy. In Walter Scheidel, editor, *Debating Roman Demography*. Brill, Leiden, NL, 2001.

[334] Walter Scheidel. Personal Communications, 2003.

[335] Rainer Schlittgen and Bernd H.J. Streitberg. *Zeitreihenanalyse. 3., durchgesehene und verbesserte Auflage*. R. Oldenbourg, München, D, 1989.

[336] Josef Schmid. *Wohlfahrtsstaaten im Vergleich*. Leske und Budrich, Opladen, D, 2nd edition, 2002.

[337] Joel Schwartz. Air Pollution and Daily Mortality: A Review and Meta Analysis. *Environmental Research*, 64:36–52, 1994.

[338] Joel Schwartz. What are People Dying of on High Pollution Days? *Environmental Research*, 64:26–35, 1994.

[339] Alex Scobie. Slums, Sanitation, and Mortality in the Roman World. *KLIO*, 68:399–433, 1986.

[340] Dimitrios Seretakis, Pagona Lagiou, Loren Lipworth, Lisa B. Signorello, Kenneth J. Rothman, and Dimitrios Trichopoulos. Changing Seasonality of Mortality From Coronary Heart Disease. *Journal of the American Medical Association*, 278:1012–1014, 1997.

[341] Todd B. Seto, Murray A. Mittleman, Roger B. Davis, Deborah A. Taira, and Ichiro Kawachi. Seasonal variation in coronary artery disease mortality in Hawaii: observational study. *British Medical Journal*, 316:1946–1947, 1998.

[342] Sunil Shah and Janet Peacock. Deprivation and excess winter mortality. *Journal of Epidemiology and Community Health*, 53:499–502, 1999.

[343] Brent D. Shaw. Seasons of Death: Aspects of Mortality in Imperial Rome. *Journal of Roman Studies*, 86:100–138, 1996.

[344] David J. Sheskin. *Handbook of Parametric and Nonparametric Statistical Procedures*. CRC Press, Boca Raton, US, 1997.

[345] Tej Sheth, Cyril Nair, James Muller, and Salim Yusuf. Increased Winter Mortality From Acute Myocardial Infarction and Stroke: The Effect of Age. *Journal of the American College of Cardiology*, 33:1916–1919, 1999.

[346] Vladimir M. Shkolnikov, Evgueni E. Andreev, and Alexander Z. Begun. Gini coefficient as a life table function: computation from discrete data, decomposition of differences and empirical examples. *Demographic Research*, 8:305–357, 2003.

[347] Maria Shkolnikova. Personal Communications, 2004.

[348] Theresa A. Singleton. The Archaeology of Slavery in North America. *Annual Review of Anthropology*, 24:119–140, 1995.

[349] Axel Skytthe. The Fundament for Danish Register Research. Civil Registration System. Presentation given at the course "The data of Denmark", Odense, DK, 30 April 2001, 2000.

[350] Paul Slack. The Disappearance of Plague: An Alternative View. *The Economic History Review*, 34:469–476, 1981.

[351] Malcolm J. Slakter. A comparison of the pearson chi-square and the kolmogorov goodness-of-fit tests with respect to validity. *Journal of the American Statistical Association*, 60:854–858, 1965.

[352] N. Smirnoff. Sur les écarts de la courbe de distribution empirique. *Recueil. Math. de Moscou*, 6:3–26, 1939.

[353] Robert S. Smith. Barcelona "Bills of Mortality" and Population 1457–1590. *The Journal of Political Economy, New Series*, 34:469–476, 1986.

[354] Robert R. Sokal and F. James Rohlf. *Biometry. The Principles and Practice of Statistics in Biological Research.* W.H. Freeman and Company, New York, N.Y., 3rd edition, 2000.

[355] Sigurd Sparr. Cold and ischaemic heart disease in the elderly. *International Journal of Circumpolar Health*, 59(3–4):192–194, 2000.

[356] Frederick A. Spencer, Robert J. Goldberg, Becker Richard C., and Joel M. Gore. Seasonal distribution of acute myocardial infarction in the second national registry of myocardial infarction. *Journal of the American College of Cardiology*, 31:1226–1233, 1998.

[357] Hans-Theo Speth. Komponentenzerlegung und Saisonbereinigung ökonomischer Zeitreihen mit dem Verfahren BV4.1. Methodenberichte, Heft 3, 2004, Statistisches Bundesamt, Wiesbaden, D, 2004.

[358] A.S. St Leger. Comparison of two tests for seasonality in epidemiological data. *Applied Statistics*, 25:280–286, 1976.

[359] E. Stoupel, J. Abramson, S. Domarkiene, M. Shimshoni, and J. Sulkes. Space proton flux and the temporal distribution of cardiovascular deaths. *International Journal of Biometeorology*, 40:113–116, 1997.

[360] Gustav Sundbärg. *Bevölkerungsstatistik Schwedens 1750–1900.* National Central Bureau of Statistics, Skriftserie utgiven av statistika centralbyrän, Urval Nummer 3, 1970.

[361] José M. Tenías Burillo, Ferran Ballester Díez, Sylvia Medina, and Antonio Daponte Codina. Revisió de los trabajos originales que analizan los effectos de la contaminacón atmosférica en la martalidad, 1994–1998. *Rev Esp Salud Pública*, 73:145–164, 1999.

[362] The Guardian. Cold killed 20,000 elderly people last winter, says charity. Available online at: http://www.guardian.co.uk, 2001.

[363] The Independent. Britain is a rich nation; its old people should not be dying of the cold. Available online at: http://www.independent.co.uk, 2003.

[364] G. Touloumi, S.J. Pocock, K. Katsouyanni, and D. Trichopoulos. Short Term Effects of Air Pollution on Daily Mortality in Athens: A Time-Series Analysis. *International Journal of Epidemiology*, 23:957–967, 1994.

[365] G. Touloumi, E. Samoli, and K. Katsouyanni. Daily mortality and "winter type" air pollution in Athens, Greece—a time series analysis within the APHEA project. *Journal of Epidemiology and Community Health*, 50 (Supp. 1):S47–S51, 1996.

[366] G. Ian Town. The health effect of particulate air pollution—a Christchurch perspective. *Biomarkers*, 6:15–18, 2001.

[367] Richard Trudeau. Monthly and daily patterns of death. *Health Reports (Statistics Canada)*, 9:43–50, 1997.

[368] A.M. Tulloch. On the Sickness and Mortality among the Troops in the West Indies. *Journal of the Statistical Society of London*, 1:428–444, 1838.

[369] Jane H. Underwood. Seasonality of vital events in a Pacific island population. *Social Biology*, 38:113–126, 1991.

[370] UNESCO. International Standard Classification of Education ISCED 1997. Available online at:
http://www.unesco.org/education/information/nfsunesco/doc/isced_1997.ht%m, 1997.

[371] Rainer Unger. *Soziale Differenzierung der aktiven Lebenserwartung im internationalen Vergleich*. Deutscher Universitätsverlag, Wiesbaden, D, 2003.

[372] U.S. Census Bureau. Historical Census of Housing Tables: House Heating Fuel. Accessible online at: http://www.census.gov/~hhes/www/housing/census/historic/fuels.html, 2002.

[373] U.S. Census Bureau. Intercensal Estimates of the Unites States Resident Population by Age and Sex: 1998. Accessible online at:
http://eire.census.gov/popest/data/national/tables/intercensal/US-EST90INT-07/US-EST90INT-07-1998.csv, 2004.

[374] Tapani Valkonen. Adult mortality and level of education: a comparison of six countries. In J. Fox, editor, *Health inequalities in European countries*. missing, 1989.

[375] Jacques Vallin and France Meslé. *Les Causes de Décès en France de 1925 a 1978*. Travaux et Documents Cahier n°115. Institut National d'Études Démographiques, 1988.

[376] Caroline T.M. van Rossum, Martin J. Shipley, Harry Hemingway, Grobbee Diederick E., Johan P. Mackenbach, and Michael J. Marmot. Seasonal variation in cause-specific mortality: Are there high-risk groups? 25-year follow-up of civil servants from the first Whitehall study. *International Journal of Epidemiology*, 30:1109–1116, 2001.

[377] James W. Vaupel. How Change in Age-Specifig Mortality Affects Life Expectancy. *Population Studies*, 40:147–157, 1986.

[378] James W. Vaupel. The remarkable improvements in survival at older ages. *Philosophical Transactions of the Royal Society of London: Biological Sciences*, 352:1799–1804, 1997.

[379] James W. Vaupel. Directions for demographic research in the 21st century. Presentation at Meeting "Perspectives of Demographic Research in Austria", Vienna, Austria, 1998.

[380] James W. Vaupel. Life expectancy at current rates vs. current conditions. a reflexion stimulated by bongaarts and feeneys "how long do we live?". *Demographic Research*, 7:365–378, 2002.

[381] James W. Vaupel. Personal Communications, 2003.

[382] James W. Vaupel and Vladimir Canudas Romo. *Analysis of Population Changes and Differences. Methods for Demographers, Statisticians, Biologists, Epidemiologists, and Reliability Engineers*. Max Planck Institute for Demographic Research, Rostock, Germany, Konrad Zuse Str. 1, D–18057 Rostock, Germany, November 18 2001.

[383] James W. Vaupel and Vladimir Canudas Romo. Decomposing demographic change into direct vs. compositional components. *Demographic Research*, 7:1–14, 2002.

[384] James W. Vaupel, James R. Carey, Kaare Christensen, Thomas E. Johnson, Niels V. Yashin, Anatoli I.and Holm, Ivan A. Iachine, Väinö Kannisto, Aziz A. Khazaeli, Pablo Liedo, Valter D. Longo, Yi Zeng, Kenneth G. Manton, and James W. Curtsinger. Biodemographic trajectories of longevity. *Science*, 280:855–860, 1998.

[385] James W. Vaupel, Kenneth G. Manton, and Eric Stallard. The Impact of Heterogeneity in Individual Frailty on the Dynamics of Mortality. *Demography*, 16:439–454, 1979.

[386] James W. Vaupel and Anatoli I. Yashin. Heterogeneity's ruses: Some Surprising Effects of Selection on Population Dynamics. *The American Statistician*, 39:176–185, 1985.

[387] James W. Vaupel and Anatoli I. Yashin. Repeated Resuscitation: How Lifesaving Alters Life Tables. *Demography*, 24:123–135, 1987.

[388] James W. Vaupel, Wang Zhenglian, Kirill F. Andreev, and Anatoli I. Yashin. *Population Data at a Glance: Shaded Contour Maps of Demographic Surfaces over Age and Time*. Odense Monographs on Population Aging 4. University Press of Southern Denmark, Odense, DK, 1997.

[389] W.N. Venables and B.D. Ripley. *Modern Applied Statistics with S-PLUS*. Springer, New York, NY, 3rd edition, 1999.

[390] H. Verdoux, N. Takei, R. Cassou de Saint-Mathurin, and M. Bourgeois. Analysis of the seasonal variation of schizophrenic births using a kolmogorov-smirnov type statistic. *European Psychiatry*, 12:111–116, 1997.

[391] S. Villa, H. Guisecafré, H. Martinez, and O Munõ. Seasonal diarrhoeal mortality among mexican children. *Bulletin of the World Health Organization*, 77:375–380, 1999.

[392] Friedrich Vogel. *Beschreibende und schließende Statistik. Formeln, Definitionen, Erläuterungen, Stichwörter und Tabellen.* Oldenbourg, München, D, 8 edition, 1995.

[393] Friedrich Vogel. *Studienskript: Parametrische und nichtparametrische (verteilungsfreie) Schätz- und Testverfahren.* Universität Bamberg, Lehrstuhl für Statistik, Bamberg, D, 1998.

[394] Sylvan Wallenstein, Clarice R. Weinberg, and Madelyn Gould. Testing for a pulse in seasonal event data. *Biometrics*, 45:817–830, 1989.

[395] S.D. Walter. Exact significance levels for Hewitt's test for seasonality. *Journal of Epidemiology and Community Health*, 34:147–149, 1980.

[396] S.D. Walter and J.M. Elwood. A test for seasonality of events with a variable population at risk. *British Journal of Preventive Social Medicine*, 29:18–21, 1975.

[397] James H. Ware. Particulate Air Pollution and Mortality—Clearing the Air (Editorial). *The New England Journal of Medicine*, 343:1798–1799, 2000.

[398] Huber R. Warner, Robert N. Butler, Richard L. Sprott, and Edward L. Schneider, editors. *Modern Biological Theories of Aging*. Aging 31. Raven Press, New York, NY, 1987.

[399] Susan Cotts Watkins and Etienne van de Walle. Nutrition, Mortality, and Population Size: Malthus' Court of Last Resort. *Journal of Interdisciplinary History*, 14:205–226, 1983.

[400] Harald Westergaard. Mortality in Remote Corners of the World. *Journal of the Statistical Society of London*, 43:509–520, 1880.

[401] Christine D. White. Isotopic Determination of Seasonality in Diet and Death from Nubian Mummy Hair. *Journal of Archaelogical Science*, 20:657–666, 1993.

[402] Kevin M. White. Cardiovascular and Tuberculosis Mortality: The Contrasting Effects of Changes in Two Causes of Death. *Population and Development Review*, 25:289–302, 1999.

[403] Michael J. White. Segregation and Diversity Measures in Population Distribution. *Population Index*, 52:198–221, 1986.

[404] Paul Wilkinson, Megan Landon, Ben Armstrong, Simon Stevenson, Sam Pattenden, Martin McKee, and Tony Fletcher. *Cold comfort. The social and environmental determinants of excess winter death in England, 1986–96.* Policy Press, Bristol, UK, 2001.

[405] Paul Wilkinson, Sam Pattenden, Ben Armstrong, Astrid Fletcher, R Sari Kovats, Punam Mangtani, and Anthony J McMichael. Vulnerability to winter mortality in elderly people in Britain: population based study. *British Medical Journal*, 329:647–650, 2004.

[406] J. Dennis Willigan and Katherine A. Lynch. *Sources and Methods of Historical Demography*. Academic Press, New York, NY, 1982.

[407] John R. Wilmoth. Preliminary Results on Seasonal Mortality in Sweden. Presentation given at the workshop "Seasonality in Mortality", Duke University, NC, 07–08 March 2002, 2002.

[408] Ursula Wittwer-Backofen. Personal Communications, 2002.

[409] Ursula Wittwer-Backofen and Helene Buba. Age estimation by tooth cementum annulation. In Robert D. Hoppa and James W. Vaupel, editors, *Paleodemography. age distributions from skeletal samples*, pages 107–128. Cambridge University Press, Cambridge, UK, 2002.

[410] Ursula Wittwer-Backofen, Jutta Gampe, and James W. Vaupel. Tooth cementum annulation for age estimation: Results from a large known-age validation study. *American Journal of Physical Anthropology*, 123:119–129, 2004.

[411] Peter Woodhouse and Kay-Tee Khaw. Seasonal variation of risk factors for cardiovascular disease and diet in older adults. *International Journal of Circumpolar Health*, 59(3–4):204–209, 2000.

[412] Peter R. Woodhouse, Kay-Tee Khaw, and Martyn Plummer. Seasonal variation of blood pressure and its relationship to ambient temperature in an elderly population. *Journal of Hypertension*, 11:1267–1274, 1993.

[413] Peter R. Woodhouse, Kay-Tee Khaw, and Martyn Plummer. Seasonal Variation of Serum Lipids in an Elderly Population. *Age and Ageing*, 22:273–278, 1993.

[414] Mark Woodward. *Epidemiology. Study Design and Data Analysis*. Chapman and Hall / CRC, Boca Raton, FL, 1999.

[415] E.A. Wrigley, R.S. Davies, J.E. Oeppen, and R.S. Schofield. *English population history from family reconstitution 1580–1837*. Cambridge University Press, Cambridge, UK, cambridge studies in population, economy and society in past time 32 edition, 1997.

[416] E.A. Wrigley and R.S. Schofield. *The Population History of England, 1541–1871*. Cambridge University Press, Cambridge, UK, 1989.

[417] Robert Yaffee. *Time Series Analysis and Forecasting with Applications of SAS and SPSS*. Academic Press, San Diego, CA, 2000.

[418] Kazuo Yamaguchi. *Event history analysis*, volume 28 of *Applied social research methods series*. SAGE Publications, Newbury Park, CA, 1991.

[419] Yuk Yee Yan. The influence of weather on human mortality in Hong Kong. *Social Science and Medicine*, 50:419–427, 2000.

[420] Chung-Jen Yen, Chia-Lun Chao, Fung-Chang Sung, Wen-Jone Chen, Chiau-Suong Liau, and Yuan-The Lee. Seasonal effects on cardiovascular mortality in older patients. *Age & Ageing*, 29:186–187, 2000.

[421] Shoshona Zevin, Sandra Saunders, Steven Gourlay, Peyton Jacob III, and Neal Benoqitz. Cardiovascular Effects of Carbon Monoxide and Cigarette Smoking. *Journal of the American College of Cardiology*, 38:1633–1638, 2001.

Printing: Krips bv, Meppel
Binding: Stürtz, Würzburg